Political Shakespeare

New essays in cultural materialism

edited by Jonathan Dollimore *and* Alan Sinfield

Political Shakespeare

New essays in cultural materialism

Manchester University Press ⏣

Manchester and New York

Distributed exclusively in the USA and Canada by St. Martin's Press

Published by Manchester University Press
Oxford Road, Manchester M13 9PL, UK

Reprinted 1986, 1988, 1989, 1992

British Library cataloguing in publication data

Political Shakespeare: new essays in cultural materialism.
  1. Shakespeare, William—Criticism and interpretation
  I. Dollimore, Jonathan   II. Sinfield, Alan 822.3'3   PR2976

  ISBN 0–7190–1794–7 *paperback*

Printed in Great Britain
by Billings Ltd, Worcester

Contents

Contents

Foreword Cultural materialism

The break-up of consensus in British political life during the 1970s was accompanied by the break-up of traditional assumptions about the values and goals of literary criticism. Initially at specialised conferences and in committed journals, but increasingly in the main stream of intellectual life, literary texts were related to the new and challenging discourses of Marxism, feminism, structuralism, psycho-analysis and poststructuralism. It is widely admitted that all this has brought a new rigour and excitement to literary discussions. At the same time, it has raised profound questions about the status of literary texts, both as linguistic entities and as ideological forces in our society.

Some approaches offer a significant alternative to traditional practice; others are little more than realignments of familiar positions. But our belief is that a combination of historical context, theoretical method, political commitment and textual analysis offers the strongest challenge and has already contributed substantial work. Historical context undermines the transcendent significance traditionally accorded to the literary text and allows us to recover its histories; theoretical method detaches the text from immanent criticism which seeks only to reproduce it in its own terms; socialist and feminist commitment confronts the conservative categories in which most criticism has hitherto been conducted; textual analysis locates the critique of traditional approaches where it cannot be ignored. We call this 'cultural materialism'.

There are (at least) two ways of using the word 'culture'. The analytic one is used in the social sciences and especially anthro-pology: it seeks to describe the whole system of significations by which a society or a section of it understands itself and its relations with the world. The evaluative use has been more common when we are thinking about 'the arts' and 'literature': to be 'cultured' is to be the possessor of superior values and a refined sensibility, both of which are manifested through a positive and fulfilling engagement with 'good' literature, art, music and so on.

Cultural materialism draws upon the analytic sense of 'culture', and it includes work on the cultures of subordinate and marginalised groups like schoolchildren and skinheads, and on forms like television and popular music and fiction. But its effects are perhaps most startling when it is applied to artefacts and practices which have traditionally been prized within the evaluative idea of culture. In brief, 'high culture' is taken as one set of signifying practices among others.

'Materialism' is opposed to 'idealism': it insists that culture does not (cannot) transcend the material forces and relations of production. Culture is not simply a reflection of the economic and political system, but nor can it be independent of it. Cultural materialism therefore studies the implication of literary texts in history. A play by Shakespeare is related to the contexts of its production – to the economic and political system of Elizabethan and Jacobean England and to the particular institutions of cultural production (the court, patronage, theatre, education, the church). Moreover, the relevant history is not just that of four hundred years ago, for culture is made continuously and Shakespeare's text is reconstructed, reappraised, reassigned all the time through diverse institutions in specific contexts. What the plays signify, how they signify, depends on the cultural field in which they are situated. That is why this book discusses also the institutions through which Shakespeare is reproduced and through which interventions may be made in the present.

Finally, cultural materialism does not pretend to political neutrality. It knows that no cultural practice is ever without political significance – not the production of *King Lear* at the Globe, or at the Barbican, or as a text in a school, popular or learned edition, or in literary criticism, or in the present volume. Cultural materialism does not, like much established literary criticism, attempt to mystify its perspective as the natural, obvious or right interpretation of an allegedly given textual fact. On the contrary, it registers its commitment to the transformation of a social order which exploits people on grounds of race, gender and class.

Jonathan Dollimore
Alan Sinfield

University of Sussex

Part I Recovering history

Introduction Shakespeare, cultural materialism and the new historicism

One of the most important achievements of 'theory' in English studies has been the making possible a truly interdisciplinary approach to – some might say exit from – the subject. Actually, such an objective had been around for a long time, though largely unrealised outside of individual and often outstanding studies. With the various structuralisms, Marxism, psychoanalysis, semiotics and post-structuralism, there occurred a significant dismantling of barriers (barriers of exclusion as well as of containment) and many critics discovered what they had wanted to know for some time – how, for example, history and philosophy could be retrieved from their 'background' status and become part of both the content and the perspective of criticism. At the same time this was possible only because quite new conceptions of philosophy and history were involved. In utilising theory in the field of literary studies we find that it has made possible far more than it has actually introduced. By this criterion alone it proves itself a major intellectual contribution. But not everyone approves, as the anti-theoretical invective of recent years has shown. We don't propose to dwell on this reaction, nor on the much vaunted 'crisis' in English studies, except to remark that if there is a crisis it has more to do with this reaction than with theory itself.

But of course 'theory' is as erroneous a title as was 'structuralism', both giving a misleading impression of unity where there is in fact enormous diversity. We are concerned here with one development of recent years, cultural materialism; it preceded the advent of theory but also derived a considerable impetus from it.

The term 'cultural materialism' is borrowed from its recent use by Raymond Williams; its practice grows from an eclectic body of work in Britain in the post-war period which can be broadly characterised as cultural analysis. That work includes the considerable output of Williams himself, and, more generally, the convergence of history, sociology and English in cultural studies, some of the major developments in feminism, as well as continental Marxist-structuralist and post-structuralist theory, especially that of Althusser, Macherey, Gramsci and Foucault.[1]

The development of cultural materialism in relation to Renaissance literature has been fairly recent although there is already a diverse and developing field of work relating literary texts to, for example, the following: enclosures and the oppression of the rural poor[2]; State power and resistance to it;[3] reassessments of what actually were the dominant ideologies of the period and the radical countertendencies to these;[4] witchcraft; the challenge and containment of the carnivalesque;[5] a feminist recovery of the actual conditions of women and the altered understanding of their literary representations which this generates;[6] conflict between class fractions within the State and, correspondingly, the importance of a non-monolithic conception of power.[7]

Much of this work is explicitly concerned with the operations of power. But it is in the United States that most attention has been given to the representations of power in Renaissance literature. This work is part of an important perspective which has come to be called the new historicism,[8] a perspective concerned generally with the interaction in this period between State power and cultural forms[9] and, more specifically, with those genre and practices where State and culture most visibly merge – for example, pastoral, the masque and the institution of patronage.[10] An analysis by the new historicism of power in early modern England as itself deeply theatrical – and therefore of the theatre as a prime location for the representation and legitimation of power – has led to some remarkable studies of the Renaissance theatre as well as of individual plays, Shakespeare's included.[11]

According to Marx, men and women make their own history but not in conditions of their own choosing.[12] Perhaps the most significant divergence within cultural analysis is that between those who concentrate on culture as this making of history, and those who concentrate on the unchosen conditions which constrain and inform that process of making. The former allows much to human agency, and tends to privilege human experience; the latter concentrates on the formative power of social and ideological structures which are both prior to experience and in some sense determining of it, and so opens up the whole question of autonomy.[13]

A similar divergence is acknowledged in Stephen Greenblatt's *Renaissance Self-Fashioning*, an outstanding instance of the new historicism. In an epilogue Greenblatt tells how he began with an intention to explore 'the role of human autonomy in the construction

[3]

of identity'. But as the work progressed the emphasis fell more and more on cultural institutions – family, religion and the State – and 'the human subject itself began to seem remarkably unfree, the ideological product of the relations of power in a particular society' (p. 256).

In the rest of this introduction I explore some of the other important and shared concerns of cultural materialism and the new historicism as they relate to Renaissance studies generally and part one of this book in particular.

History versus the human condition

Materialist criticism refuses to privilege 'literature' in the way that literary criticism has done hitherto; as Raymond Williams argued in an important essay, 'we cannot separate literature and art from other kinds of social practice, in such a way as to make them subject to quite special and distinct laws'. This approach necessitates a radical contextualising of literature which eliminates the old divisions between literature and its 'background', text and context. The arts 'may have quite specific features as practices, but they cannot be separated from the general social process' (Williams, *Problems*, p. 44). This attention to social process has far-reaching consequences. To begin with it leads us beyond idealist literary criticism – that preoccupied with supposedly universal truths which find their counterpart in 'man's' essential nature; the criticism in which history, if acknowledged at all, is seen as inessential or a constraint transcended in the affirmation of a transhistorical human condition.

It would be wrong to represent idealist criticism as still confidently dominant in Shakespeare studies; in fact it is a vision which has been failing for some time, and certainly before the advent of theory. In recent decades its advocates have tended to gesture towards this vision rather than confidently affirm it; have hesitated over its apparent absence, often then to become preoccupied with the tragic sense of life as one which recuperated the vision *as* absence, which celebrated not man's transcendent consciousness but his will to endure and to know why transcendence was itself an illusion. In short, an existentialist-tragic sense of life was in tension with a more explicitly spiritual one, the former trying to break with the latter but being unable to because it had nowhere to go; a diminished metaphysic, aetiolation became the condition of its survival.

Materialist criticism also refuses what Stephen Greenblatt calls the monological approach of historical scholarship of the past, one 'concerned with discovering a single political vision, usually identical to that said to be held by the entire literate class or indeed the entire population' (*The Power of Forms*, p. 5). E. M. W. Tillyard's very influential *The Elizabethan World Picture*, first published in 1943 and still being reprinted, is perhaps the most notorious instance. Tillyard was concerned to expound an idea of cosmic order 'so taken for granted, so much part of the collective mind of the people, that it is hardly mentioned except in explicitly didactic passages'.[14]

The objection to this is not that Tillyard was mistaken in identifying a metaphysic of order in the period, nor even that it had ceased to exist by the turn of the century (two criticisms subsequently directed at him). The error, from a materialist perspective, is falsely to unify history and social process in the name of 'the collective mind of the people'. And such a perspective would construe the 'didactic passages' referred to by Tillyard in quite different terms: didacticism was not the occasional surfacing, the occasional articulation, of the collective mind but a strategy of ideological struggle. In other words, the didactic stress on order was in part an anxious reaction to emergent and (in)-subordinate social forces which were perceived as threatening. Tillyard's world picture, to the extent that it did still exist, was not shared by all; it was an ideological legitimation of an existing social order, one rendered the more necessary by the apparent instability, actual *and* imagined, of that order. If this sounds too extreme then we need only recall Bacon's remark to some circuit judges in 1617: 'There will be a perpetual defection, except you keep men in by preaching, as well as law doth by punishing'.[15] Sermons were not simply the occasion for the collective mind to celebrate its most cherished beliefs but an attempt to tell sectors of an unruly populace what to think 'in order' to keep them in their place.

Historians who have examined the effects of social change and reactions to it present a picture quite opposite to Tillyard's:

> In the late sixteenth and early seventeenth centuries ... this almost hysterical demand for order at all costs was caused by a collapse of most of the props of the medieval world picture. The unified dogma and organisation of the Catholic Church found itself challenged by a number of rival creeds and institutional structures ... the reliance upon the intellectual authority of the Ancients was threatened by new scientific discoveries. Moreover in England there occurred a phase of unprecedented social and geographical mobility which at the higher levels transformed the composition and size of the gentry and professional classes, and at the lower levels tore hundreds of thousands of individuals loose from their traditional kinship and neighbourhood backgrounds.[16]

In making sense of a period in such rapid transition, and of the contradictory interpretations of that transition from within the period itself, we might have recourse to Raymond Williams's very important distinction between residual, dominant, and emergent aspects of culture (*Marxism and Literature*, pp. 121–7). Tillyard's world picture can then be seen as in some respects a dominant ideology, in others a residual one, with one or both of these perhaps being confronted and displaced by new, emergent cultural forms. Nor is this threefold distinction exhaustive of cultural diversity: there will also be levels of culture appropriately described as subordinate, repressed and marginal. Non-dominant elements interact with the dominant forms, sometimes coexisting with, or being absorbed or even destroyed by them, but also challenging, modifying or even displacing them. Culture is not by any stretch of the imagination – not even the literary imagination – a unity.

Tillyard was not entirely unaware of this, though it is presumably with unwitting irony that he writes of 'the educated nucleus that *dictated* the current beliefs of the Elizabethan Age' and of cosmic order as 'one of the genuine *ruling* ideas of the age' (pp. 22, 7; italics added). Because, for Tillyard, the process of ideological legitimation was itself more or less legitimate, it is a process which in his book – and much more so than his claims about the Elizabethan world picture itself – is accepted to the point of being barely recognised. Further, because Tillyard revered the period ('the "real" Elizabethan age – the quarter century from 1580–1605 – was after all the great age', p. 130) what he discerned as its representative literature is presented as the legitimate object of study. And those literary forms wherein can be glimpsed the transgression of the world picture – where, that is, we glimpse subordinate cultures resisting or contesting the dominant – these are dismissed as unworthy of study because unrepresentative: '[Hooker] represents far more truly the background of Elizabethan literature than do the coney-catching pamphlets or the novel of low-life' (p. 22). But whose literature, and whose background? In different respects all the essays in Part I of this book are concerned with the marginalised and subordinate of Elizabethan and Jacobean culture. Their exploitation is in part secured ideologically and this deserves some preliminary consideration.

There are several ways of deploying the concept of ideology, and these correspond to its complex history.[17] One which in particular concerns materialist criticism traces the cultural connections between signification and legitimation: the way that beliefs, practices and institutions legitimate the dominant social order or *status quo* – the existing relations of domination and subordination. Such legitimation is found (for example) in the representation of sectional interests as universal ones. Those who rule may in fact be serving their own interests and those of their class, but they, together with the institutions and practices through which they exercise and maintain power, are understood as working in the interests of the community as a whole. Secondly, through legitimation the existing social order – that is, existing social relations – are 'naturalised', thus appearing to have the unalterable character of natural law. History also tends to be invested with a law of development (teleology) which acts as the counterpart of natural law, a development leading 'inevitably' to the present order and thereby doubly ratifying it. Legitimation further works to efface the fact of social contradiction, dissent and struggle. Where these things present themselves unavoidably they are often demonised as attempts to subvert the social order. Therefore, if the very conflicts which the existing order generates from within itself are construed as attempts to subvert it from without (by the 'alien'), that order strengthens itself by simultaneously repressing dissenting elements and eliciting consent for this action: the protection of society from subversion. (See especially Chapters 3 and 4 below).

This combined emphasis on universal interests, society as a 'reflection' of the 'natural' order of things, history as a 'lawful' development leading up to and justifying the present, the demonising of dissent and otherness, was central to the age of Shakespeare.

The politics of Renaissance theatre

I want to consider next why the socio-political perspective of materialist criticism is especially appropriate for recovering the political dimension of Renaissance drama. This entails a consideration of the theatre as an institution and, more generally, literature as a practice.

Analysts of literature in the Renaissance were much concerned with its effect. The almost exclusive pecoccupation in traditional English studies with the intrinsic meaning of texts leads us to miss, ignore or underestimate the importance of this fact. Effect was considered not at the level of the individual reader in abstraction, but of actual readers – and, of course, audiences. Rulers and preachers were only two groups especially concerned to determine, regulate, and perhaps exploit these effects.

As regards the theatre there were two opposed views of its effectiveness. The one view stressed its capacity to instruct the populace – often, and quite explicitly, to keep them obedient. Thus

[7]

Heywood, in an *Apology for Actors*, claimed that plays were written and performed to teach 'subjects obedience to their king' by showing them 'the untimely end of such as have moved tumults, commotions and insurrections'.[18] The other view claimed virtually the opposite, stressing the theatre's power to demystify authority and even to subvert it; in 1605 Samuel Calvert had complained that plays were representing 'the present Time, not sparing either King, State or Religion, in so great Absurdity, and with such Liberty, that any would be afraid to hear them'.[19] In an often cited passage from *Basilikon Doron* James I likened the king to 'one set on a stage, whose smallest actions and gestures, all the people gazingly do behold'; any 'dissolute' behaviour on his part breeds contempt in his subjects and contempt is 'the mother of rebellion and disorder'.[20] The theatre could encourage such contempt by, as one contemporary put it in a description of Shakespeare's *Henry VIII*, making 'greatness very familiar, if not ridiculous'.[21] A year after *Basilikon Doron* appeared, a French ambassador recorded in a despatch home that James was being held in just the contempt that he feared and, moreover, that the theatre was encouraging it.[22]

A famous attempt to use the theatre to subvert authority was of course the staging of a play called *Richard II* (probably Shakespeare's) just before the Essex rising in 1601; Queen Elizabeth afterwards anxiously acknowledged the implied identification between her and Richard II, complaining also that 'this tragedy was played 40 times in open streets and houses'.[23] As Stephen Greenblatt points out, what was really worrying for the Queen was both the repeatability of the representation – and hence the multiplying numbers of people witnessing it – and the locations of these repetitions: '*open* streets and houses'. In such places the 'conventional containment' of the playhouses is blurred and perhaps relinquished altogether with the consequence that the 'safe' distinction between illusion and reality itself blurs: 'are the "houses" to which Elizabeth refers public theatres or private dwellings where her enemies plot her overthrow? Can "tragedy" be a strictly literary term when the Queen's own life is endangered by the play?' (*The Power of Forms*, p. 4)

Jane P. Tompkins has argued that the Renaissance inherited from the classical period a virtually complete disregard of literature's meaning and a correspondingly almost exclusive emphasis on its effect: what mattered, ultimately, was action not signification, behaviour not discourse. In a sense yes: Tompkins's emphasis on effect is both correct and important, especially when she goes on to show that this pragmatic view of literature made its socio-political dimension *obviously* significant at the time.[24] But Tompkins draws a distinction between effect and signification which is too extreme, even for this period: effectivity is both decided and assessed in the practice of signification. If we ignore this then we are likely to ignore also the fact that socio-political effects of literature are in part achieved in and through the practice of appropriation. Thus what made Elizabeth I so anxious was not so much a retrospectively and clearly ascertained effect of the staging of *Richard II* (the uprising was, after all, abortive and Essex was executed) but the fact of the play having been appropriated – been given significance for a particular cause and in certain 'open' contexts. This period's pragmatic conception of literature meant that such appropriations were not a perversion of true literary reception, they were its reception.

This applies especially to tragedy, that genre traditionally thought to be most capable of transcending the historical moment of inception and of representing universal truths. Contemporary formulations of the tragic certainly made reference to universals but they were also resolutely political, especially those which defined it as a representation of tyranny. Such accounts, and of course the plays themselves, were appropriated as both defences of *and* challenges to authority.

Thomas Elyot, in *The Governor*, asserted that, in reading tragedies, a man shall be led to 'execrate and abhor the intollerable life of tyrants', and for Sidney tragedy made 'Kings fear to be tyrants'. Puttenham in *The Art of English Poesy* had said that tragedy revealed tyranny to 'all the world', while the downfall of the tyrant disclosed (perhaps incongruously) both historical vicissitude ('the mutability of fortune') and God's providential order (his 'just punishment'). In contrast Fulke Greville explicitly disavowed that his own tragedies exemplified God's law in the form of providential retribution. Rather, they were concerned to 'trace out the high ways of ambitious governors'. He further stressed that the 'true stage' for his plays was not the theatre but the reader's own life and times – 'even the state he lives in'. This led Greville actually to destroy one of his tragedies for fear of incrimination – it could, he said, have been construed as 'personating ... vices in the present Governors, and government'. (It seems he had in mind the events of the Essex rebellion.)[25] Raleigh, in his *History of the World*, warns of the danger of writing in general when the subject is contemporary history: if the writer follows it too closely 'it may happily strike out his teeth'.[26] Those like Greville and Raleigh knew then that the idea

of literature passively reflecting history was erroneous; literature
was a practice which intervened in contemporary history in the very
act of representing it. This recognition is partly responsible for the
form of contextualising attempted by the contributors to Part I of
this book. The essays here aim to give not so much new readings of
Shakespeare's texts as a historical relocation of them, one which
radically alters the meanings traditionally ascribed to them by a
criticism preoccupied with their textual integrity. Thus Leonard
Tennenhouse proposes that the opposition between a political and a
literary use of language is largely a modern invention and that
Shakespeare's plays, like Renaissance 'literature' generally, 'displayed its politics as it idealized or demystified specific forms of
power' and that 'such a display rather than the work's transcendence
or referentiality was what made it aesthetically successful' (p. 110).
Especially illuminating is the way Tennenhouse relates the textual
representations of authority to each other and to the institutions and
actual power struggles of Elizabethan and Jacobean England without thereby assuming a simple correspondence of the text to the pre-
existent real. The recovery of history becomes, inescapably, a
'theoretical' procedure too.

Consolidation, subversion, containment

Three aspects of historical and cultural process figure prominently in
materialist criticism: consolidation, subversion and containment.
The first refers, typically, to the ideological means whereby a dominant order seeks to perpetuate itself; the second to the subversion of
that order, the third to the containment of ostensibly subversive
pressures.

The metaphysic of order in the Elizabethan period has already been
briefly considered. Those of Tillyard's persuasion saw it as consoli-
dating, that is socially cohesive in the positive sense of transcending
sectional interests and articulating a genuinely shared culture and
cosmology, characterised by harmony, stability and unity. In contrast, materialist criticism is likely to consider the ideological dimension of consolidation – the way, for example, that this world picture
reinforces particular class and gender interests by presenting the
existing social order as natural and God-given (and therefore im-
mutable). Interestingly, ideas approximating to these contrasting
positions circulated in the period. Those Elizabethan sermons which
sought to explain social hierarchy as a manifestation of Divine Law,
and which drew analogies between hierarchy in the different levels of
cosmos, nature and society, would be an example of the first, and the

assertion in Ben Jonson's *Sejanus* that "tis place,/Not blood, discerns the noble, and the base'[27] of the second.

Important differences exist within materialist criticism of Renaissance literature between those who emphasise the process of consolidation and those who discover resistances to it. Here the disagreement tends to be at distinct but overlapping levels: actual historical process and its discursive representation in literature. So, for example, within feminist criticism of the period, there are those who insist on its increasing patriarchal oppressiveness, and, moreover, insist that the limiting structures of patriarchy are also Shakespeare's. Kathleen McLuskie summarises this perspective as follows: 'Shakespeare ... gave voice to the social views of his age. His thoughts on women were necessarily bounded by the parameters of hagiography and misogyny'.[28] Conversely, other feminist critics want to allow that there were those in the period, including Shakespeare, who could and did think beyond these parameters, and participated in significant resistance to such constructions of women.[29] But this second perspective, at least in its materialist version, is united with the first in rejecting a third position, namely that which sees Shakespeare's women as exemplifying the transhistorical (universal) qualities of 'woman', with Shakespeare's ability to represent these being another aspect of a genius who transcends not only his time but also his sex. McLuskie's essay in this book insists on the constraints of the literary tradition, the ideological and material conditions from which the plays emerge. A materialist feminism, rather than simply co-opting or writing off Shakespeare, follows the unstable constructions of, for example, gender and patriarchy back to the contradictions of their historical moment. Only thus can the authority of the patriarchal bard be understood and etfectively challenged.

In considering in that same historical moment certain representations of authority, along with those which ostensibly subvert it, we discover not a straightforward opposition but a process much more complex. Subversiveness may for example be apparent only, the dominant order not only containing it but, paradoxical as it may seem, actually producing it for its own ends. An important article arguing this position is that by Stephen Greenblatt, who takes as his example the Machiavellian proposition that religion was a kind of false consciousness perpetuated by the rulers to keep the ruled in their place. If authority does indeed depend on such mystifications for its successful operation, then the Machiavellian demystification of such a process is also a subversion of authority. Yet, in Thomas Harriot's account of the first Virginia colony the reverse seems to be the case. One conclusion in a sophisticated argument extended to

Shakespeare's history plays is that 'the power Harriot both serves and embodies not only produces its own subversion but is actively built upon it: in the Virginia colony, the radical undermining of Christian order is not the negative limit but the positive condition for the establishment of that order' (below, p. 24).

To some extent the paradox disappears when we speak not of a monolithic power structure producing its effects but of one made up of different, often competing elements, and these not merely producing culture but producing it through appropriations. The importance of this concept of appropriation is that it indicates a process of making or transforming. If we talk only of power producing the discourse of subversion we not only hypostatise power but also efface the cultural differences – and context – which the very process of containment presupposes. Resistance to that process may be there from the outset or itself produced by it. Further, although subversion may indeed be appropriated by authority for its own purposes, once installed it can be used against authority as well as used by it. Thus the demonised elements in Elizabethan culture – for example, masterless men – are, quite precisely, *identified* as such in order to ratify the exercise of power, but once identified they are also there as a force to be self-identified. But this didn't make them a power in their own right; on the contrary, for masterless men to constitute a threat to order it was usually – though not always – necessary that they first be mobilised or exploited by a counter-faction within the dominant.

But appropriation could also work the other way: subordinate, marginal or dissident elements could appropriate dominant discourses and likewise transform them in the process. I have already suggested what Essex may have been trying to do with *Richard II*: another recently rediscovered instance is recounted in Carlo Ginzburg's *The Cheese and the Worms*.[30] This book relates how Menocchio, an Italian miller and isolated heretic, interpreted seemingly very orthodox texts in a highly challenging way – construing from them, for example, a quite radical materialist view of the universe. Ginzburg emphasises the 'one sided and arbitrary' nature of Menocchio's reading, and sees its source as being in a peasant culture, oral, widespread and at once sceptical, materialist and rationalist. It is this culture and not at all the intrinsic nature of the texts which leads Menocchio to appropriate them in a way subversive enough to incur torture and eventually death by burning for heresy.

The subversion-containment debate is important for other reasons. It is in part a conceptual or theoretical question: what, for example, are the criteria for distinguishing between, say, that which subverts and that which effects change? Stephen Greenblatt provides a useful working definition here: radical subversiveness is defined as not merely the attempt to seize existing authority, but as a challenge to the principles upon which authority is based.[31] But we are still faced with the need for interpretation simply in making this very distinction: theoretical clarification of necessity involves historical enquiry and vice versa. And the kind of enquiry at issue is inextricably bound up with the question of perspective: which one, and whose? How else for example can we explain why what is experienced as subversive at the time may retrospectively be construed as a crucial step towards progress? More extremely still, how is it that the same subversive act may be later interpreted as having contributed to either revolutionary change or anarchic disintegration?

Nothing can be intrinsically or essentially subversive in the sense that prior to the event subversiveness can be more than potential; in other words it cannot be guaranteed a priori, independent of articulation, context and reception. Likewise the mere thinking of a radical idea is not what makes it subversive: typically it is the context of its articulation: to whom, how many and in what circumstances; one might go further and suggest that not only does the idea have to be conveyed, it has also actually to be used to refuse authority *or* be seen by authority as capable and likely of being so used. It is, then, somewhat misleading to speak freely and only of 'subversive thought'; what we are concerned with (once again) is a *social process*. Thus the 'Machiavellian' demystification of religion was circulating for centuries before Machiavelli; what made it actually subversive in the Renaissance was its being taken up by many more than the initiated few. Even here interpretation and perspective come into play: we need to explain why it was taken up, and in so doing we will almost certainly have to make judgements about the historical changes it helped precipitate. Explicitness about one's own perspective and methodology become unavoidable in materialist criticism and around this issue especially: as textual, historical, sociological and theoretical analysis are drawn together, the politics of the practice emerges.

The essays by Leonard Tennenhouse, Paul Brown and Jonathan Dollimore all attend to representations of subversiveness. Tennenhouse's is partly concerned with the complex relations in the Henry plays and *A Midsummer Night's Dream* between authority and the figures of misrule, carnival and festival. Concentrating on *The Tempest*, Brown, like Greenblatt, addresses the power and complexity of colonial discourse. His analysis of the way it constructs the threatening 'other' is especially revealing. This production of otherness is seen as essential to colonialism yet fraught with internal contradiction since 'it produces the possibility of ... resistance in the other precisely at the moment when it seeks to impose its captivating power' (p. 59). The radical ambiguity of the colonial stereotype, and the instability of the civil / savage opposition so central to the colonial project, help to focus the ideological contradictions of the play's political unconscious. If, then, as Jonathan Goldberg has argued, contradictions are the very means by which power achieves its aims (*James I*, esp. pp. 12, 55, 186), they also generate an instability which can be its undoing.

Dollimore also considers the construction of the other, now in the form of the sexual deviant. In this period deviancy is regarded by many as radically subversive. Yet here too, especially in *Measure for Measure*, that which apparently threatens authority seems to be produced by it. An apparent crisis in the State is attributed to its deviant population whose transgressions, far from undermining authority, enable its relegitimation. At the same time those whose exploitation permits this reaction are endlessly spoken of and for, yet never themselves speak; they have no voice, no part.

All the contributors to this book would endorse Frank Lentricchia's contention that 'Ruling culture does not define the whole of culture, though it tries to, and it is the task of the oppositional critic to re-read culture so as to amplify and strategically position the marginalised voices of the ruled, exploited, oppressed, and excluded'.[32] Lentricchia, here quoting Raymond Williams, rightly insists that cultural domination is not a static unalterable thing; it is rather a *process*, one always being contested, always having to be renewed. As Williams puts it: 'alternative political and cultural emphases, and the many forms of opposition and struggle, are important not only in themselves but as indicative features of what the hegemonic process has in practice had to work to control' (*Marxism and Literature*, p. 113). At the same time, 'the mere pluralization of voices and traditions (a currently fashionable and sentimental gesture) is inadequate to the ultimate problem of linking repressed and master voices as the agon of history, their abiding relation of class conflict' (Lentricchia, *Criticism and Social Change*, p. 131). Arguably an oppositional criticism will always be deficient, always liable to despairing collapse, if it underestimates the extent, strategies and flexible complexity of domination.[33] The instance of low-life sexuality in *Measure for Measure* suggests that we can never find in a repressed sub-culture that most utopian of fantasies: an alternative to the

dominant which is simultaneously subversive of it and self-authenticating. Of course one can, sometimes, recover history from below.
But to piece together its fragments may be eventually to disclose not
the self-authenticating other, but the self-division intrinsic to (and
which thereby perpetuates) subordination. At other times we will
listen in vain for voices from the past or search for their traces in a
'history' they never officially entered. And in the case of those who
sexually trangressed in the early seventeenth century, what we
recover may well tell us more about the society that demonised than
about the demonised themselves. But even to be receptive to that fact
involves a radical shift in awareness which is historically quite
recent. And it is a shift which means that if we feel - as do several of
the contributors to this book – the need to disclose the effectiveness
and complexity of the ideological process of containment, this by no
means implies a fatalistic acceptance that it is somehow inevitable
and that all opposition is hopeless. On the contrary the very desire to
disclose that process is itself oppositional and motivated by the
knowledge that, formidable though it be, it is a process which is
historically contingent and partial – never necessary or total. It did
not, and still does not, have to be so.

Notes

1 Raymond Williams, *Problems in Materialism and Culture* (London: Verso, 1980),
  Marxism and Literature (Oxford University Press, 1977), *Culture* (Glasgow:
  Fontana, 1981); Janet Wolff, *The Social Production of Art* (London: Macmillan,
  1981); Terry Lovell, *Pictures of Reality: Aesthetics, Politics, Pleasure* (London:
  British Film Institute, 1980); Terry Eagleton, *Literary Theory: an Introduction*
  (Oxford: Blackwell, 1983); Tony Bennett et al., *Culture, Ideology and Social
  Process: a Reader* (Batsford and the Open University, 1981), Alan Sinfield,
  'Literary Theory and the 'Crisis' in English Studies',*CQ*, 25, no 3, 1983, 35–47.
2 Raymond Williams, *The Country and the City* (London: Chatto, 1973).
3 J. W. Lever, *The Tragedy of State* (London: Methuen, 1971); Franco Moretti,
  Signs Taken for Wonders: Essays in the Sociology of Literary Forms (London:
  Verso, 1983), chs. 1 and 2.
4 David Aers, Bob Hodge and Gunther Kress, *Literature, Language and Society in
  England, 1580–1680* (Dublin: Gill and Macmillan, 1981); Margot Heinemann,
  *Puritanism and Theatre: Thomas Middleton and Opposition Drama Under the
  Early Stuarts* (Cambridge University Press, 1980); Alan Sinfield, *Literature in
  Protestant England 1560–1660* (London: Croom Helm, 1982), 'The Cultural
  Politics of Sidney's *Defence of Poetry*', in *Sir Philip Sidney in His Time and Ours*,
  ed. Gary Waller and Michael Moore (London: Croom Helm, 1984); Jonathan
  Dollimore, *Radical Tragedy: Religion, Ideology and Power in the Drama of
  Shakespeare and His Contemporaries* (Brighton: Harvester, 1984, University of
  Chicago Press, 1984); Marie Axton, 'The Tudor Mask and Elizabethan Court
  Drama', in *English Drama: Forms and Development*, ed. Marie Axton and
  Raymond Williams (Cambridge University Press, 1977), pp. 24–47; Graham
  Holderness, *Shakespeare's History* (Dublin: Gill and Macmillan, forthcoming).

5 Peter Stallybrass, 'Macbeth and Witchcraft', in Focus on 'Macbeth' ed. John Russell Brown (London: Routledge, 1982), pp. 189–209; Stallybrass and Allon White, The Politics and Poetics of Trangression (forthcoming).

6 Lisa Jardine, Still Harping on Daughters: Women and Drama in the Age of Shakespeare (Brighton: Harvester, 1983); Simon Shepherd, Amazons and Warrior Women: Varieties of Feminism in Seventeenth Century Drama (Brighton: Harvester, 1981).

7 Alan Sinfield, 'Power and Ideology: an Outline Theory and Sidney's Arcadia' (forthcoming); Alan Sinfield and Jonathan Dollimore, 'History and Ideology: the Instance of Henry V', in Alternative Shakespeares, ed. John Drakakis (London: Methuen, 1985).

8 The Power of Forms in the English Renaissance, ed. Stephen Greenblatt (Norman: Pilgrim Books, 1982), Introduction; for two important reviews of the new historicism and its relations with other recent work see Jonathan Goldberg, 'The Politics of Renaissance Literature: a Review Essay', ELH, 49 (1982), 514–42, 'Recent Studies in the English Renaissance', SEL, 24 (1984), 157–99.

9 Stephen Greenblatt, Renaissance Self Fashioning: From More to Shakespeare (University of Chicago Press, 1980); Jonathan Goldberg, James I and the Politics of Literature: Jonson, Shakespeare, Donne and Their Contemporaries (Baltimore and London: Johns Hopkins University Press, 1983).

10 Louis Adrian Montrose, ' "Eliza, Queene of Shepheardes" and the Pastoral of Power', English Literary Renaissance, 10 (1980), 153–82; 'Celebration and Insinuation: Sir Philip Sidney and the Motives of Elizabethan Courtship', Renaissance Drama, n.s. 8 (1977), 3–35; Stephen Orgel, The Illusion of Power: Political Theatre in the English Renaissance (Berkeley and Los Angeles: University of California Press, 1975); Patronage in the Renaissance, ed. Guy Fitch Lytle and Stephen Orgel (Princeton University Press, 1981).

11 See especially Greenblatt, Renaissance Self Fashioning; Goldberg, James I and the Politics of Literature, chs. 3–5; Steven Mullaney, 'Lying Like Truth: Riddle, Representation and Treason in Renaissance England', ELH, 47 (1980), 32–47; Louis Adrian Montrose, 'The Purpose of Playing: Reflections on Shakespearean Anthropology', Helios, n.s. 7 (1980), 51–74; Walter Cohen, 'The Merchant of Venice and the Possibilities of Historical Criticism', ELH, 49 (1982), 765–89; Steven Mullaney, 'Strange Things, Gross Terms, Curious Customs: The Rehearsal of Cultures in the Late Renaissance', Representations, 2 (Spring 1983).

12 Karl Marx, Selected Works, One Volume (London: Lawrence and Wishart, 1968), p. 96.

13 Stuart Hall, 'Cultural Studies: Two Paradigms', in Bennett et al. pp. 19–37; see also the Editor's introduction, pp. 9–15.

14 E. M. W. Tillyard, The Elizabethan World Picture (Harmondsworth: Penguin, 1963), p. 18.

15 Francis Bacon, Works, 14 vols., ed. J. Spedding, R. L. Ellis and D. D. Heath, 1857–61 (Stuttgart: Frommann, 1961–3), XIII, 213.

16 Lawrence Stone, The Family, Sex and Marriage in England 1500–1800 (London: Weidenfeld and Nicolson, 1977), pp. 653–4.

17 See Centre for Contemporary Cultural Studies, On Ideology (London: Hutchinson, 1978); Jorge Larrain, The Concept of Ideology (London: Hutchinson, 1979); Göran Therborn, The Ideology of Power and the Power of Ideology (London: Verso, 1980); on this period in particular see Dollimore, Radical Tragedy, ch 1.

18 Thomas Heywood, An Apology for Actors, reprinted for the Shakespeare Society (London, 1841), p. 53.

19 Quoted in V. C. Gildersleeve, Government Regulation of the Elizabethan Drama (New York, 1961), p. 101.

20 The Political Works of James I, reprinted from the edition of 1616, ed. Charles H. McIlwain (New York: Russell and Russell, 1965), p. 43.

21 Sir Henry Wotton, quoted from Stephen Orgel's article on the same theme, 'Making Greatness Familiar', in *The Power of Forms*, ed. Greenblatt, pp. 41–8, p. 47.

22 E. K. Chambers, *The Elizabethan Stage*, 4 vols. (Oxford: Clarendon, 1923), I, 325.

23 *Richard II*, ed. P. Ure (London: Methuen, 1966), p. lix.

24 Jane P. Tompkins, 'The Reader in History: the Changing Shape of Literary Response', in *Reader Response Criticism: From Formalism to Post-Structuralism*, ed. Jane P. Tompkins (Baltimore and London: Johns Hopkins University Press, 1980), pp. 201–26, especially pp. 205–10.

25 Elyot, *The Boke Named the Gouernour*, ed. H. H. S. Croft, 2 vols. (1883; New York: 1967), I, 71; Philip Sidney, *A Defence of Poetry*, ed. J. A. van Dorsten (Oxford University Press, 1966), p. 45; George Puttenham, in *Elizabethan Critical Essays*, 2 vols., ed. G. Gregory Smith (Oxford: Clarendon, 1904), II, 35; Fulke Greville, quoted from Dollimore, *Radical Tragedy*, pp. 79 and 121; see also Moretti, *Signs*, pp. 49–56.

26 Sir Walter Raleigh, *History of the World*, ed. C. A. Patrides (London: Macmillan, 1971), p. 80.

27 Ben Jonson, *Sejanus*, ed. W. F. Bolton (London: Benn, 1966), V.11–12.

28 Kathleen McLuskie, 'Feminist Deconstruction: the Example of Shakespeare's "Taming of the Shrew",' *Red Letters* 12, pp. 33–40.

29 Compare Shepherd, *Amazons and Warrior Women*; Jardine, *Still Harping on Daughters*; Juliet Dusinberre, *Shakespeare and the Nature of Women* (London: Macmillan, 1975); *The Woman's Part: Feminist Criticism of Shakespeare*, eds. G. Greene *et al.* (Urbana: Illinois University Press, 1980); Coppelia Kahn, *Man's Estate: Masculine Identity in Shakespeare* (Berkeley and Los Angeles: University of California Press: 1981); Linda Woodbridge, *Women and the English Renaissance: Literature and the Nature of Womankind 1540–1620* (forthcoming, Brighton: Harvester).

30 Carlo Ginzburg, *The Cheese and the Worms: the Cosmos of a 16th-Century Miller* (London: Routledge, 1980).

31 Stephen Greenblatt, 'Invisible Bullets: Renaissance Authority and Its Subversion', *Glyph*, 8 (1981), 40–61, p. 41.

32 Frank Lentricchia, *Criticism and Social Change* (University of Chicago Press, 1983), p. 15.

33 For an exemplary instance of oppositional criticism, one which faces directly and without despair the tragic conditions of contemporary history, see Raymond Williams, *Modern Tragedy* (London: Chatto, 1966; revised second edn., London: Verso, 1979), especially the chapter 'Tragedy and Revolution' and the chillingly prophetic *Afterword*, added to the second edition. Also important are Williams's reflections on this work in *Politics and Letters: Interviews with New Left Review* (London: New Left Books, 1979).

Invisible bullets: Renaissance authority and its subversion, *Henry IV* and *Henry V*

In his notorious police report of 1593 on Christopher Marlowe, the Elizabethan spy Richard Baines informed his superiors that Marlowe had declared, among other monstrous opinions, that 'Moses was but a juggler, and that one Heriots, being Sir Walter Ralegh's man, can do more than he'.[1] The 'Heriots' cast for a moment in this lurid light is Thomas Harriot, the most profound Elizabethan mathematician, an expert in cartography, optics, and navigational science, an adherent of atomism, the first Englishman to make a telescope and turn it on the heavens, the author of the first original book about the first English colony in America, and the possessor throughout his career of a dangerous reputation for atheism.[2] In all of his extant writings, private correspondence as well as public discourse, Harriot professes the most reassuringly orthodox religious faith, but the suspicion persisted. When he died of cancer in 1621, one of his contemporaries, persuaded that Harriot had challenged the doctrinal account of creation *ex nihilo*, remarked gleefully that 'a *nihilum* killed him at last: for in the top of his nose came a little red speck (exceeding small), which grew bigger and bigger, and at last killed him'.[3]

Charges of atheism levelled at Harriot or anyone else in this period are extremely difficult to assess, for such accusations were smear tactics, used with reckless abandon against anyone whom the accuser happened to dislike. At a dinner party one summer evening in 1593, Sir Walter Ralegh teased an irascible country parson named Ralph Ironside and found himself the subject of a state investigation; at the other end of the social scale, in the same Dorsetshire parish, a drunken servant named Oliver complained that in the Sunday sermon the preacher had praised Moses excessively but had neglected to mention his fifty-two concubines, and Oliver too found himself under official scrutiny.[4] Few if any of these investigations turned up what we would call atheists, even muddled or shallow ones; the stance that seems to come naturally to the greenest college freshman in late twentieth-century America seems to have been almost unthinkable to the most daring philosophical minds of late sixteenth-century England.

The historical evidence, of course, is unreliable; even in the absence of substantial social pressure, people lie quite readily about their most intimate beliefs. How much more must they have lied in an atmosphere of unembarrassed repression. Still, there is probably more than politic concealment involved here. After all, treason was punished as harshly as atheism, and yet, while the period abounds in documented instances of treason in word and deed, there are virtually no professed atheists. If ever there were a place to confirm the proposition that within a given social construction of reality certain interpretations of experience are sanctioned and others excluded, it is here, in the boundaries that contained sixteenth-century scepticism. Like Machiavelli and Montaigne, Thomas Harriot professed belief in God, and there is no justification, in any of these cases, for a simple dismissal of the profession of faith as mere hypocrisy.

I am not, of course, arguing that atheism was literally unthinkable in the late sixteenth century; rather that it was almost always thinkable only as the thought of another. This is, in fact, one of its attractions as a smear; atheism is one of the characteristic marks of otherness. Hence the ease with which Catholics can call Protestant martyrs atheists, and Protestants routinely make similar charges against the Pope.[5] The pervasiveness and frequency of these charges then does not signal the probable existence of a secret society of freethinkers, a School of Night, but rather registers the operation of a religious authority that, whether Catholic or Protestant, characteristically confirms its power in this period by disclosing the threat of atheism. The authority is secular as well as religious; hence at Raleigh's 1603 treason trial, Justice Popham solemnly warned the accused not to let 'Harriot, nor any such Doctor, persuade you there is no eternity in Heaven, lest you find an eternity of hell-torments'.[6] Nothing in Harriot's writings suggests that he held the position attributed to him here, but of course the charge does not depend upon evidence: Harriot is invoked as the archetypal corrupter, Achitophel seducing his glittering Absolom. If he did not exist, he would have to be invented.

Yet atheism is not the only mode of subversive religious doubt, and we cannot entirely discount the persistent rumors of Harriot's heterodoxy by pointing to his perfectly conventional professions of faith and to the equal conventionality of the attacks upon him. Indeed I want to suggest that if we look closely at A Brief and True

Stephen Greenblatt

Report of the New Found Land of Virginia, the only work Harriot published in his lifetime and hence the work in which he was presumably the most cautious, we can find traces of exactly the kind of material that could lead to the remark attributed to Marlowe, that 'Moses was but a juggler, and that one Heriots, being Sir Walter Ralegh's man, can do more than he'. Further, Shakespeare's Henry plays, like Harriot in the New World, can be seen to confirm the Machievellian hypothesis of the origin of princely power in force and fraud even as they draw their audience irresistibly toward the celebration of that power.

The apparently feeble wisecrack attributed to Marlowe finds its way into a police file because it seems to bear out one of the Machiavellian arguments about religion that most excited the wrath of sixteenth-century authorities: Old Testament religion, the argument goes, and by extension the whole Judeo-Christian tradition, originated in a series of clever tricks, fraudulent illusions perpetrated by Moses, who had been trained in Egyptian magic, upon the 'rude and gross' (and hence credulous) Hebrews.[7] This argument is not actually to be found in Machiavelli, nor does it originate in the sixteenth century; it is already fully formulated in early pagan polemics against Christianity. But it seems to acquire a special force and currency in the Renaissance as an aspect of a heightened consciousness, fuelled by the period's prolonged crises of doctrine and church governance, of the social function of religious belief.

Here Machiavelli's writings are important, for *The Prince* observes in its bland way that if Moses's particular actions and methods are examined closely, they do not appear very different from those employed by the great pagan princes, while the *Discourses* treat religion as if its primary function were not salvation but the achievement of civic discipline and hence as if its primary justification were not truth but expediency. Thus Romulus's successor, Numa Pompilius, 'finding a very savage people, and wishing to reduce them to civil obedience by the arts of peace, had recourse to religion as the most necessary and assured support of any civil society'.[8] For although 'Romulus could organize the Senate and establish other civil and military institutions without the aid of divine authority, yet it was very necessary for Numa, who feigned that he held converse with a nymph, who dictated to him all that he wished to persuade the people to' (147). In truth, continues Machiavelli, 'there never was any remarkable lawgiver amongst any people who did not resort to divine authority, as otherwise his laws would not have been accepted by the people' (147).

From here it was only a short step, in the minds of Renaissance authorities, to the monstrous opinions attributed to the likes of Marlowe and Harriot. Kyd, under torture, testified that Marlowe had affirmed that 'things esteemed to be done by divine power might have as well been done by observation of men', and the Jesuit Robert Parsons claimed that in Ralegh's 'school of Atheism', 'both Moses and our Savior, the Old and the New Testament, are jested at'.[9] On the eve of Ralegh's treason trial, some 'hellish verses' were lifted from an anonymous tragedy written ten years earlier and circulated as Ralegh's own confession of atheism. (The movement here is instructive: the fictional text returns to circulation as the missing confessional language of real life.) At first the earth was held in common, the verses declare, but this golden age gave way to war, kingship, and property:

> Then some sage man, above the vulgar wise,
> Knowing that laws could not in quiet dwell,
> Unless they were observed, did first devise
> The names of Gods, religion, heaven, and hell ...
> Only bug-bears to keep the world in fear.[10]

Now Harriot does not give voice to any of these speculations, but if we look attentively at his account of the first Virginia colony, we find a mind that seems interested in the same set of problems, a mind indeed that seems to be virtually testing the Machiavellian hypotheses. Sent by Ralegh to keep a record of the colony and to compile a description of the resources and inhabitants of the area, Harriot took care to learn the North Carolina Algonkian dialect and to achieve what he calls a 'special familiarity with some of the priests'.[11] The Indians believe, he writes, in the immortality of the soul and in otherworldly punishments and rewards for behaviour in this world; 'What subtlety soever be in the *Wiroances* and Priests, this opinion worketh so much in many of the common and simple sort of people that it maketh them have great respect to their Governors, and also great care what they do, to avoid torment after death and to enjoy bliss' (374). The split between the priests and the people implied here is glimpsed as well in the description of the votive images: 'They think that all the gods are of human shape, and therefore they represent them by images in the forms of men, which they call Kewasowak. ... The common sort think them to be also gods' (373).

We have then, as in Machiavelli, a sense of religion as a set of beliefs manipulated by the subtlety of the priests to help ensure social order and cohesion. To this we may add a still more telling observation not of the internal function of native religion but of the impact of

European culture upon the Indians: 'Most things they saw with us', Harriot writes, 'as mathematical instruments, sea compasses, the virtue of the loadstone in drawing iron, a perspective glass whereby was showed many strange sights, burning glasses, wildfire works, guns, books, writing and reading, spring clocks that seem to go of themselves, and many other things that we had, were so strange unto them, and so far exceeded their capacities to comprehend the reason and means how they should be made and done, that they thought they were rather the works of gods then of men, or at the leastwise they had been given and taught us of the gods' (375–6). The effect of this delusion, born of what Harriot supposes to be the vast techno-logical superiority of the European, is that the savages began to doubt that they possessed the truth of God and religion and to suspect that such truth 'was rather to be had from us, whom God so specially loved than from a people that were so simple, as they found themselves to be in comparison of us' (376).

What we have here, I suggest, is the very core of the Machiavellian anthropology that posited the origin of religion in a cunning imposi-tion of socially coercive doctrines by an educated and sophisticated lawgiver upon a simple people. And in Harriot's list of the marvels – from wildfire to reading – with which he undermined the Indian's confidence in their native understanding of the universe, we have the core of the claim attributed to Marlowe: that Moses was but a juggler and that Ralegh's man Harriot could do more than he. It was, we may add, supremely appropriate that this hypothesis should be tested in the encounter of the Old world and the New, for though vulgar Machiavellianism implied that all religion was a sophisticated confidence trick, Machiavelli himself saw that trick as possible only at a radical point of origin: 'if any one wanted to establish a republic at the present time', he writes, 'he would find it much easier with the simple mountaineers, who are almost without any civilization, than with such as are accustomed to live in cities' (*Discourses*, p. 148).

In Harriot then we have one of the earliest instances of a highly significant phenomenon: the testing upon the bodies and minds of non-Europeans or, more generally, the non-civilised, of a hypothesis about the origin and nature of European culture and belief. Such testing could best occur in this privileged anthropological moment, for the comparable situations in Europe itself tended to be already contaminated by prior contact. Only in the forest, with a people ignorant of Christianity and startled by its bearers' technological potency, could one hope to reproduce accurately, with live subjects, the relation imagined between Numa and the primitive Romans, Moses and the Hebrews. And the testing that could then take place could only happen once, for it entails not detached observation but radical change, the change Harriot begins to observe in the priests who 'were not so sure grounded, nor gave such credit to their traditions and stories, but through conversing with us they were brought into great doubts of their own' (375). I should emphasise that I am speaking here of events as reported by Harriot. The history of subsequent English–Algonkian relations casts doubts upon the depth, extent, and irreversibility of the supposed Indian crisis of belief. In the *Brief and True Report*, however, the tribe's stories begin to *collapse* in the minds of their traditional guardians, and the coercive power of the European beliefs begins to show itself almost at once in the Indians' behaviour: 'On a time also when their corn began to wither by reason of a drought which happened extraordinarily, fearing that it had come to pass by reason that in some thing they had displeased us, many would come to us and desire us to pray to our God in England, that he would preserve their corn, promising that when it was ripe we also should be partakers of the fruit' (377). If we remember that, like virtually all sixteenth-century Europeans in the New World, the English resisted or were incapable of provisioning themselves and were in consequence dependent upon the Indians for food, we may grasp the central importance for the colonists of this dawning Indian fear of the Christian God.[12] As Machiavelli understood, physical compulsion is essential but never sufficient; the survival of the rulers depends upon a supplement of coercive belief.

The Indians must be persuaded that the Christian God is all-powerful and committed to the survival of his chosen people, that he will wither the corn and destroy the lives of savages who displease him by disobeying or plotting against the English. We have then a strange paradox: Harriot tests and seems to confirm the most radically subversive hypothesis in his culture about the origin and function of religion by imposing his religion – with all of its most intense claims to transcendence, unique truth, inescapable coercive force – upon others. Not only the official purpose but the survival of the English colony depends upon this imposition. This crucial circumstance is what has licensed the testing in the first place; it is only as an agent of the English colony, dependent upon its purposes and committed to its survival, that Harriot is in a position to disclose the power of human achievements – reading, writing, gunpowder and the like – to appear to the ignorant as divine and hence to promote belief and compel obedience.

Thus the subversiveness which is genuine and radical – sufficiently disturbing so that to be suspected of such beliefs could lead to imprisonment and torture – is at the same time contained by the power it would appear to threaten. Indeed the subversiveness is the very product of that power and furthers its ends. One may go still further and suggest that the power Harriot both serves and embodies not only produces its own subversion but is actively built upon it: in the Virginia colony, the radical undermining of Christian order is not the negative limit but the positive condition for the establishment of the order. And this paradox extends to the production of Harriot's text: *A Brief and True Report*, with its latent heterodoxy, is not a reflection upon the Virginia colony nor even a simple record of it – not, in other words, a privileged withdrawal into a critical zone set apart from power – but a continuation of the colonial enterprise.

By October 1586, there were rumours in England that there was little prospect of profit in Virginia, that the colony had been close to starvation, and that the Indians had turned hostile. Harriot accordingly begins with a descriptive catalogue in which the natural goods of the land are turned into social goods, that is, into 'merchantable commodities': 'Cedar, a very sweet wood and fine timber; whereof if nests of chests be there made, or timber thereof fitted for sweet and fine bedsteads, tables, desks, lutes, virginals, and many things else, ... [it] will yield profit ' (329–30).[13] The inventory of these commodities is followed by an inventory of edible plants and animals, to prove to readers that the colony need not starve, and then by the account of the Indians, to prove that the colony could impose its will upon them. The key to this imposition, as I have argued, is the coercive power of religious belief, and the source of this power is the impression made by advanced technology upon a 'backward' people.

Hence Harriot's text is committed to record what we have called his confirmation of the Machiavellian hypothesis, and hence too this confirmation is not only inaccessible as subversion to those on whom the religion is supposedly imposed but functionally inaccessible to most readers and quite possibly to Harriot himself. It may be that Harriot was demonically conscious of what he was doing – that he found himself situated exactly where he could test one of his culture's darkest fears about its own origins, that he used the Algonkians to do so, and that he wrote a report on his findings, a coded report, of course, since as he wrote to Kepler years later, 'our situation is such that I still may not philosophize freely'.[14] But we do not need such a biographical romance to account for the phenomenon: the subversiveness, as I have argued, was produced by the colonial power in its own interest, and *A Brief and True*

Report was, with perfect appropriateness, published by the great Elizabethan exponent of missionary colonialism, the Reverend Richard Hakluyt.

Yet it is misleading, I think, to conclude without qualification that the radical doubt implicit in Harriot's account is *entirely* contained. Harriot was, after all, hounded through his whole life by charges of atheism and, more tellingly, the remark attributed to Marlowe suggests that it was fully possible for a contemporary to draw the most dangerous conclusions from the Virginia report. Moreover, the 'Atlantic Republican Tradition', as Pocock has argued, does grow out of the 'Machiavellian moment' of the sixteenth century, and that tradition, with its transformation of subjects into citizens, its subordination of transcendent values to capital values, does ultimately undermine, in the interests of a new power, the religious and secular authorities that had licensed the American enterprise in the first place. What we have in Harriot's text is a relation between orthodoxy and subversion that seems, in the same interpretive moment, to be perfectly stable and dangerously volatile.

We can deepen our understanding of this apparent paradox if we consider a second mode of subversion and its containment in Harriot's account. Alongside the *testing* of a subversive interpretation of the dominant culture, we find the *recording* of alien voices or, more precisely, of alien interpretations. The occasion for this recording is another consequence of the English presence in the New World, not in this case the threatened extinction of the tribal religion but the threatened extinction of the tribe: 'There was no town where we had any subtle device practiced against us', Harriot writes, 'but that within a few days after our departure from every such town, the people began to die very fast, and many in short space; in some towns about twenty, in some forty, in some sixty and in one six score, which in truth was very many in respect of their numbers. The disease was so strange, that they neither knew what it was, nor how to cure it; the like by report of the oldest man in the country never happened before, time out of mind' (378).[15] Harriot is writing, of course, about the effects of measles, smallpox, or perhaps simply the common cold upon people with no resistence to them, but a conception of the biological basis of epidemic disease lies far, far in the future. For the English the deaths must be a moral phenomenon – the notion is for them as irresistible as the notion of germs for ourselves – and hence the 'facts' as they are observed are already moralised: the deaths only occurred 'where they used some practice against us', that is, where the Indians conspired secretly against the English. And, with the wonderful self-validating circularity that characterises virtually all powerful constructions of reality, the evidence for these secret conspiracies is precisely the deaths of the Indians.

Now it is not surprising that Harriot seems to endorse the idea that God is protecting his chosen people by killing off untrustworthy Indians; what is surprising is that Harriot is interested in the Indians's own anxious speculations about the unintended but lethal biological warfare that was destroying them. Drawing upon his special familiarity with the priests, he records a remarkable series of conjectures, almost all of which assume – correctly, as we now know – that their misfortune was linked to the presence of the strangers. 'Some people', observing that the English remained healthy while the Indians died, 'could not tell', Harriot writes, 'whether to think us gods or men'; others, seeing that the members of the first colony were all male, concluded that they were not born of women and therefore must be spirits of the dead returned to mortal form (an Algonkian 'Night of the Living Dead'). Some medicine men learned in astrology blamed the disease on a recent eclipse of the sun and on a comet – a theory Harriot considers seriously and rejects – while others shared the prevailing English interpretation and said 'that it was the special work of God' on behalf of the colonists. And some who seem in historical hindsight eerily prescient prophesied 'that there were more of [the English] generation yet to come, to kill theirs and take their places'. The supporters of this theory even worked out a conception of the disease that in some features uncannily resembles our own: 'Those that were immediately to come after us [the first English colonists], they imagined to be in the air, yet invisible and without bodies, and that they by our entreaty and for the love of us did make the people to die ... by shooting invisible bullets into them' (380).

For a moment, as Harriot records these competing theories, it may seem to a reader as if there were no absolute assurance of God's national interest, as if the drive to displace and absorb the other had given way to conversation among equals, as if all meanings were provisional, as if the signification of events stood apart from power. This impression is intensified for us by our awareness that the theory that would ultimately triumph over the moral conception of epidemic disease was already at least metaphorically present in the conversation. In the very moment that the moral conception is busily authorising itself, it registers the possibility (indeed from our vantage point, the inevitability) of its own destruction.

But why, we must ask ourselves, should power record other voices, permit subversive inquiries, register at its very centre the transgressions that will ultimately violate it? The answer may be in part that power, even in a colonial situation, is not perfectly monolithic and hence may encounter and record in one of its functions materials that can threaten another of its functions; in part that power thrives on vigilance, and human beings are vigilant if they sense a threat; in part that power defines itself in relation to such threats or simply to that which is not identical with it. Harriot's text suggests an intensification of these observations: English power in the first Virginia colony *depends* upon the registering and even the production of such materials. 'These their opinions I have set down the more at large', Harriot tells the 'Adventurers, Favorers, and Wellwishers' of the colony to whom his report is addressed, 'that it may appear unto you that there is good hope they may be brought through discrete dealing and government to the embracing of the truth, and consequently to honor, obey, fear, and love us' (318). The recording of alien voices, their preservation in Harriot's text, is part of the process whereby Indian culture is constituted as a culture and thus brought into the light for study, discipline, correction, trans- formation. The momentary sense of instability or plenitude – the existence of other voices – is produced by the monological power that ultimately denies the possibility of plenitude, just as the subver- sive hypothesis about European religion is tested and confirmed only by the imposition of that religion.

We may add that the power of which we are speaking is in effect an allocation method – a way of distributing resources to some and denying them to others, critical resources (here primarily corn and game) that prolong life or, in their absence, extinguish it. In a remarkable study of how societies make 'tragic choices' in the allocation of scarce resources (e.g. kidney machines) or in the determination of high risks (e.g. the military draft), Guido Calabresi and Philip Bobbitt observe that by complex mixtures of approaches, societies attempt to avert 'tragic results, that is, results which imply the rejection of values which are proclaimed to be fundamental'. These approaches may succeed for a time, but it will eventually become apparent that some sacrifice of fundamental values has taken place, whereupon 'fresh mixtures of methods will be tried, structured . . . by the shortcomings of the approaches they replace'. These too will in time give way to others in a 'strategy of successive moves' that comprises an 'intricate game', a game that reflects the simultaneous perception of an inherent flaw and the determination to 'forget' that perception in an illusory resolution.[16] Hence the simple operation of any systematic order, any allocation method, will inevitably run the risk of exposing its own limitations, even (or perhaps especially) as it asserts its underlying moral principle.

This exposure is as its most intense at moments in which a

comfortably established ideology confronts unusual circumstances, moments when the moral value of a particular form of power is not merely assumed but explained. We may glimpse such a moment in Harriot's account of a visit from the colonists' principal Indian ally, the chief Wingina. Wingina was persuaded that the disease decimating his people was indeed the work of the Christian God and had come to request the English to ask their God to direct his lethal magic against an enemy tribe. The colonists tried to explain that such a prayer would be 'ungodly', that their God was indeed responsible for the disease but that, in this as in all things, he would only act 'according to his good pleasure as he had ordained' (379). Indeed if men asked God to make an epidemic he probably would not do it; the English could expect such providential help only if they made sincere 'petition for the contrary,' that is, for harmony and good fellowship in the service of truth and righteousness.

The problem with these assertions is not that they are self-consciously wicked (in the manner of Richard III or Iago) but that they are highly moral and logically coherent; or rather, what is unsettling is one's experience of them, the nasty sense that they are at once irrefutable ethical propositions and pious humbug designed to conceal from the English themselves the rapacity and aggression that is implicit in their very presence. The explanatory moment manifests the self-validating, totalising character of Renaissance political theology – its ability to account for almost every occurrence, even (or above all) apparently perverse or contrary occurrences – and at the same time confirms for us the drastic disillusionment that extends from Machiavelli to its definitive expression in Hume and Voltaire. In his own way, Wingina himself clearly thought his lesson in Christian ethics was polite nonsense. When the disease had in fact spread to his enemies, as it did shortly thereafter, he returned to the English to thank them – I presume with the Algonkian equivalent of a sly wink – for their friendly help, for 'although we satisfied them not in promise, yet in deeds and effect we had fulfilled their desires' (379). For Harriot, this 'marvelous accident', as he calls it, is another sign of the colony's great expectations.

Once again a disturbing vista – a sceptical critique of the function of Christian morality in the New World – is glimpsed only to be immediately closed off. Indeed we may feel at this point that subversion scarcely exists and may legitimately ask ourselves how our perception of the subversive and orthodox is generated. The answer, I think, is that 'subversive' is for us a term used to designate those elements in Renaissance culture that contemporary authorities tried to contain or, when containment seemed impossible, to destroy and that now conform to our own sense of truth and reality. That is, we locate as 'subversive' in the past precisely those things that are *not* subversive to ourselves, that pose no threat to the order by which we live and allocate resources: in Harriot's *Brief and True Report*, the function of illusion in the establishment of religion, the displacement of a providential conception of disease by one focused on 'invisible bullets', the exposure of the psychological and material interests served by a certain conception of divine power. Conversely, we identify as the principle of order and authority in Renaissance texts things that we would, if we took them seriously, find subversive for ourselves: religious and political absolutism, aristocracy of birth, demonology, humoral psychology, and the like. That we do not find such notions subversive, that we complacently identify them as principles of aesthetic or political order, is a version of the process of containment that licensed what we call the subversive elements in Renaissance texts: that is, our own values are sufficiently strong for us to contain almost effortlessly alien forces. What we find then in Harriot's *Brief and True Report* can best be described by adapting a remark about the possibility of hope that Kafka once made to Max Brod: There is subversion, no end of subversion, only not for us.

I want now to consider the relevance of what I've been saying to our understanding of more complex literary works. It is tempting to focus such remarks on Shakespeare's *Tempest* where Caliban, Prospero's 'salvage and deformed slave' enters cursing the expropriation of his island and exits declaring that he will 'be wise hereafter, / And seek for grace'.[17] What better instance, in the light of Harriot's Virginia, of the containment of a subversive force by the authority that has created that force in the first place: 'This thing of darkness', Prospero says of Caliban at the close, 'I acknowledge mine.'

But I do not want to give the impression that the process I have been describing is applicable only to works that address themselves directly or allusively to the New World. Shakespeare's plays are centrally and repeatedly concerned with the production and containment of subversion and disorder, and the three modes that we have identified in Harriot's text – testing, recording, and explaining – all have their recurrent theatrical equivalents. I am speaking not solely of plays like *Measure for Measure* and *Macbeth*, where authority is obviously subjected to open, sustained, and radical questioning before it is reaffirmed, with ironic reservations, at the close, but of a play like *1 Henry IV* in which authority seems far less problematical. 'Who does not all along see', wrote Upton in the mid eighteenth century, 'that when prince Henry comes to be king he will assume a character suitable to his dignity?' My point is not to dispute this interpretation of the prince as, in Maynard Mack's words, 'an ideal image of the potentialities of the English character',[18] but to observe that such an ideal image involves as its positive condition the constant production of its own radical subversion and the powerful containment of that subversion.

We are continually reminded that Hal is a 'juggler', a conniving hypocrite, and that the power he both serves and comes to embody is glorified usurpation and theft; yet at the same time, we are drawn to the celebration of both the prince and his power. Thus, for example, the scheme of Hal's moral redemption is carefully laid out in his soliloquy at the close of the first tavern scene, but as in the act of *explaining* that we have examined in Harriot, Hal's justification of himself threatens to fall away at every moment into its antithesis. 'By how much better than my word I am', Hal declares, 'By so much shall I falsify men's hopes' (I.ii.210–11). To falsify men's hopes is to exceed their expectations, and it is also to disappoint their expectations, to deceive men, to turn their hopes into fictions, to betray them. Not only are the competing claims of Bolingbroke and Falstaff at issue but our own hopes, the fantasies continually aroused by the play of absolute friendship and trust, limitless playfulness, innate grace, plenitude. But though all of this is in some sense at stake in Hal's soliloquy and though we can perceive at every point, through our own constantly shifting allegiances, the potential instability of the structure of power that has Henry IV at the pinnacle and Robin Ostler, who 'never joy'd since the price of oats rose' (II.i.12), near the bottom, Hal's 'redemption' is as inescapable and inevitable as the outcome of those practical jokes the madcap prince is so fond of playing. Indeed, the play insists, this redemption is not something toward which the action moves but something that is happening at every moment of the theatrical representation.

The same yoking of the unstable and the inevitable may be seen in the play's acts of *recording*, that is, the moments in which we hear voices that seem to dwell in realms apart from that ruled by the potentates of the land. These voices exist and have their apotheosis in Falstaff, but their existence proves to be utterly bound up with Hal, contained politically by his purposes as they are justified aesthetically by his involvement. The perfect emblem of this containment is Falstaff's company, marching off to Shrewsbury: 'discarded unjust servingmen, younger sons to younger brothers, revolted tapsters, and ostlers trade-fall'n, the cankers of a calm world and a long peace' (IV.ii.27–30). These are, as many a homily would tell us, the very types of Elizabethan subversion – masterless men, the natural enemies of social discipline – but they are here pressed into service as defenders of the established order, 'good enough to toss,' as Falstaff tells Hal, 'food for powder, food for powder' (IV.ii.65–6). For power as well as powder, and we may add that this food is produced as well as consumed by the great.

Shakespeare gives us a glimpse of this production in the odd little scene in which Hal, with the connivance of Poins, reduces the puny tapster Francis to the mechanical repetition of the word 'Anon':

> *Prince.* Nay, but hark you, Francis: for the sugar thou gavest me, 'twas a pennyworth, was't not?
> *Francis.* O Lord, I would it had been two!
> *Prince.* I will give thee for it a thousand pound. Ask me when thou wilt, and thou shalt have it.
> *Poins.* [*Within*] Francis!
> *Francis.* Anon, anon.
> *Prince.* Anon, Francis? No Francis; but tomorrow, Francis; or, Francis, a' Thursday; or indeed, Francis, when thou wilt.
>   (II.iv.58–67)

The Bergsonian comedy in such a moment resides in Hal's exposing a drastic reduction of human possibility: 'That ever this fellow should have fewer words than a parrot,' he says at the scene's end, 'and yet the son of a woman!' (II.iv.98). But the chief interest for us resides in the fact that Hal has himself produced the reduction he exposes. The fact of this production, its theatrical demonstration, implicates Hal not only in the linguistic poverty upon which he plays but in the poverty of the five years of apprenticeship Francis has yet to serve: 'Five year!' Hal exclaims, 'by'r lady, a long lease for the clinking of pewter' (II.iv.45–6). And as the Prince is implicated in the production of this oppressive order, so is he implicated in the impulse to abrogate it: 'But, Francis, darest thou be so valiant as to play the coward with thy indenture, and show it a fair pair of heels and run from it?' (II.iv.46–8). It is tempting to think of this peculiar moment – the Prince awakening the apprentice's discontent – as linked darkly with some supposed uneasiness in Hal about his own apprenticeship,[19] but if so the momentary glimpse of a revolt against authority is closed off at once with a few words of calculated obscurity designed to return Francis to his trade without enabling him to understand why he must do so:

> *Prince.* Why then your brown bastard is your only drink! for look you, Francis, your white canvas doublet will sully. In Barbary, sir, it cannot come to so much.
> *Francis.* What, sir?
> *Poins.* [*Within*] Francis!
> *Prince.* Away, you rogue, dost thou not hear them call? (II.iv.73–9)

If Francis takes the earlier suggestion, robs his master and runs away, he will find a place for himself, the play implies, as one of the 'revolted tapsters' in Falstaff's company, men as good as dead long before they march to their deaths as upholders of the crown. Better that he should follow the drift of Hal's deliberately mystifying words and continue to clink pewter. As for the prince, his interest in the brief exchange, beyond what we have already sketched, is suggested by his boast to Poins moments before Francis enters: 'I have sounded the very base-string of humility. Sirrah, I am sworn brother to a leash of drawers and can call them all by their christen names, as Tom, Dick, and Francis' (II.iv.5–8). The prince must sound the basestring of humility if he is to know how to play all of the chords and hence to be the master of the instrument, and his ability to conceal his motives and render opaque his language offers assurance that he himself will not be played on by another.

I have spoken of such scenes in *1 Henry IV* as resembling what in Harriot's text I have called *recording*, a mode that culminates for Harriot in a glossary, the beginnings of an Algonkian–English dictionary, designed to facilitate further acts of recording and hence to consolidate English power in Virginia. The resemblance may be seen most clearly perhaps in Hal's own glossary of tavern slang: 'They call drinking deep, dyeing scarlet: and when you breathe in your watering, they cry 'hem!' and bid you play it off. To conclude, I am so good proficient in one quarter of an hour that I can drink with any tinker in his own language during my life' (II.iv.15–20). The potential value of these lessons, the functional interest to power of recording the speech of an 'under-skinker' and his mates, may be glimpsed in the expressions of loyalty that Hal laughingly recalls: 'They take it already upon their salvation that ... when I am King of England I shall command all the good lads in Eastcheap' (II.iv.9–15).

There is, it may be objected, something slightly absurd in likening such moments to aspects of Harriot's text; *1 Henry IV* is a play, not a tract for potential investors in a colonial scheme, and the only values we may be sure that Shakespeare had in mind, the argument would go, were theatrical values. But theatrical values do not exist in a realm of privileged literariness, of textual or even institutional self-referentiality. Shakespeare's theatre was not isolated by its wooden walls, nor was it merely the passive reflector of social and ideological forces that lay entirely outside of it : rather the Elizabethan and Jacobean theatre was itself a *social event*. Drama, and artistic expression in general, is never perfectly self-contained and abstract, nor can it be derived satisfactorily from the subjective consciousness of an isolated creator. Collective actions, ritual gestures, paradigms of relationship, and shared images of authority penetrate the work of art, while conversely the socially overdetermined work of art, along with a multitude of other institutions and utterances, contributes to the formation, realignment, and transmission of social practices.

Works of art are, to be sure, marked off in our culture from ordinary utterances, but this demarcation is itself a communal event and signals not the effacement of the social but rather its successful absorption into the work by implication or articulation. This absorption – the presence within the work of its social being – makes it possible, as Bakhtin has argued, for art to survive the disappearance of its enabling social conditions, where ordinary utterance, more dependent upon the extraverbal pragmatic situation, drifts rapidly toward insignificance or incomprehensibility.[20] Hence art's genius for survival, its delighted reception by audiences for whom it was never intended, does not signal its freedom from all other domains of life, nor does its inward articulation of the social confer upon it a formal coherence independent of the world outside its boundaries. On the contrary, artistic form itself is the expression of social evaluations and practices.

One might add that *1 Henry IV* itself insists that it is quite impossible to keep the interests of the theatre hermetically sealed off from the interests of power. Hal's characteristic activity is playing or, more precisely, theatrical improvisation – his parts include his father, Hotspur, Hotspur's wife, a thief in buckram, himself as prodigal and himself as penitent – and he fully understands his own behaviour through most of the play as a role that he is performing. We might expect that this role-playing gives way at the end to his true identity – 'I shall hereafter', Hal has promised his father, 'be more myself' (III.ii.92–3) – but with the killing of Hotspur, Hal clearly does not reject all theatrical masks but rather replaces one with another. 'The time will come', Hal declares midway through the play, 'That I shall make this northern youth exchange / His glorious deeds for my indignities' (III.ii.144–6); when that time *has* come, at the play's close, Hal hides with his 'favours' (that is, a scarf or other emblem, but the word also has in the sixteenth century the sense of 'face') the dead Hotspur's 'mangled face' (V.iv.96), as if to mark the completion of the exchange.

Theatricality then is not set over against power but is one of power's essential modes. In lines that anticipate Hal's promise, the angry Henry IV tells Worcester, 'I will from henceforth rather be myself, / Mighty and to be fear'd, than my condition' (I.iii.5–6). 'To be oneself' here means to perform one's part in the scheme of power as opposed to one's natural disposition, or what we would normally designate as the very core of the self. Indeed it is by no means clear that such a thing as a natural disposition exists in the play as anything more than a theatrical fiction; we recall that in Falstaff's hands 'instinct' itself becomes a piece of histrionic rhetoric, an improvised excuse when he is confronted with the shame of his flight from the masked prince: 'Beware instinct – the lion will not touch the true prince. Instinct is a great matter; I was now a coward on instinct. I shall think the better of myself, and thee, during my life; I for a valiant lion, and thou for a true prince' (II.iv.271–5). Both claims – Falstaff's to natural valour, Hal's to legitimate royalty – are, the lines darkly imply, of equal merit.

Again and again in *1 Henry IV* we are tantalised by the possibility of an escape from theatricality and hence from the constant pressure of improvisational power, but we are, after all, in the theatre, and our pleasure depends upon the fact that there is no escape, and our applause ratifies the triumph of our confinement. The play then operates in the manner of its central character, charming us with its visions of breadth and solidarity, 'redeeming' itself in the end by betraying our hopes, and earning with this betrayal our slightly anxious admiration. Hence the odd balance in this play of spaciousness – the constant multiplication of separate, vividly realised realms – and claustrophobia – the absorption of all of these realms by a power at once vital and impoverished. The balance is almost eerily perfect, as if Shakespeare had somehow reached through in *1 Henry IV* to the very centre of the system of opposed and interlocking forces that held Tudor society together.

When we turn, however, to the plays that continue the chronicle of Hal's career, *2 Henry IV* and *Henry V*, not only do we find that the forces balanced in the earlier play have pulled apart – the claustrophobia triumphant in *2 Henry IV*, the spaciousness triumphant in *Henry V* – but that from this new perspective the familiar view of *1 Henry IV* as a perfectly poised play must be revised. What appeared as 'balance' may on closer inspection seem like radical instability tricked out as moral or aesthetic order; what appeared as clarity may seem now like a conjurer's trick concealing confusion in order to buy time and stave off the collapse of an illusion. Not waving but drowning.

2 Henry IV makes the characteristic operations of power less equivocal than they had been in the preceding play: there is no longer even the lingering illusion of distinct realms, each with its own system of values, its soaring visions of plenitude, and its bad dreams. There is manifestly a single system now, one based on predation and betrayal. Hotspur's intoxicating dreams of honour are dead, replaced entirely by the cold rebellion of cunning but impotent schemers. The warm, roistering sounds overheard in the tavern – sounds that seemed to signal a subversive alternative to rebellion – turn out to be the noise of a whore and bully beating a customer to death. And Falstaff, whose earlier larcenies were gilded by fantasies of innate grace, now talks of turning diseases to commodity (I.ii.234–5).

Only Prince Hal seems, in comparison to the earlier play, less meanly calculating, subject now to fits of weariness and confusion, though this change serves less, I think, to humanise him (as Auerbach argued in a famous essay) than to make it clear that the betrayals are systematic. They happen to him and for him. He needn't any longer soliloquise his intention to 'Falsify men's hopes' by selling his wastrel friends: the sale will be brought about by the structure of things, a structure grasped in this play under the twinned names of time and necessity. So too there is no longer any need for heroic combat with a dangerous, glittering enemy like Hotspur (the only reminder of whose voice in this play is Pistol's parody of Marlovian swaggering); the rebels are deftly if ingloriously dispatched by the false promises of Hal's younger brother, the primly virtuous John of Lancaster. To seal his lies, Lancaster swears fittingly 'by the honour of my blood' – the cold blood, as Falstaff observes of Hal, that he inherited from his father.

The 'recording' of alien voices – the voices of those who have no power to leave literate traces of their existence – continues in this play, but without even the theatrical illusion of princely complicity. The king is still convinced that his son is a prodigal and that the kingdom will fall to ruin after his death – there is a certain peculiar consolation in the thought – but it is no longer Hal alone who declares (against all appearances) his secret commitment to disciplinary authority. Warwick assures the king that the prince's interests in the good lads of Eastcheap are entirely what they should be:

> The Prince but studies his companions
> Like a strange tongue, wherein, to gain the language,
> 'Tis needful that the most immodest word
> Be look'd upon and learnt, which once attain'd,
> Your Highness knows, comes to no further use
> But to be known and hated. So, like gross terms,
> The Prince will in the perfectness of time
> Cast off his followers, and their memory
> Shall as a pattern or a measure live,
> By which his Grace must mete the lives of other,
> Turning past evils to advantages. (IV.iv.68–78)

At first the language analogy likens the prince's low-life excursions to the search for proficiency: perfect linguistic competence, the 'mastery' of a language, requires the fullest possible vocabulary. But the darkness of Warwick's words – 'to be known and hated' – immediately pushes the goal of Hal's linguistic researches beyond proficiency. When in *1 Henry IV* Hal boasts of his mastery of tavern slang, we are allowed for a moment at least to imagine that we are witnessing a social bond, the human fellowship of the extremest top and bottom of society in a homely ritual act of drinking together. The play may make it clear, as I have argued, that there are well-defined political interests involved, but these interests may be bracketed, if only briefly, for the pleasure of imagining what Victor Turner calls 'communitas' – a union based on the momentary breaking of the hierarchical order that normally governs a community.[21] And even when we pull back from this spacious sense of union, we are permitted for much of the play to take pleasure at the least in Hal's surprising skill, the proficiency he rightly celebrates in himself.

To learn another language is to acknowledge the existence of another people and to acquire the ability to function, however crudely, within its social world. Hal's remark about drinking with any tinker in his own language suggests, if only jocularly, that for him the lower classes are virtually another people, an alien tribe – immensely more populous than his own – within the kingdom. That this perception extended beyond the confines of Shakespeare's play is suggested by the evidence that middle- and upper-class English settlers in the New World regarded the American Indians less as another race than as a version of their own lower classes; one man's tinker is another man's Indian.[22]

If Hal's glossary initially seems to resemble Harriot's, Warwick's account of Hal's practice quickly drives it past the functionalism of the word-list in the *Brief and True Report*, with its Algonkian equivalents for fire, food, shelter, and toward a different kind of glossary, one more specifically linked to the attempt to understand and control the lower classes. I refer to the sinister glossaries appended to sixteenth-century accounts of criminals and vagabonds. 'Here I set before the good reader the lewd, lousy language of these loitering lusks and lazy lorels', announces Thomas Harman, as he introduces (with a comical flourish designed to display his own rhetorical gifts) what he claims is an authentic list, compiled at great personal cost.[23] His pamphlet, *A Caveat for Common Cursitors*, is the fruit, he declares, of personal research, difficult because his informants are 'marvellous subtle and crafty'. But 'with fair flattering words, money, and good cheer', he has learned much about their ways, 'not without faithful promise made unto them never to discover their names or anything they showed me' (82). Harman cheerfully goes on to publish what they showed him, and he ends his work not only with a glossary of 'peddlar's French' but with an alphabetical list of names, so that the laws made for 'the extreme punishment' of these wicked idlers may be enforced.

It is not at all clear that Harman's subjects – upright men, doxies, Abraham men, and the like – bear any relation to social reality, any more than it is clear in the case of Doll Tearsheet or Mistress Quickly. Much of the *Caveat*, like the other cony-catching pamphlets of the period, has the air of a jest book: time-honoured tales of tricksters and rogues, dished out cunningly as realistic observation. (It is not encouraging that the rogues' term for the stocks in which they were punished, according to Harman, is 'the harmans'.) But Harman is quite concerned to convey at least the impression of accurate observation and recording – clearly, this was among the book's selling points – and one of the principal rhetorical devices he uses to do so is the spice of betrayal: he repeatedly calls attention to his solemn promises never to reveal anything that he has been told, for his breaking of his word serves as an assurance of the accuracy and importance of what he reveals.

A middle-class Prince Hal, Harman claims that through dissembling he has gained access to a world normally hidden from his kind, and he will turn that access to the advantage of the kingdom by helping his readers to identify and eradicate the dissemblers in their midst. Harman's own personal interventions – the acts of detection and apprehension he proudly reports (or invents) – are not enough: only his book can fully expose the cunning sleights of the rogues and thereby induce the justices and shrieves to be more vigilant and punitive. Just as theatricality is thematised in the *Henry IV* plays as one of the crucial agents of royal power, so in the *Caveat for Common Cursitors* (and in much of the cony-catching literature of the period in England and France) printing is represented in the text itself as a force for social order and the detection of criminal fraud. The printed book can be widely disseminated and easily revised, so that the vagabonds' names and tricks may be known before they themselves arrive at an honest citizen's door; as if this mobility weren't quite tangible enough, Harman claims that when his pamphlet was only half-way printed, his printer helped him apprehend a particularly cunning 'counterfeit crank' – a pretended epileptic. In Harman's account the printer turns detective, first running down the street to apprehend the dissembler, then on a subsequent occasion luring him 'with fair allusions' (116) and a show of charity into the

[37]

hands of the constable. With such lurid tales Harman literalises the power of the book to hunt down vagabonds and bring them to justice.

The danger of such accounts, of course, is that the ethical charge will reverse itself: the forces of order – the people, as it were, of the book – will be revealed as themselves dependent on dissembling and betrayal, and the vagabonds either as less fortunate and well-protected imitators of their betters or, alternatively, as primitive rebels against the hypocrisy of a cruel society. Exactly such a reversal seems to occur again and again in the rogue literature of the period, from the doxies and morts who answer Harman's rebukes with unfailing if spare dignity to the more articulate defenders of vice elsewhere who insist that their lives are at worst imitations of the lives of the great:

> Though your experience in the world be not so great as mine [says a cunning cheater at dice], yet am I sure ye see that no man is able to live an honest man unless he have some privy way to help himself withal, more than the world is witness of. Think you the noblemen could do as they do, if in this hard world they should maintain so great a port only upon their rent? Think you the lawyers could be such purchasers if their pleas were short, and all their judgements, justice and conscience? Suppose ye that offices would be so dearly bought, and the buyers so soon enriched, if they counted not pillage an honest point of purchase? Could merchants, without lies, false making their wares, and selling them by a crooked light, to deceive the chapman in the thread or colour, grow so soon rich and to a baron's possessions, and make all their posterity gentlemen?[24]

Yet though these reversals are at the very heart of the rogue literature, it would be as much of a mistake to regard their final effect as subversion as it would be to regard in a similar light the comparable passages – most often articulated by Falstaff – in Shakespeare's histories. The subversive voices are produced by the affirmations of order, and they are powerfully registered, but they do not undermine that order. Indeed as the example of Harman – so much cruder than Shakespeare – suggests, the order is neither possible nor fully convincing without both the presence and perception of betrayal.

This dependence on betrayal does not prevent Harman from levelling charges of hypocrisy and deep dissembling at the rogues and from urging his readers to despise and prosecute them. On the contrary, Harman's moral indignation seems paradoxically heightened by his own implication in the deceitfulness that he condemns, as if the rhetorical violence of the condemnation cleansed him of any guilt. His broken promises are acts of civility, necessary strategies for securing social well-being. The 'rowsy, ragged rabblement of rakehells' has put itself outside the bounds of civil conversation; justice consists precisely in taking whatever measures are necessary to eradicate them. Harman's false oaths are the means of identifying and ridding the community of the purveyors of false oaths. The pestilent few will 'fret, fume, swear, and stare at this my book' in which their practices, disclosed after they had received fair promises of confidentiality, are laid open, but the majority will band together in righteous reproach: 'the honourable will abhor them, the worshipful will reject them, the yeomen will sharply taunt them, the husbandmen utterly defy them, the labouring men bluntly chide them, the women with clapping hands cry out at them' (84). To like reading about vagabonds is to hate them and to approve of their ruthless betrayal.

'The right people of the play', a gifted critic of 2 *Henry IV* observes, 'merge into a larger order; the wrong people resist or misuse that larger order'.[25] True enough, but like Harman's happy community of vagabond-haters, the 'larger order' of the Lancastrian State seems, in this play, to batten on the breaking of oaths. Shakespeare does not shrink from any of the felt nastiness implicit in this sorting out of the right people and the wrong people; he takes the discursive mode that he could have found in Harman and a hundred other texts and intensifies it, so that the founding of the modern State, like the founding of the modern prince, is shown to be based upon acts of calculation, intimidation, and deceit. And the demonstration of these acts is rendered an entertainment for which an audience, subject to just this State, will pay money and applaud.

There is, thoughout 2 *Henry IV* a sense of constriction that the obsessive enumeration of details – 'Thou didst swear to me upon a parcel-gilt goblet, sitting in my Dolphin chamber, at the round table by a sea-coal fire, upon Wednesday in Wheeson week. ...' – only intensifies. We may find, in Justice Shallow's garden, a few twilight moments of release from this oppressive circumstantial and strategic constriction, but Falstaff mercilessly deflates them – and the puncturing is so wonderfully adroit, so amusing, that we welcome it: 'I do remember him at Clement's Inn, like a man made after supper of a cheese-paring. When 'a was naked, he was for all the world like a forked radish, with a head fantastically carv'd upon it with a knife' (III.ii.308–12).

What is left is the law of nature: the strong eat the weak. Yet this is not quite what Shakespeare invites the audience to affirm through its applause. Like Harman, Shakespeare refuses to endorse so baldly cynical a conception of the social order; instead actions that should

Stephen Greenblatt

have the effect of radically undermining authority turn out to be the
props of that authority. In this play, even more cruelly than in *1
Henry IV*, moral values – justice, order, civility – are secured
paradoxically through the apparent generation of their subversive
contraries. Out of the squalid betrayals that preserve the State
emerges the 'formal majesty' into which Hal at the close, through a
final, definitive betrayal – the rejection of Falstaff – merges himself.

There are moments in *Richard II* in which the collapse of kingship
seems to be confirmed in the discovery of the physical body of the
ruler, the pathos of his creatural existence:

> ... throw away respect,
> Tradition, form, and ceremonious duty,
> For you have but mistook me all this while.
> I live with bread like you, feel want,
> Taste grief, need friends: subjected thus,
> How can you say to me I am a king? (III.ii.172–7)

By the close of *2 Henry IV* such physical limitations have been
absorbed into the ideological structure, and hence justification, of
kingship. It is precisely because Prince Hal lives with bread that we
can understand the sacrifice that he and, for that matter, his father,
have made. Unlike Richard II, Henry IV's articulation of this
sacrifice is rendered by Shakespeare not as a piece of histrionic
rhetoric but as a private meditation, the innermost thoughts of a
troubled, weary man:

> Why rather, sleep, liest thou in smoky cribs,
> Upon uneasy pallets stretching thee,
> And hush'd with buzzing night-flies to thy slumber,
> Than in the perfum'd chambers of the great,
> Under the canopies of costly state,
> And lull'd with sound of sweetest melody? (III.i.9–14)

Who knows? perhaps it is even true; perhaps in a society in which
the overwhelming majority of men and women had next to nothing,
the few who were rich and powerful did lie awake at night. But we
should understand that this sleeplessness was not a well-kept secret:
the sufferings of the great are one of the familiar themes in the
literature of the governing classes in the sixteenth century. Henry IV
speaks in soliloquy, but as is so often the case in Shakespeare his
isolation only intensifies the sense that he is addressing a large
audience: the audience of the theatre. We are invited to take measure
of his suffering, to understand – here and elsewhere in the play – the
costs of power. And we are invited to understand these costs in order
to ratify the power, to accept the grotesque and cruelly unequal

distribution of possessions: everything to the few, nothing to the many. The rulers earn, or at least pay for, their exalted position through suffering, and this suffering ennobles, if it does not exactly cleanse, the lies and betrayals upon which this position depends.

As so often Falstaff parodies this ideology, or rather – and more significantly – presents it as humbug *before* it makes its appearance as official truth. Called away from the tavern to the court, Falstaff turns to Doll and Mistress Quickly and proclaims sententiously: 'You see, my good wenches, how men of merit are sought after. The undeserver may sleep when the man of action is called on' (II.iv. 374–7). Seconds later this rhetoric – marked out as something with which to impress whores and innkeepers to whom one owes money one does not intend to pay – recurs in the speech, and by convention of the soliloquy, the innermost thoughts of the king.

At such moments 2 *Henry IV* seems to be testing and confirming an extremely dark and disturbing hypothesis about the nature of monarchical power in England: that its moral authority rests upon a hypocrisy so deep that the hypocrites themselves believe it. 'Then (happy) low, lie down! / Uneasy lies the head that wears a crown' (III.i.30–1): so the old pike tells the young dace. But the old pike actually seems to believe in his own speeches, just as he may believe that he never really sought the crown, 'But that necessity so bow'd the state / That I and greatness were compell'd to kiss' (III.i.72–3). We who have privileged knowledge of the network of State betrayals and privileged access to Falstaff's cynical wisdom can make this opaque hypocrisy transparent. And yet even in 2 *Henry IV*, where the lies and the self-serving sentiments are utterly inescapable, where the illegitimacy of legitimate authority is repeatedly demonstrated, where the whole State seems – to adapt More's phrase – a conspiracy of the great to enrich and protect their interests under the name of commonwealth, even here the audience does not leave the theatre in a rebellious mood. Once again, though in a still more iron-age spirit than at the close of 1 *Henry IV*, the play appears to ratify the established order, with the new-crowned Henry V merging his body into 'the great body of our state', with Falstaff despised and rejected, and with Lancaster – the cold-hearted betrayer of the rebels – left to admire his still more cold-hearted brother: 'I like this fair proceeding of the King's' (V.v.97).

The mood at the close remains, to be sure, an unpleasant one – the rejection of Falstaff has been one of the nagging 'problems' of Shakespearean criticism – but the discomfort only serves to verify Hal's claim that he has turned away his former self. If there is frustration at the harshness of the play's end, the frustration is confirmation of a carefully plotted official strategy whereby subversive perceptions are at once produced and contained:

> My father is gone wild into his grave;
> For in his tomb lie my affections,
> And with his spirits sadly I survive,
> To mock the expectation of the world,
> To frustrate prophecies, and to rase out
> Rotten opinion. ... (V.ii.123–8)

The first part of *Henry IV* enables us to feel at moments that we are like Harriot, surveying a complex new world, testing upon it dark thoughts without damaging the order that those thoughts would seem to threaten. The second part of *Henry IV* suggests that we are still more like the Indians, compelled to pay homage to a system of beliefs whose fraudulence somehow only confirms their power, authenticity, and truth. The concluding play in the series, *Henry V*, insists that we have all along been both coloniser and colonised, king and subject. The play deftly registers every nuance of royal hypocrisy, ruthlessness, and bad faith, but it does so in the context of a celebration, a collective panegyric to 'This star of England', the charismatic leader who purges the commonwealth of its incorrigibles and forges the martial national State.

By yoking together diverse peoples – represented in the play by the Welshman Fluellen, the Irishman Macmorris, and the Scotsman Jamy, who fight at Agincourt alongside the loyal Englishmen – Hal symbolically tames the last wild areas in the British Isles, areas that in the sixteenth century represented, far more powerfully than any New World people, the doomed outposts of a vanishing tribalism. He does so, obviously, by launching a war of conquest against the French, but his military campaign is itself depicted as carefully founded upon acts of what I have called 'explaining'. The play opens with a notoriously elaborate account of the king's genealogical claim to the French throne, and, as we found in the comparable instances in Harriot, this ideological justification of English policy is an unsettling mixture of 'impeccable' reasoning[26] (once its initial premises are accepted) and gross self-interest. The longer the Archbishop of Canterbury continues to spin out the public justifications for an invasion he has privately said would relieve financial pressure on the Church, the more the audience is driven toward scepticism. None of the subsequent attempts at explanation and justification offers much relief: Hal continually warns his victims that they are bringing pillage and rape upon themselves by resisting him, but from the head of an invading army these arguments lack a certain moral force.

Similarly, Hal's meditation on the sufferings of the great – 'What infinite heart's ease / Must kings neglect that private men enjoy!' – suffers a bit from the fact that he is almost single-handedly responsible for a war that by his own account and that of the enemy is causing immense civilian misery. And after watching a scene in which anxious, frightened troops sleeplessly await the dawn, it is difficult to be fully persuaded by Hal's climactic vision of the 'slave' and 'peasant' sleeping comfortably, little knowing 'What watch the King keeps to maintain the peace' (IV.i.283).

This apparent subversion of the glorification of the monarch has led some recent critics to view the panegyric as bitterly ironic or to argue, more plausibly, that Shakespeare's depiction of Henry V is radically ambiguous.[27] But in the light of Harriot's *Brief and True Report*, we may suggest that the subversive doubts the play continually awakens serve paradoxically to intensify the power of the king and his war, even while they cast shadows upon this power. The shadows are real enough, but they are deferred – deferred until after Essex's campaign in Ireland, after Elizabeth's reign, after the monarchy itself as a significant political institution. Deferred indeed even today, for in the wake of full-scale ironic readings and at a time in which it no longer seems to matter very much, it is not at all clear that *Henry V* can be successfully performed as subversive. For the play's enhancement of royal power is not only a matter of the deferral of doubt: the very doubts that Shakespeare raises serve not to rob the king of his charisma but to heighten it, precisely as they heighten the theatrical interest of the play; the doubt-less celebrations of royal power with which the period abounds have no theatrical force and have long since fallen into oblivion.

The audience's tension then enhances its attention; prodded by constant reminders of a gap between real and ideal, facts and values, the spectators are induced to make up the difference, to invest in the illusion of magnificence, to be dazzled by their own imaginary identification with the conqueror. The ideal king must be in large part the invention of the audience, the product of a will to conquer which is revealed to be identical to a need to submit. *Henry V* is remarkably self-conscious about this dependence upon the audience's powers of invention. The prologue's opening lines invoke a form of theatre radically unlike the one that is about to unfold: 'A kingdom for a stage, princes to act, / And monarchs to behold the swelling scene!' (3–4). In such a theatre-State there would be no social distinction between the king and the spectator, the performer and the audience; all would be royal, and the role of the performance would be to transform not an actor into a king but a king into a god:

'Then should the warlike Harry, like himself, / Assume the port of Mars' (5–6). This is in effect the fantasy acted out in royal masques, but Shakespeare is intensely aware that his theatre is not a courtly entertainment, that his actors are 'flat unraised spirits,' and that his spectators are hardly monarchs – 'gentles all', he calls them, with fine flattery. 'Let us', the prologue begs the audience, 'On your imaginary forces work . . . For 'tis your thoughts that now must deck our kings' (18, 28). This 'must' is cast in the form of an appeal and an apology – the consequence of the miserable limitations of 'this unworthy scaffold' – but the necessity extends, I suggest, beyond the stage: all kings are 'decked' out by the imaginary forces of the spectators, and a sense of the limitations of king or theatre only excites a more compelling exercise of those forces.

To understand Shakespeare's whole conception of Hal, from rakehell to monarch, we need in effect a poetics of Elizabethan power, and this in turn will prove inseparable, in crucial respects, from a poetics of the theatre. Testing, recording, and explaining are elements in this poetics that is inseparably bound up with the figure of Queen Elizabeth, a ruler without a standing army, without a highly developed bureaucracy, without an extensive police force, a ruler whose power is constituted in theatrical celebrations of royal glory and theatrical violence visited upon the enemies of that glory. Power that relies upon a massive police apparatus, a strong, middle-class nuclear family, an elaborate school system, power that dreams of a panopticon in which the most intimate secrets are open to the view of an invisible authority, such power will have as its appropriate aesthetic form the realist novel;[28] Elizabethan power, by contrast, depends upon its privileged visibility. As in a theatre, the audience must be powerfully engaged by this visible presence while at the same time held at a certain respectful distance from it. 'We princes', Elizabeth told a deputation of Lords and Common in 1586, 'are set on stages in the sight and view of all the world.'[29]

Royal power is manifested to its subjects as in a theatre, and the subjects are at once absorbed by the instructive, delightful, or terrible spectacles, and forbidden intervention or deep intimacy. The play of authority depends upon spectators – 'For 'tis your thoughts that now must deck our kings' – but the performance is made to seem entirely beyond the control of those whose 'imaginary forces' actually confer upon it its significance and force. These matters, Thomas More imagines the common people saying of one such spectacle, 'be king's games, as it were stage plays, and for the more part played upon scaffolds. In which poor men be but the lookers-on. And they that wise be will meddle no farther'.[30] Within this theatrical setting, there is a remarkable insistence upon the paradoxes, ambiguities, and tensions of authority, but this apparent production of subversion is, as we have already seen, the very condition of power. I should add that this condition is not a theoretical necessity of theatrical power in general but an historical phenomenon, the particular mode of this particular culture. 'In sixteenth century England', writes Clifford Geertz, comparing Elizabethan and Majapahit royal progresses, 'the political centre of society was the point at which the tension between the passions that power excited and the ideals it was supposed to serve was screwed to its highest pitch.... In fourteenth century Java, the centre was the point at which such tension disappeared in a blaze of cosmic symmetry.'[31]

It is precisely because of the English form of absolutist theatricality that Shakespeare's drama, written for a theatre subject to State censorship, can be so relentlessly subversive: the form itself, as a primary expression of Renaissance power, contains the radical doubts it continually provokes. There are moments in Shakespeare's career – *King Lear* is the greatest example – in which the process of containment is strained to the breaking point, but the histories consistently pull back from such extreme pressure. And we are free to locate and pay homage to the plays' doubts only because they no longer threaten us. There is subversion, no end of subversion, only not for us.

Notes

1 John Bakeless, *The Tragicall History of Christopher Marlowe*, 2 vols. (Cambridge, Mass.: Harvard University Press, 1942), I, 111.
2 On Harriot see especially *Thomas Harriot, Renaissance Scientist*, ed. John W. Shirley (Oxford University Press, 1974); also Muriel Rukeyser, *The Traces of Thomas Harriot* (New York: Random House, 1970), and Jean Jacquot, 'Thomas Harriot's Reputation for Impiety', *Notes and Records of the Royal Society*, 9 (1952), 164–87.
3 John Aubrey, *Brief Lives*, ed. Andrew Clark, 2 vols. (Oxford University Press, 1898), I, 286.
4 For the investigation of Ralegh, see *Willobie His Avisa* (1594), ed. G. B. Harrison (London: John Lane, 1926), appendix 3, pp. 255–71.
5 See, for example, *The Historie of Travell into Virginia Britania* (1612), ed. Louis B. Wright and Virginia Freund (London: Hakluyt Society, 2nd. ser., no. 103, 1953), p. 101.
6 Jacquot, 'Thomas Harriot's Reputation for Impiety', p. 167.
7 See for instance Richard Baines's version of Marlowe's version of this argument: C. F. Tucker Brooke, *The Life of Marlowe* (London: Methuen, 1930), appendix 9, p. 98.
8 Niccolò Machiavelli, *Discourses*, trans. Christian Detmold (New York: Random House, 1950), p. 146. See also *The Prince* in *Tutte le opere di Niccolò Machiavelli*, ed. Francesco Flora and Carlo Cordiè, 2 vols. (Rome: Arnoldo Mondadori, 1949), I, 18.

9 Kyd is quoted in Brooke, *Life of Marlowe*, appendix 12, p. 107; Parsons in Ernest A. Strathmann, *Sir Walter Ralegh* (New York: Columbia University Press, 1951), p. 25.

10 Quoted in Jean Jacquot, 'Ralegh's "Hellish Verses" and the "Tragicall Raigne of Selimus"', *Modern Language Review*, 48 (1953), 1.

11 Thomas Harriot, *A Briefe and True Report of the New Found Land of Virginia* (1588), in *The Roanoke Voyages, 1584–1590*, ed. David Beers Quinn, 2 vols. (London: Hakluyt Society, 2nd ser., no. 104, 1955), p. 375. (Quotations are modernised here.) On the Algonkians of southern New England see Bruce G. Trigger, ed., *Handbook of North American Indians*: vol. 15, *Northeast* (Washington, D.C.: Smithsonian, 1978).

12 Cf. Richard Hakluyt, *The Principal Navigations, Voyages, Traffiques, & Discoveries of the English Nation*, 12 vols. (Glasgow: James Maclehose, 1903–5), X, 54, 56.

13 On these catalogues, see Wayne Franklin, *Discoverers, Explorers, Settlers: the Diligent Writers of Early America* (University of Chicago Press, 1979), pp. 69–122.

14 Quoted by Edward Rosen, 'Harriot's Science: the Intellectual Background', in *Thomas Harriot*, ed. Shirley, p. 4.

15 Cf. Walter Bigges's account of Drake's visit to Florida in 1586, in *The Roanoke Voyages*, I, 306.

16 Guido Calabresi and Philip Bobbitt, *Tragic Choices* (New York: Norton, 1978), p. 195. The term *tragic* is, I think, misleading.

17 V.i.295–6. All citations of Shakespeare are to *The Riverside Shakespeare*, ed. G. Blakemore Evans (Boston: Houghton Mifflin, 1974).

18 John Upton, *Critical Observations on Shakespeare* (1748), in *Shakespeare: the Critical Heritage*, ed. Brian Vickers, vol. 3: *1733–1752* (London: Routledge, 1975), p. 297; Maynard Mack, introduction to Signet Classic edition of *1 Henry IV* (New York: New American Library, 1965), p. xxxv.

19 See S. P. Zitner, 'Anon, Anon: or, a Mirror for a Magistrate', *Shakespeare Quarterly*, 19 (1968), 63–70.

20 See V. N. Volosinov, *Freudianism: a Marxist Critique*, trans. I. R. Titunik, ed. Neal H. Bruss (New York: Academic Press, 1976), pp. 93–116; the book was written by Bakhtin and published under Volosinov's name.

21 See, for example, Victor Turner, *Drama, Fields, and Metaphors: Symbolic Action in Human Society* (Ithaca: Cornell University Press, 1974).

22 See Karen Ordahl Kupperman, *Settling with the Indians: the Meeting of English and Indian Cultures in America, 1580–1640* (Totawa, N.J.: Rowman and Littlefield, 1980).

23 Thomas Harman, *A Caveat of Warening, for Commen Cursetors Vulgarely Called Vagabones* (1566), in Gāmini Salgādo, ed., *Cony-Catchers and Bawdy Baskets* (Harmondsworth: Penguin, 1972), p. 146.

24 Gilbert Walker?, *A manifest detection of the moste vyle and detestable use of Diceplay* (c. 1552), in Salgādo, *Cony-Catchers*, pp. 42–3.

25 Norman N. Holland, in the Signet Classic edition of *2 Henry IV* (New York: New American Library, 1965). p. xxxvi.

26 So says J. H. Walter in the New Arden edition of *Henry V* (London: Methuen, 1954), p. xxv.

27 See the illuminating discussion in Norman Rabkin, *Shakespeare and the Problem of Meaning* (University of Chicago Press, 1981), pp. 33–62.

28 For a brilliant exploration of this hypothesis, see D. A. Miller, 'The Novel and the Police', *Glyph*, 8 (1981), 127–47.

29 Quoted in J. E. Neale, *Elizabeth I and her Parliaments, 1584–1601*, 2 vols. (London: Cape, 1965), II, 119.

30 *The History of King Richard III*, ed. R. S. Sylvester, in *The Complete Works of*

St Thomas More, vol. 3 (New Haven: Yale University Press, 1963), p. 80.
31 Clifford Geertz, 'Centers, Kings and Charisma: Reflections on the Symbolics of Power', in *Culture and its Creators: Essays in Honour of Edward Shils*, ed. Joseph Ben-David and Terry Nichols Clark (University of Chicago Press, 1977), p. 160.

Sections of this article orginally appeared in *Glyph* 8: *Johns Hopkins Textual Studies* (Baltimore: Johns Hopkins University Press, 1981), pp. 40–61.

'This thing of darkness I acknowledge mine': *The Tempest* and the discourse of colonialism

It has long been recognised that *The Tempest* bears traces of the contemporary British investment in colonial expansion. Attention has been drawn to Shakespeare's patronal relations with prominent members of the Virginia Company and to the circumstances of the play's initial production at the expansionist Jacobean court in 1611 and 1612–13. Borrowings from a traditional and classical stock of exotic stereotypes, ranging from the wild man, the savage and the masterless man to the tropology of the pastoral *locus amoenus* and the wilderness, have been noted. Semi-quotations from contemporary propagandist pamphlets and Montaigne's essay on cannibals have been painstakingly logged.[1] However, a sustained historical and theoretical analysis of the play's involvement in the colonialist project has yet to be undertaken.[2] This chapter seeks to demonstrate that *The Tempest* is not simply a reflection of colonialist practices but an intervention in an ambivalent and even contradictory discourse.[3] This intervention takes the form of a powerful and pleasurable narrative which seeks at once to harmonise disjunction, to transcend irreconcilable contradictions and to mystify the political conditions which demand colonialist discourse. Yet the narrative ultimately fails to deliver that containment and instead may be seen to foreground precisely those problems which it works to efface or overcome. The result is a radically ambivalent text which exemplifies not some *timeless* contradiction internal to the discourse by which it inexorably undermines or deconstructs its 'official' pronouncements, but a moment of *historical* crisis. This crisis is the struggle to produce a coherent discourse adequate to the complex requirements of British colonialism in its initial phase. Since accounts of the miraculous survival of members of the company of the Sea Adventure, wrecked off Bermuda in 1609, are said to have provided Shakespeare with an immediate source for his production, let an incident in the later life of one of those survivors serve as a ground for this analysis.

In 1614 John Rolfe, a Virginia planter, wrote a letter seeking the Governor's blessing for his proposed marriage with Pocahontas, abducted daughter of Powhatan, chief-of-chiefs. This remarkable document announces a victory for the colonialist project, confirming Rolfe in the position of coloniser and Pocahontas in the position of a savage other. The letter is an exposure of Rolfe's inner motives to public scrutiny, a production of his civilised 'self' as a text to be read by his superiors, that is, his Governor and his God. What lurks in Rolfe's 'secret bosome' is a desire for a savage female. He has had 'to strive with all my power of body and minde, in the undertaking of so mightie a matter, no way led (so farre forth as mans weaknesse may permit) with the unbridled desire of carnall affection: but for the good of this plantation, for the honour of our countrie, for the glory of God, for my own salvation, and for the converting to the true knowledge of God and Jesus Christ, an unbeleeving creature, namely Pokahuntas'.[4] As the syntax of the sentence indicates, the whole struggle, fought on the grounds of psychic order, social cohesion, national destiny, theological mission, redemption of the sinner and the conversion of the pagan, is conducted in relation to the female body. 'Carnall affection' would appear, despite Rolfe's disavowal, to have been a force which might disrupt commitments to conscience, Governor and God.

Pocahontas had posed a problem that was 'so intricate a laborinth, that I was even awearied to unwinde my selfe thereout'. Yet whether good or evil, Pocahontas cannot fail to operate as a sign of Rolfe's election, since if reformable, she is the space to be filled with the saintly seed of civility, if obdurately irreformable, she assures the godliness of him who is called to trial (the whole ethos of the godly community in the wilderness depended upon such proximity and exposure to evil). Rolfe's supposedly problematic letter may therefore be said to *produce* Pocahontas as an other in such a way that she will always affirm Rolfe's sense of godly duty and thus confirm him as a truly civil subject.

Inexorably, the text moves from the possible beleaguerments of carnality – variously constituted as the threat of the tempting wilderness, the charge that Rolfe's own interests in this matter are purely sexual, and the possible detraction of 'depravers and turbulent spirits' within the colony – towards a more positive presentation. Now the carnal affection which might fracture Rolfe's sense of duty becomes re-encoded as a vital part of God's commandments: 'why was I created? If not for transitory pleasures and worldly vanities, but to labour in the Lord's vineyard, there to sow and plant, to nourish and increase the fruites thereof, daily adding with the

Paul Brown

good husbandman in the Gospell, somewhat to the tallent, that in the end the fruites may be reaped, to the comfort of the laborer in this life, and his salvation in the world to come?' Given this imperative, mutual sexual desire, including the female's 'own inticements', can be admitted. Now it would be unmasterly not to desire her, as husbandman. The other incites the godly project: the godly project is embodied in the other. With the word thus made flesh and with Rolfe's self-acquittal in the court of conscience, all that remains to be achieved is the reorientation of those potential detractors into public witnesses of Rolfe's heroism, that 'all the world may truly say: this is the work of God, and it is marvelous in our eies'.

The threats of disruption to Rolfe's servitude to conscience, Governor and God have thus become the site of the affirmation of psychic, social and cosmic order. The encounter with the savage other serves to confirm the civil subject in that self-knowledge which ensures self-mastery. Of his thoughts and desires he can say: 'I know them all, and have not rashly overslipped any'. The letter, then, rehearses the power of the civil subject to maintain self-control and to bring the other into his service, even as it refers to a desire which might undermine that mastery.

After his initial calls for Rolfe to be denounced as a traitor, James I allowed the 'princess', newly christened 'Lady Rebecca', into court as visible evidence of the power of civility to transform the other. Pocahontas was to die in England a nine day's wonder; Rolfe returned to his tobacco plantation, to be killed in the great uprising of the Indians in 1622. The Pocahontas myth was only beginning, however.[5]

Even this partial analysis of one aspect of such myth-making serves to demonstrate the characteristic operations of the discourse of colonialism. This complex discourse can be seen to have operated in two main areas: they may be called 'masterlessness' and 'savagism'. Masterlessness analyses wandering or unfixed and un-supervised elements located in the internal margins of civil society (in the above example, Rolfe's subjective desire and potential detractors within the colony). Savagism probes and categorises alien cultures on the external margins of expanding civil power (in the same example, the Amerindian cultures of Virginia). At the same time as they serve to define the other, such discursive practices refer back to those conditions which constitute civility itself. Masterlessness reveals the mastered (submissive, observed, supervised, deferential) and masterful (powerful, observing, supervising, teleological) nature of civil society. Savagism (a-sociality and untrammelled libidinality) reveals the necessity of psychic and institutional order and direction in the civil regime. In practice these two concepts are intertwined and mutually reinforcing. Together they constitute a powerful discourse in which the non-civil is represented to the civil subject to produce for Rolfe a 'laborinth' out of which, like Theseus escaping from the Minotaur's lair, he is to 'unwinde' his 'selfe'.

That such an encounter of the civil and non-civil should be couched in terms of the promulgation/resistance of fulfilling/destructive sexual desire, as it is in Rolfe's case, deserves careful attention, as this strategy is common in colonialist discourse. Such tropes as that of the coloniser as husbandman making the land fruitful, or of the wilderness offering a dangerous libidinal attraction to the struggling saint, are ubiquitous. The discourse of sexuality in fact offers the crucial nexus for the various domains of colonialist discourse which I have schematised above. Rolfe's letter reorients potentially truant sexual desire within the confines of a duly ordered and supervised civil relationship. *The Tempest* represents a politicisation of what for Rolfe is experienced as primarily a crisis of his individual subjectivity. For example, the proof of Prospero's power to order and supervise his little colony is manifested in his capacity to control not *his*, but his *subjects'* sexuality, particularly that of his slave and his daughter. Rolfe's personal triumph of reason over passion or soul over body is repeated publicly as Prospero's triumphant ordering of potentially truant or subversive desires in his body politic. Similarly, Prospero's reintegration into the political world of Milan and Naples is represented, in Prospero's narrative, as an elaborate courtship, a series of strategic manoeuvres with political as well as 'loving' intentions and effects. This will be examined further in due course. For the moment I am simply seeking to show connection between a class discourse (masterlessness), a race discourse (savagism) and a courtly and politicised discourse on sexuality. This characteristically produces an encounter with the other involving the coloniser's attempts to dominate, restrict, and exploit the other even as that other offers allurements which might erode the order obtaining within the civil subject or the body politic. This encounter is truly a labyrinthine situation, offering the affirmation or *ravelling up* of the civil subject even as it raises the possibility of its undoing, its erosion, its *unravelling*.[6] A brief survey of British colonial operations will help us to establish a network of relations or discursive matrix *within and against which* an analysis of *The Tempest* becomes possible.

Geographically, the discourse operated upon the various domains of British world influence, which may be discerned roughly, in the terms of Immanuel Wallerstein, as the 'core', 'semiperiphery' and 'periphery'.[7] Colonialism therefore comprises the expansion of royal hegemony in the English-Welsh mainland (the internal colonialism of the core), the extension of British influence in the semiperiphery of Ireland, and the diffuse range of British interests in the extreme periphery of the New World. Each expansive thrust extended British power beyond existing spheres of influence into new margins. In the core, these areas included the North, Wales and other 'dark corners' such as woods, wastes and suburbs. In the semiperiphery, the Pale around Dublin was extended and other areas subdued and settled. In America, official and unofficial excursions were made into 'virgin' territory. I have given one example of the production of an American other; the production of core and Irish others will exemplify the enormous scope of contemporary colonialist discourse.

In his 'archaeology' of the wild man type, Hayden White discusses the threat to civil society posed by the very proximity of anti-social man: 'he is just out of sight, over the horizon, in the nearby forest, desert, mountains, or hills. He sleeps in crevices, under great trees, or in the caves of wild animals'.[8] Many of these characteristics are shared by the more socially specific production of the 'masterless man', the ungoverned and unsupervised man without the restraining resources of social organisation, an embodiment of directionless and indiscriminate desire. Masterless types were discerned in royal proclamations to exist in the very suburbs of the capital.[10] These and other texts produce a counter-culture within the margins of civility, living in disorder, requiring surveillance, classification, expulsion and punishment. A typical example is Richard Johnson's *Look Upon Me London* (1613) in which warnings against the city's many 'alectives to unthriftinesse' are given. To counter such traps for the ingenuous sons of the gentry, Johnson produces a taxonomy of bad houses, hierarchically arranged according to the social standing of their clientele, of which the worst are 'out of the common walkes of the magistrates'.[11] These are 'privy houses', privy in that they are hidden and secret and also in that they attract the dirt or excremental elements of the body politic. Such dirt is continually viewed as a dire threat to civil order in this literature. Johnson specifically warns that 'if the shifters in, and within the level of London, were truly mustered, I dare boldly say they would amaze a good army' (p. 20). The masterless are, here, produced as an other, that 'many-headed multitude' common in such writing.[12]

This other is a threat around which the governing classes might mobilise, that is, around which they might recognise their common class position, as governors, over and against the otherwise ungoverned and dangerous multitudes. In *The Tempest* Stephano the 'drunken butler' and the 'jester' Trinculo obviously represent such masterless men, whose alliance with the savage Caliban provides an antitype of order, issuing in a revolt requiring chastisement and ridicule. The assembled aristocrats in the play, and perhaps in the original courtly audiences, come to recognise in these figures their own common identity – and the necessity for a solidarity among the ruling class in face of such a threat. This solidarity must take priority over any internecine struggles; the masterless therefore function to bind the rulers together in hegemony. They were produced as a counter-order, sometimes classified according to rigid hierarchies of villainy in some demonic parody of good order,[13] sometimes viewed as a reserve army of potential recruits for rebellion (see Chapter 4 in the present volume), sometimes offered as a mere negative principle, the simple absence of the requirements of civility, attracting the sons of the gentry through its very spaciousness, irresponsibility and dirtiness.

Johnson's text produces a complex pleasure beyond the simple production of an instrumental knowledge of the masterless other. This knowledge is certainly offered for the services of magistracy and no doubt produces the antitype by which good order might be defined. Yet this moral and serviceable discourse displays in its descriptive richness precisely the intense and voyeuristic fascination for the other which it warns the gentry against. The text ostensibly avoids the taint of voyeurism by declaring that since this probing and exposing of dirt is required for the sober gaze of magistracy, a certain specular pleasure may be allowed. Again, at least officially, a potentially disruptive desire provoked by the 'alective' other of masterlessness is channelled into positive civil service. This encoding of pleasure within the production of useful knowledge for the advantage of civil power is specifically described by Francis Bacon in his essay 'Of Truth' as an erotic and courtly activity: the pursuit of knowledge is a 'love-making or wooing'.[14] Bacon implicitly offers an ideal of Renaissance sovereignty which can unite what Foucault terms 'power-knowledge-pleasure'.[15] Here pleasure is not simply disruptive, something produced by the other to deform or disturb the civil subject; it is a vital adjunct to power, a utilisation of the potentially disruptive to further the workings of power. In courtly fictions we can see this movement in operation: the other is incorporated into the service of sovereignty by reorienting *its* desires.

Such fictions include celebrations which centre upon the figure of the good sovereign. In these, the mere presence of the royal personage and the power of the royal gaze are able to transmute hitherto recalcitrant elements of the body politic, engendering in the place of disorderly passion a desire for service that is akin to an erotic courtship. In progresses, processions and masques such powers were continually complimented. In 1575, for example, at Kenilworth, Elizabeth I was confronted by an 'Hombre Salvagio'. In dangerous marginal space, beyond the confines of the great house, at the edge of the wild woods, at a most dangerous hour (nine o'clock in the evening), the Virgin Queen encountered the very emblem of marginality. But at this moment of maximum threat the wild man is metamorphosed into her eloquent and loving subject. He says:

> O queen, I must confesse it is not without cause
> These civile people so rejoice, that you should give them lawes.
> Since I, which live at large, a wilde and savage man,
> And have ronne out a wilfull race, since first my life began,
> Do here submit my selfe, beseeching yow to serve.[16]

The Hombre's entry into a loving relationship with Elizabeth is also his entry into interpersonal language (he has hitherto only spoken to his echo) and into subjection to a lawful sovereign: his very capacity to represent himself as 'I' is in the gift of the sovereign. She confers on him the status of a linguistic and a legal subject, he now operates in a courtly idiom and in the 'sentence' of the sovereign law.[17] Such taming of the wild man by a courtly virgin is a ubiquitous trope in medieval and Renaissance literature, as Richard Bernheimer has shown.[18] It serves as an emblem of courtly power, of the capacity to reorient masterlessness and savagism into service without recourse to the naked exercise of coercive power. This tropology is of great importance in the delineation of the Miranda–Caliban relationship, as I shall show later.

The discourse of masterlessness was embodied also in proclamations and statutes requiring that the bodies of vagrant classes, for example, should be modified.[19] Those condemned as persistent vagrants could literally be marked (whipped, bored, branded) with public signs announcing their adulteration, the hallmark of vice. Alternatively they could suffer the discipline of the work-house or the Bridewell. Yet no apparatus seemed sufficient to keep their numbers down. The constant vilification and punishment of those designated masterless by the ruling classes was not simply a strategy designed to legitimate civil rule: it also evidences a genuine anxiety. This took several forms: a real fear of the power of the governed classes should they mobilise against their betters; a complex displacement of the fear of aristocratic revolt on to the already vilified; a realisation that the increasing numbers of mobile classes evidenced a fundamental social change and a great threat to traditional modes of deference; and, finally, perhaps, a recognition of the restrictive nature of that deference society registered precisely in the continuous fascination for the disorderly other.

The thrust into Ireland from the 1530s sought to consolidate and expand British political control and economic exploitation of a strategic marginal area previously only partially under British authority.[20] D. B. Quinn has shown that the major policies of this expansion included plantation of British settlements in key areas, the establishment of a docile landed elite, the fossilisation of the social order in areas under British control, the conversion of Gaelic customs into their 'civil' counterparts and the introduction of English as the sole official language.[21] These policies were exercised partly through a vast discursive production of Ireland and the Irish. The virtuous and vicious potentialities that were attributed to Pocahontas predominate in such discourse. Ireland was therefore a savage land that might yet be made to flow with milk and honey like a new Canaan. Similarly the Irish were seen as both savage Gaels and lapsed civil subjects. This arose out of historic claims that the land was *both* a feudal fief under British lordship (then, under the Tudors, under direct British sovereignty), whose truant subjects needed reordering and pacification *and* also a colony, where the savage other needed to be civilised, conquered, dispossessed.[22] The discourse afforded a flexible ensemble to be mobilised in the service of the varying fortune of the British in their semiperiphery.

In this highly complex discourse an 'elementary ethnology' was formulated in which the various cultures of Ireland might be examined, and evidence gathered to show their inferiority to civility even as their potential for exploitation was assessed (Quinn, p. 20). As with the Negro or Amerindian, the Irish might be constituted as bestial or only marginally human and, as such, totally irreformable. For example, in 1594 Dawtrey drew upon a whole stock of commonplaces to give his opinion of the possibility of change in the Irish: 'an ape will be an ape though he were clad in cloth of gold' (quoted in Quinn, pp. 36–7). It should be noted that Stephano's and Trinculo's masterless aping of the aristocrats in IV.i, where they steal rich clothes off a line, bears the weight of this stereotypicality – and their subsequent punishment, being hunted with dogs, draws full attention to their bestiality.

Even if granted human status, Gaelic modes of social behaviour were viewed as the antithesis of civil codes. In Spenser's account of booleying (the seasonal migration of livestock and owners to summer pasture), this wandering and unsupervised operation enables its practioners to 'grow thereby the more barbarous and live more licentiously than they could in towns, ... for there they think themselves half exempted from law and obedience, and having once tasted freedom do, like a steer that hath long been out of his yoke, grudge and repine ever after to come under rule again.²³ Barbarity is opposed to the life of the town or *polis*, and the booleyers evade the law, conferring upon themselves the status of truants or outlaws – masterless men. Each social relegation marks the Irish off again as beast-like, requiring the management of the British husbandman.

Within this general delineation of masterless barbarity, particular classes of footloose Irish were specifically targeted, especially jesters (again notice how Trinculo is related to such exemplary antitypes), 'carrows' (or gamblers), wolvine 'kernes' (or foot soldiers) and bards. Such figures literally embodied the masterless/savage threat and their suppression became a symbolic statement of British intent for the whole of uncivil Ireland.

More positive versions of Ireland were also produced, particularly in those texts which advocated plantation of the English beyond the Pale. Such versions produce Irish culture, generally, along the lines of a 'negative formula', in which the alien is afforded no positive terms but merely displays the absence of those qualities that connote civility, for example, no law, no government, no marriage, no social hierarchy, no visible mode of production, no permanent settlement.²⁴ Again *The Tempest* is implicated in such a strategy. Gonzalo's description of his imagined island kingdom in II.i, culled from Montaigne, rehearses the standard formula by which the colonised is denigrated even as it appears to be simply the idle thoughts of a stranded courtier.

At its most optimistic the negative formula represents the other as a natural simplicity against which a jaded civility might be criticised, yet even here the other is produced for the use of civility, to gauge *its* present crisis. Nevertheless, the other's critical function must not be overlooked, as I hope to demonstrate with *The Tempest*. The more typical orientation of the other around the negative formula, however, is the production of a *tabula rasa*. Eden's translation of Peter Martyr's *Decades* (1555) provides a central statement of such a strategy. The Amerindians are 'Gentiles' who 'may well be likened to a smooth, bare table unpainted, or a white paper unwritten, upon the which you may at the first paint or write what you list, as you cannot upon tables already painted, unless you raze or blot out the first forms'.²⁵ Here the other is an empty space to be inscribed at will by the desire of the coloniser. In some accounts of Ireland the land and the bulk of its peasantry were this unpainted table. Yet contradictorily, for instance in the version of Sir John Davies, before it could be painted at will certain obdurate forms, tyrannical lords and customs had to be razed.[26]

So vacuous or vicious, docile or destructive, such stereotypical production announced the triumph of civility or declared the other's usefulness for its purposes. But a dark countertruth needed to be acknowledged. The inferior culture of the Gaels had absorbed the Old English invaders, as Davies noted with horror: 'The English, who hoped to make a perfect conquest of the Irish, were by them perfectly and absolutely conquered' (p. 290). The possibility of 'going native' was constantly evidenced in this example, which Davies likened to the vicious transformation of Nebudchadnezzar or the Circean swine (p. 297). The supposed *binary* division of civil and other into virtue/vice, positive/negative, etc, was shown to be erodable as the forces of the subordinate term of the opposition seeped back into the privileged term. The blank spaces of Ireland provided not only an opportunity for the expansion of civility; they were also sites for the possible undoing of civil man, offering a 'freedom' (Spenser's term for the avoidance of civility in the quotation above) in which he might lapse into masterlessness and savagism. The same discourse which allows for the transformation of the savage into the civil also raises the possibility of a reverse transformation. As Davies could announce a hope for the homogen-isation of the Irish into civility 'so that we may conceive an hope that the next generation will in tongue and heart and every way else become English' (Davies, p. 335), so Spenser could remark of civil man: 'Lord, how quickly doth that country alter men's natures' (p. 51).

Given the importance of the colonisation of Ireland for British expansionism, together with its complex discursive formation which I have outlined briefly, it is surprising that such scant attention has been paid to such material in relation to *The Tempest*. I am not suggesting that Irish colonial discourse should be ransacked to find possible sources for some of the play's phraseology. Rather (as Hulme and Barker suggest) we should note a general analogy between text and context; specifically, between Ireland and Prospero's island. They are both marginally situated in semiperiph-eral areas (Ireland is geographically semiperipheral, its subjects both truant civilians and savages, as Prospero's island is ambiguously placed between American and European discourse). Both places are described as 'uninhabited' (that is, connoting the absence of civility) and yet are peopled with a strange admixture of the savage and masterless other, powerfully controlling and malcontentedly lapsed civil subjects. Both locations are subject to powerful organising narratives which recount the beleaguerments, loss and recovery – the ravelling and unravelling – of colonising subjects. Such discourse provides the richest and the most fraught discussion of colonialism at the moment of the play's inception.

Much of my analysis above has been theoretically informed by Edward Said's account of orientalist discourse.[27] Orientalism is not simply a discourse which produces a certain knowledge of the East, rather it is a 'western style for dominating, restructuring and having authority over the Orient' (p. 3). Although it cannot be simply correlated with the process of *material* exploitation of the East, the discourse produces a form of knowledge which is of great utility in aiding this process – serving to define the West as its origin, serving to relegate alien cultures, serving even the voyeuristic and libidinal desire of the western man who is denied such expression elsewhere.

Homi K. Bhabha's recent account of the colonialist stereotype effects a critique of Said, suggesting that even in the stereotype there is something which prevents it from being *totally* useful for the coloniser.[28] Bhabha says the stereotype 'connotes rigidity and an unchanging order as well as disorder, degeneracy and demonic repetition' (p. 18). This is to say that at the heart of the stereotype, a discursive strategy designed to locate or 'fix' a colonial other in a position of inferiority to the coloniser, the potentiality of a disruptive threat must be admitted. For example, if a stereotype declares the black to be rapacious, then even as it marks him as inferior to the self-controlled white, it announces his power to violate, and thus requires the imposition of restraint if such power is to be curtailed: so the stereotype cannot rest, it is always impelled to *further* action.

To summarise, I have begun to suggest that colonialist discourse voices a demand both for order and disorder, producing a disruptive other in order to assert the superiority of the coloniser. Yet that production is itself evidence of a struggle to restrict the other's disruptiveness to that role. Colonialist discourse does not simply announce a triumph for civility, it must continually *produce* it, and this work involves struggle and risk. It is this complex relation between the intention to produce colonialist stereotypicality, its beleaguerements and even its possible erosion in the face of the other that I now wish to trace through *The Tempest*.

The play begins in an apparent disruption of that social deference and elemental harmony which characterise the representation of courtly authority in Renaissance dramaturgy. Yet this initial 'tempest' becomes retroactively a kind of antimasque or disorderly prelude to the assertion of that courtly authority which was supposedly in jeopardy. From Prospero's initial appearance it becomes clear that disruption was produced to create a series of problems precisely in order to effect their resolution. The dramatic conflict of the opening of the play is to be reordered to declare the mastery of Prospero in being able to initiate and control such dislocation and dispersal. This narrative intention is a correlate of the courtly masque proper, in which, conflict having been eradicated, elaborate and declarative compliment might be made to the supervising sovereign (as in the Hombre Salvagio episode, above). Prospero's problems concerning the maintenance of his power on the island are therefore also problems of representation, of his capacity to 'forge' the island in his own image. The production of narrative, in this play, is always related to questions of power.

In his powerful narrative, Prospero interpellates the various listeners – calls to them, as it were, and invites them to recognise themselves as subjects of his discourse, as beneficiaries of his civil largesse. Thus for Miranda he is a strong father who educates and protects her; for Ariel he is a rescuer and taskmaster; for Caliban he is a coloniser whose refused offer of civilisation forces him to strict discipline; for the shipwrecked he is a surrogate providence who corrects errant aristocrats and punishes plebeian revolt. Each of these subject positions confirms Prospero as master.

The second scene of the play is an extended demonstration of Prospero's powerful narration as it interpellates Miranda, Ariel and Caliban. It is recounted as something importantly rescued out of the 'dark backward and abysm of time' (I.ii.50), a remembrance of things past soon revealed as a mnemonic of power. This is to say, Prospero's narrative demands of its subjects that they should accede to *his* version of the past. For Miranda, Prospero's account of her origins is a tale of the neglect of office, leading to a fraternal usurpation and a banishment, followed by a miraculous landfall on the island. Prospero first tells of his loss of civil power and then of its renewal, in magic, upon the marginal space of the island. This reinvestiture in civil power through the medium of the non-civil is an essentially colonialist discourse. However, the narrative is fraught because it reveals internal contradictions which strain its ostensible project and because it produces the possibility of sites of resistance in the other precisely at the moment when it seeks to impose its captivating power.

In the recitation to Miranda, for example, Prospero is forced to remember his own past *forgetfulness*, since it was his devotion to private study that allowed his unsupervised brother, masterlessly, to seize power. He is forced to recall a division between liberal and stately arts which are ideally united in the princely magus of masquing fiction. However as the recitation continues, this essentially political disjunction becomes simply the pretext or initial disruption that is replaced by a mysterious account of the recovery of civil power, the reunification of the liberal artist and the politic sovereign. It is re-presented as a *felix culpa*, a fortunate fall, in which court intrigue becomes reinscribed in the terms of romance, via a shift from the language of courtiership to that of courtship, to a rhetoric of love and charity.

This is marked by a series of tropes deriving from courtly love conventions, as Kermode notes (p. 18). The deposed duke becomes a helpless exile who cries into the sea, which charitably responds, as does the wind, with pity (148–50). The deposition becomes a 'loving wrong' (151) – again the very form of oxymoron is typical of Petrarchan love sonnetry. These romance tropes effect a transition from a discourse of power to one of powerlessness. This mystifies the origin of what is after all a colonialist regime on the island by producing it as the result of charitable acts (by the sea, the wind and the honest courtier, Gonzalo, alike) made out of pity for powerless exiles. Recent important work on pastoral and amatory sonnet sequences has shown how such a rhetoric of love, charity and romance is always already involved in the mediation of power relations.[29] Prospero's mystifying narrative here has precisely these effects. Further, his scheme for the resumption of his dukedom and his reintegration with the larger political world is also inscribed in such terms, as a courtship of 'bountiful Fortune', his 'dear lady', or of an auspicious star which 'If now I court her not, but omit, my fortunes / Will ever after droop' (see 179–84). And, of course, a major strategy of this scheme is to engineer another courtship, between Miranda and the son of his old enemy – his daughter having been duly educated for such a role in the enclosed and enchanted space of the island. The entire production of the island here, ostensibly an escape or exile from the world of statism, is thoroughly instrumental, even if predicated upon an initial loss of power.

In the same scene Prospero reminds Ariel of his indebtedness to the master, an act of memory which it is necessary to repeat monthly (261–3). This constant reminding operates as a mode of 'symbolic violence':[30] What is really at issue is the underlining of a power relation. Ariel is, paradoxically, *bound* in service by this constant reminder of Prospero's gift of *freedom* to him, in releasing him from imprisonment in a tree. That bondage is reinforced by both a promise to repeat the act of release when a period of servitude has expired and a promise to repeat the act of incarceration should service not be forthcoming. In order to do this, Prospero utilises the previous regime of Sycorax as an evil other. Her black, female magic ostensibly contrasts with that of Prospero in that it is remembered as viciously coercive, yet beneath the apparent voluntarism of the white, male regime lies the threat of precisely this coercion. This tends to produce an identification between the regimes, which is underscored by biographical similarities such as that both rulers are magicians, both have been exiled because of their practices, both have nurtured children on the isle. The most apparent distinction between black and white regimes[31] would seem to be that the latter is simply more powerful and more flexible. Part of its flexibility is its capacity to produce and utilise an other in order to obtain the consent of Ariel to his continued subjugation.

Caliban, on the other hand, is nakedly enslaved to the master. The narrative of I.ii legitimises this exercise of power by representing Caliban's resistance to colonisation as the obdurate and irresponsible refusal of a simple educative project. This other, the offspring of a witch and a devil, the wild man and savage, the emblem of morphological ambivalence (see Hulme, 'Hurricans in the Caribbees,' p. 67ff), was even without language before the arrival of the exiles. It was Miranda, the civil virgin, who, out of pity, taught Caliban to 'know thine own meaning' (358). Yet, as with the Hombre Salvagio above, the 'gift' of language also inscribes a power relation as the other is hailed and recognises himself as a linguistic subject of the master language. Caliban's refusal marks him as obdurate yet he must voice this in a curse in the language of civility, representing himself as a subject of what he so accurately describes as '*your* language' (367, my stress). Whatever Caliban does with this gift announces his capture by it.

Yet within the parameters of this capture Caliban is able to create a resistance. Ostensibly *produced* as an other to provide the pretext for the exercise of naked power, he is also a *producer*, provoking reaction in the master. He does not come when called, which makes Prospero angry (315–22). Then he greets the colonisers with a curse, provoking the master to curse in reply, reducing the eloquent master of civil language to the raucous registers of the other (323–32). Third, he ignores the civil curse and proceeds with his own narrative, in which Prospero himself is designated as usurping other to Caliban's initial monarchy and hospitality (333–46). Such discursive strategies show that Caliban has indeed mastered enough of the lessons of civility to ensure that its interpellation of him as simply savage, 'a born devil, on whose nature / Nurture can never stick' (IV.i.188–9), is inadequate. Paradoxically, it is the eloquent power of civility which allows him to know his *own* meaning, offering him a site of resistance even as civility's coercive capacities finally reduce him to silence (373–5).

The island itself is an 'uninhabited' spot, a *tabula rasa* peopled fortuitously by the shipwrecked. Two children, Miranda and Caliban, have been nurtured upon it. Prospero's narrative operates to produce in them the binary division of the other, into the malleable and the irreformable, that I have shown to be a major strategy of colonialist discourse. There is Miranda, miraculous courtly lady, virgin prospect (cf. Virginia itself) and there is Caliban, scrambled 'cannibal', savage incarnate. Presiding over them is the cabalist Prospero, whose function it is to divide and demarcate these potentialities, arrogating to the male all that is debased and rapacious, to the female all that is cultured and needs protection.

Such a division of the 'children' is validated in Prospero's narrative by the memory of Caliban's attempted rape of Miranda (I.ii.347–53), which immediately follows Caliban's own account of his boundless hospitality to the exiles on their arrival (333–46). The issue here is not whether Caliban is actually a rapist or not, since Caliban accepts the charge. I am rather concerned with the political effects of this charge at this moment in the play. The first effect is to circumvent Caliban's version of events by reencoding his boundlessness as rapacity: his inability to discern a concept of private, bounded property concerning his own dominions is reinterpreted as a desire to violate the chaste virgin, who epitomises courtly property. Second, the capacity to divide and order is shown to be the prerogative of the courtly ruler alone. Third, the memory legitimises Prospero's takeover of power.

Such a sexual division of the other into rapist and virgin is common in colonialist discourse. In *The Faerie Queene*, for example, Ireland is presented as both Irene, a courtly virgin, and Grantorto, a rapacious woodkerne from whom the virgin requires protection, thus validating the intervention of the British knight, Artegall, and his killing machine, Talus.[32] Similarly, in Purchas's *Virginia's Verger* of 1625 the uprising of 1622 is shown to be an act of incestuous rape by native sons upon a virgin land, and this declares the rightfulness of the betrothal of that land to duly respectful civil husbandmen, engaged in 'presenting her as a chaste virgin to Christ' (see Porter, *The Inconstant Savage*, p. 480). Miranda is represented as just such a virgin, to be protected from the rapist native and presented to a civil lover, Ferdinand. The 'fatherly' power of the coloniser, and his capacity to regulate and utilise the sexuality of his subject 'children', is therefore a potent trope as activated in the *The Tempest* and again demonstrates the crucial nexus of civil power and sexuality in colonial discourse. The other is here presented to legitimate the seizure of power by civility and to define by antithesis (rape) the proper course of civil courtship – a channelling of desire into a series of formal tasks and manoeuvres and, finally, into courtly marriage. Such a virtuous consummation is predicated upon the disruptive potential of carnality, embodied in the rapist other and in the potentially truant desires of the courtly lovers themselves, which Prospero constantly warns them against (as at IV.i.15–23 and 51–4). With little evidence of such truancy, Prospero's repeated warnings reassert his power to regulate sexuality just at the point when such regulatory power is being transferred from father to husband. Yet his continued insistence on the power of desire to disrupt courtly form surely also evidences an unease, an anxiety, about the power of civility to deliver control over a force which it locates both in the other and in the civil subject.

A capacity to divide and demarcate groups of subjects along class lines is also demonstrated. The shipwrecked courtiers are dispersed on the island into two groups, aristocrats and plebians. The usurping 'men of sin' in the courtly group are first maddened, then recuperated; the drunken servants, unmastered, are simply punished and held up to ridicule. This division of masterless behaviour serves a complex hegemonic function: the unselfmastered aristocrats are reabsorbed, after correction, into the governing class, their new solidarity underscored by their collective laughter at the chastened revolting plebians. The class joke acts as a recuperative and defusive strategy which celebrates the renewal of courtly hegemony and displaces its breakdown on to the ludicrous revolt of the masterless.

Such binarism is also apparent in productions such as Ben Jonson's *Irish Masque at Court* (first put on in December, 1613).[33] Here indecorous stage-Irish plebeians are banished from the royal presence, to be replaced with the courtly exemplars of newly-converted Anglo-Irish civility. In this James I's coercive power is celebrated as music. Now Ireland has stooped to 'the music of his peace, / She need not with the spheres change harmony'. This harmonics of power causes the Irish aristocrats to slough off their former dress and customs to emerge as English court butterflies; the ant-like rabble are precluded from such a metamorphosis.

This last example demonstrates another strategy by which sovereign power might at once be praised and effaced *as power* in colonialist discourse. In this masque, power is represented as an *aesthetic* ordering. This correlates with Prospero's investment in the power of narrative to maintain social control and with *The Tempest*'s production of the origins of colonialism through the rhetoric of romance, its representation of colonial power as a gift of freedom or of education, its demonstration of colonialist organisation as a 'family romance' involving the management and reordering of disruptive desire. The play's observation of the classical unities (of space, time and action), its use of harmonious music to lead, enchant, relax, restore, its constant reference to the leisured space of pastoral[34] and the dream, all underline this aesthetic and disinterested, harmonious and non-exploitative representation of power. In a sermon of Richard Crashaw (1610), the latent mechanisms of power which actually promote the metamorphosis of jaded civil subjects is acknowledged: the transplanted, if 'subject to some pinching miseries and to a strict form of government and severe discipline, do often become new men, even as it were cast in a new mould' (quoted in Porter, pp. 369–70). *The Tempest* is, therefore, fully implicated in the process of 'euphemisation', the effacement of power – yet, as I have begun to demonstrate, the play also reveals precisely 'the strict form of government' which actually underpins the miraculous narrative of 'sea change'. The play oscillates uneasily between mystification and revelation and this is crucially demonstrated in the presentation of the plebeian revolt.

The process of euphemisation depends upon the rebellious misalliance of Caliban and Stephano and Trinculo being recognised as a kind of antimasque, yet there are features of this representation which disrupt such a recognition. Ostensibly the 'low' scenes of the play ape courtly actions and demonstrate the latter's superiority. The initial encounter of the masterless and the savage, for example, is analogous to the encounter between the civil and the savage narrated by Prospero, and to the encounter of the New World virgin and the gallant courtier enacted before the audience. Caliban's hospitality to Prospero is repeated as an act of voluntary subjection to the actually powerless exile, Stephano. This act is a bathetic version of the idealised meeting of civil and savage epitomised in the Hombre Salvagio episode – Caliban misrecognises *true* sovereignty and gives his fealty rather to a drunken servant. Unlike the immediate recognition of a common courtly bond which Miranda and Ferdinand experience, the savage and the masterless reveal a spontaneous *non-civil* affinity. More locally, as the courtly exiles brought Caliban the gift of language, so the masterless donate 'that which will give language to you, cat' – a bottle (II.ii.84–5); the former imposes linguistic capture and restraint, the latter offers release.

Yet the issue is more complex, for what this misalliance mediates, in 'low' terms, is precisely a colonising situation. Only here can the colonising process be viewed as nakedly avaricious, profiteering, perhaps even pointless (the expense of effort to no end rather than a proper teleological civil investment). Stephano, for example, contemplates taming and exhibiting Caliban for gain (II.ii.78–80). Also, the masterless do not lead but are led around by the savage, who must constantly remind them of their rebellious plans (see IV.i.231–2). This low version of colonialism serves to displace possibly damaging charges which might be levied against properly-constituted civil authority on to the already excremental products of civility, the masterless. This allows those charges to be announced and defused, transforming a possible anxiety into pleasure at the ludicrous antics of the low who will, after all, be punished in due course.

This analysis still produces the other as being in the (complex) service of civility, even if the last paragraph suggests that a possible anxiety is being displaced. Yet there is a manifest contradiction in the representation of the misalliance which I have not considered so far: in denigrating the masterless, such scenes foreground more positive qualities in the savage. The banter of the drunkards serves to counterpoint moments of great eloquence in the obdurate slave. Amid all the comic business, Caliban describes the effects of the island music:

> the isle is full of noises,
> Sounds and sweet airs, that give delight, and hurt not.
> Sometimes a thousand twangling instruments
> Will hum about mine ears; and sometimes voices,
> That, if I then had wak'd after long sleep,
> Will make me sleep again: and then, in dreaming,
> The clouds methought would open, and show riches
> Ready to drop upon me: that, when I wak'd,
> I cried to dream again (III.ii.133–41)

Here the island is seen to operate not for the coloniser but for the colonised. Prospero utilises music to charm, punish and restore his various subjects, employing it like James I in a harmonics of power. For Caliban, music provokes a dream wish for the riches which in reality are denied him by colonising power. There seems to be a quality in the island beyond the requirements of the coloniser's powerful harmonics, a quality existing for itself, which the other may use to resist, if only in dream, the repressive reality which hails him as villain – both a feudalised bonded workhorse and evil incarnate.

This production of a site beyond colonial appropriation can only be represented through colonialist discourse, however, since

Paul Brown

Caliban's eloquence is after all 'your language', the language of the coloniser. Obviously the play itself, heavily invested in colonialist discourse, can only represent this moment of excess through that very discourse: and so the discourse itself may be said to produce this site of resistance. Yet what precisely is at stake here?

The answer I believe is scandalously simple. Caliban's dream is not the *antithesis* but the *apotheosis* of colonialist discourse. If this discourse seeks to efface its own power, then here at last is an eloquent spokesman who is powerless; here such eloquence represents not a desire to control and rule but a fervent wish for release, a desire to escape reality and return to dream. Caliban's production of the island as a pastoral space, separated from the world of power, takes *literally* what the discourse in the hands of a Prospero can only mean *metaphorically*. This is to say, the colonialist project's investment in the processes of euphemisation of what are really powerful relations here has produced a utopian moment where powerlessness represents *a desire for powerlessness*. This is the danger that any metaphorical system faces, that vehicle may be taken for tenor and used against the ostensible meanings intended. The play registers, if only momentarily, a radical ambivalence at the heart of colonialist discourse, revealing that it is a site of *struggle* over meaning.

Prospero's narrative can be seen, then, to operate as a reality principle, ordering and correcting the inhabitants of the island, subordinating their discourse to his own. A more potent metaphor, however, might be the concept of dreamwork[35] – that labour undertaken to represent seamlessly and palatably what in reality is a contest between a censorship and a latent drive. The masterful operations of censorship are apparent everywhere in *The Tempest*. In the terminology of the analysis of dreamwork developed by Freud, these political operations may be discerned as displacement (for example, the displacement of the fear of noble insurrection on to the easily defeated misalliance), condensation (the condensation of the whole colonial project into the terms of a patriarchal demarcation of sexuality), symbolisation (the emblems of the vanishing banquet, the marriage masque, the discovery of the lovers at chess) and secondary revision (the ravelling up of the narrative dispersal of the storm scene, the imposition of Prospero's memory over that of his subjects, etc.). As I have attempted to show above with specific examples, such operations encode struggle and contradiction even as they, or *because* they, strive to insist on the legitimacy of colonialist narrative.

Further, as this narrative progresses, its master appears more and more to divest himself of the very power he has so relentlessly sought.

As Fiedler brilliantly notes, in the courtship game in which Miranda is a pawn, even as Prospero's gameplan succeeds he himself is played out, left without a move as power over his daughter slips away (Fiedler, *The Stranger in Shakespeare*, p. 206). So the magus abjures his magic, his major source of coercive power (V.i.33–57). This is ostensibly replaced by civil power as Prospero resorts to his 'hat and rapier', twin markers of the governor (the undoffed hat signifying a high status in a deference society, as the rapier signifies the aristocratic right to carry such weaponry). Yet this resumption of power entails the relinquishing of revenge upon the usurpers, an end to the exploitation and punishment of the masterless and the savage, even an exile from the island. Further, he goes home not to resume public duty but to retire and think of death (see V.i.310–11). The completion of the colonialist project signals the banishment of its supreme exponent even as his triumph is declared.

Is this final distancing of the master from his narrative an unravelling of his project? Or is this displacement merely the final example of that courtly euphemisation of power outlined above? One last example must serve to demonstrate that the 'ending' of the play is in fact a struggle between the apotheosis and the aporia of colonialist discourse. The marriage masque of IV.i demonstrates Prospero's capacity to order native spirits to perform a courtly narrative of his own design. In addition, this production is consented to by the audience of the two courtly lovers, whose pleasure itself shows that they are bound by the narrative. As such, the masque is a model of ideological interpellation, securing chastity, a state which the master continually *demands* of the lovers, through active consent rather than coercive power. Further, Prospero's instructions to his audience before the masque begins implicitly rehearse his ideal subject-audience: 'No tongue! All eyes! be silent' (IV.i.59). Yet the masque is disrupted, as Prospero is drawn back from this moment of the declaration of his triumph into the realm of struggle, for Caliban's plot must be dealt with. Although the plot is allowed for in his timetable (see IV.i.141–2) and is demonstrably ineffectual, this irruption of the antimasque into the masque proper has a totally disproportionate effect to its actual capacity to seize power. The masque is dispelled and Prospero utters a monologue upon the illusory nature of all representation, even of the world itself (IV.i.153–8). Hitherto he has insisted that his narrative be taken as real and powerful – now it is collapsed, along with everything else, into the 'stuff' of dreams. The forging of colonialist narrative is, momentarily, revealed as a forgery. Yet, Prospero goes on to meet the threat and triumph over it, thus completing his narrative. What is profoundly ambivalent here is the relation between narrative declaration and dramatic struggle. Prospero requires a struggle with the forces of the other in order to show his power: struggle is therefore the precondition for the announcement of his victory. Yet here the moment of declaration is disrupted as a further contest arises: Prospero must repeat the process of struggle. It is *he* who largely produces the ineffectual challenge as a dire threat. This is to say, the colonialist narrative requires and produces the other – an other which continually destabilises and disperses the narrative's moment of conviction. The threat must be present to validate colonialist discourse; yet if present it cannot but impel the narrative to further action. The process is interminable. Yet the play has to end.

Given this central ambivalence in the narrative, and given Prospero's problematic relationship to the restitution of civil power, it falls upon the honest old courtier, Gonzalo, actually to announce the closure of the narrative. He confirms that all is restored, includ-ing 'all of us ourselves / When no man was his own' (see V.i.206–13). True civil subjectivity is declared: the encounter with the forces of otherness on the island produces a signal victory. Yet the architect of that victory is to retire and die, his narrative a mere entertainment to while away the last night on the isle, his actor reduced in the epilogue to beg for the release of applause. When apportioning the plebeians to the masters, he assigns Caliban to himself, saying 'this thing of darkness I / Acknowledge mine' (V.i.275–6). Even as this powerfully designates the monster as his property, an object for his own utility, a darkness from which he may rescue self-knowledge, there is surely an ironic identification *with* the other here as both become interstitial. Only a displacement of the narrating function from the master to a simpler, declarative civilian courtier can hope to term-inate the endless struggle to relate self and other so as to serve the colonialist project. At the 'close' of the play, Prospero is in danger of becoming the other to the narrative declaration of his own project, which is precisely the ambivalent position Caliban occupies.

The Tempest, then, declares no all-embracing triumph for colonialism. Rather it serves as a limit text in which the characteristic operations of colonialist discourse may be discerned – as an instru-ment of exploitation, a register of beleaguerment and a site of radical ambivalence. These operations produce strategies and stereotypes which seek to impose and efface colonialist power; in this text they are also driven into contradiction and disruption. The play's 'ending' in renunciation and restoration is only the final ambivalence, being at once the apotheosis, mystification and potential erosion of the colonialist discourse. If this powerful discourse, thus mediated, is finally reduced to the stuff of dreams, then it is still dreamwork, the site of a struggle for meaning. My project has been to attempt a repunctuation of the play so that it may reveal its involvement in colonial practices, speak something of the ideological contradictions of its *political* unconscious.[36]

Notes

1 Such scholarship is summarised in Frank Kermode's Introduction to his edition of William Shakespeare, *The Tempest* (London: Methuen, 6th ed., corrected, 1964), *passim*. All quotations of the play are taken from this edition.

2 Some of the major incursions into this field are to be found in the notes below. At a late stage in the production of this paper I learnt of Peter Hulme's and Francis Barker's collaboration on an analysis of *The Tempest* in the forthcoming *Alternative Shakespeares*, ed. John Drakakis (London: Methuen, 1985). I was very pleased to see a draft of this important intervention which, unfortunately, I have not space to comment fully upon here. However, I hope I have begun to answer their call for a historical 'con-textual' analysis of the play.

3 By 'discourse' I refer to a domain or field of linguistic strategies operating within particular areas of social practice to effect knowledge and pleasure, being produced by and reproducing or reworking power relations between classes, genders and cultures.

4 The text is reproduced in Warren M. Billings, ed., *The Old Dominion in the Seventeenth Century: a Documentary History of Virginia* (Chapel Hill: University of North Carolina Press, 1975), pp. 216–19.

5 See Grace Steele Woodward, *Pocahontas* (Norman: University of Oklahoma Press, 1969), especially pp. 153–89.

6 Actually 'ravelling' is a radically ambivalent term, meaning both to entangle and disentangle. It has peculiar descriptive relevance for my analysis of *The Tempest*.

7 See Immanuel Wallerstein, *The Modern World System: vol. I* (New York: Academic Press, 1974), ch. 2, *passim*.

8 Hayden White, 'The Forms of Wildness: Archaeology of an Idea', in Edward Dudley and Maximillian Novak, eds., *The Wild Man Within: an image in Western Thought from the Renaissance to Romanticism* (Pittsburgh University Press, 1972), pp. 20–1.

9 On the masterless classes see particularly Christopher Hill, *The World Turned Upside Down* (1972; rpt. Harmondsworth: Penguin, 1975), ch. 3, *passim*.

10 See Paul L. Hughes and James F. Larkin, ed., *Tudor Royal Proclamations* (New Haven: Yale University Press, 1969), vol. II, no. 622 and vol. III, nos. 762 and 809, for examples.

11 Richard Johnson, 'Look Upon Me London ...' in J. Payne Collier, ed., *Illustrations of Early English Popular Literature* (1863; rpt. New York: Benjamin Blom, 1966), part 7, p. 19. Jonathan Dollimore, above p. 76, quotes a remarkably similar phrase in George Whetstone's *Mirror for Magistrates*, which is undoubtedly the most important immediate source for Johnson's plagiarism and serves to underline the chronic ubiquity of such a trope.

12 See Christopher Hill, 'The Many-Headed Monster in late Tudor and Early Stuart Political Thinking', in Charles H. Carter, ed., *From the Renaissance to the Counter-Reformation* (New York: Random House, 1965), pp. 296–324.

13 See for example the collection of A. V. Judges, ed., *The Elizabethan Underworld* (1930; rpt. London: Routledge, 1965).

Paul Brown

14 In Francis Bacon, *Essays (1625)*, ed. Michael Hawkins (London: Dent, 1973), p. 4.

15 See the theorisation of power–knowledge–pleasure in Michel Foucault, *The History of Sexuality: vol. I: An Introduction*, trans. Robert Hurley (Harmondsworth: Penguin, 1981), *passim*.

16 In John Nichols, ed., *The Progresses and Public Processions of Queen Elizabeth* (1823; rpt. New York: Burt Franklin, 1966), vol. I, pp. 436–8.

17 On the assimilation of the language of the other for the service of colonialism see Stephen J. Greenblatt, 'Learning to Curse: Aspects of Linguistic Colonialism in the Sixteenth Century,' in Fredi Chiapelli, ed., *First Images of America: The Impact of the New World on the Old* (Berkeley and Los Angeles: University of California Press, 1970), 561–80. This article and that of Peter Hulme, 'Hurricans in the Caribbees: the Constitution of the Discourse of English Colonialism', in Francis Barker *et al.*, eds., *Literature and Power in the Seventeenth Century: Proceedings of the Essex Conference on the Sociology of Literature, July 1980* (Colchester: University of Essex, 1981), pp. 55–83, offer important commentary on Caliban and civil language.

18 Richard Bernheimer, *Wild Men in the Middle Ages: a Study in Art, Sentiment and Demonology* (1952; rpt. New York: Octagon Press, 1970), pp. 136–55.

19 For a listing of the acts relating to vagrancy see Ken Powell and Chris Cook, *English Historical Facts: 1485–1603* (London: Macmillan, 1977), pp. 56–8.

20 For a short account of this bloody history see Grenfell Morton, *Elizabethan Ireland* (London: Longmans, 1971), *passim*.

21 See David Beers Quinn, *The Elizabethans and the Irish* (Ithaca: Cornell University Press, 1966), especially ch. 10; and Michael Hechter, *Internal Colonialism: the Celtic Fringe in British Colonial Development 1536–1966* (London: Routledge and Kegan Paul, 1975), especially part 2.

22 Hence the discourses regarding the Irish and the Amerindians were mutually reinforcing. See on this issue Nicholas P. Canny, 'The Ideology of English Colonization', *William and Mary Quarterly*, 30 (1973), 575–98. Throughout this section I am indebted to the work of Bernard W. Sheehan, *Savagism and Civility: Indians and Englishmen in Colonial Virginia* (Cambridge University Press, 1980), *passim*.

23 Edmund Spenser, *A View of the Present State of Ireland* (1596), ed. W. L. Renwick (Oxford: Clarendon Press, 1970), p. 50.

24 See Sheehan, ch. 1, *passim* and Margaret T. Hogden, *Early Anthropology in the Sixteenth and Seventeenth Centuries* (Philadelphia: University of Pennsylvania Press, 1964), *passim*.

25 Quoted in H. C. Porter, *The Inconstant Savage: Englishmen and the North American Indian* (Duckworth, 1979), p. 28.

26 Sir John Davies, 'A Discovery of the True Causes Why Ireland Was Never Subdued ... Until the Beginning of His Majesty's Happy Reign', in Henry Morley, ed., *Ireland Under Elizabeth and James I* (London: George Routledge, 1890), p. 341.

27 Edward W. Said, *Orientalism* (London: Routledge, 1978), p. 2.

28 Homi K. Bhabha, 'The Other Question', *Screen* 24 (1983), no. 6, pp. 18–36.

29 On the relation of courtship and courtiership see Peter Stallybrass and Ann Rosalind Jones, 'The Politics of *Astrophil and Stella*', *Studies in English Literature*, 24 (1984), 53–68. On the mediation and effacement of power relations in courtly discourse see Louis A. Montrose, '"Eliza, Queene of Shepheardes", and the Pastoral of Power', *English Literary Renaissance*, 10 (1980), 153–82. For a short account of courtly theatre see Stephen Orgel, *The Illusion of Power: Political Theatre in the English Renaissance* (Berkeley and Los Angeles: University of California Press, 1975), *passim*.

30 On this concept see Pierre Bourdieu, *Outline of a Theory of Practice*, trans. Richard Nice (Cambridge University Press, 1977), pp. 190–7.
31 As noted in Leslie A. Fiedler, *The Stranger in Shakespeare* (St Albans: Paladin, 1974), p. 64.
32 Edmund Spenser, *The Faerie Queene*, ed. T. P. Roche and C. P. O'Donnell (Harmondsworth: Penguin, 1978), book V, cantos xi–xii, *passim*.
33 Ben Jonson, *The Complete Masques*, ed. Stephen Orgel (New Haven: Yale University Press, 1968), p. 206–12.
34 For the use of pastoral in colonialist discourse see Howard Mumford Jones, *O Strange New World: American Culture: the Formative Years* (New York: Viking Press, 1964), pp. 185–93.
35 On dreamwork see Sigmund Freud, *Introductory Lectures in Psychoanalysis: The Pelican Freud Library Vol. I*, trans. James Strachey, ed. James Strachey and Angela Richards (Harmondsworth: Penguin, 1973), especially chs. 9–11. Stephen Greenblatt notes in his *Renaissance Self-Fashioning: From More to Shakespeare* (University of Chicago Press, 1980), p. 173, that it was Freud who first drew the analogy between the political operations of colonialism and the modes of psychic repression. My use of Feudian terms does not mean that I endorse its ahistorical, Europocentric and sexist models of psychical development. However, a materialist criticism deprived of such concepts as displacement and condensation would be seriously impoverished in its analysis of the complex operations of colonialist discourse and its addressing of subjects of its power. This paper attempts to utilise psychoanalytic concepts for a strictly historical analysis of a particular text, foregrounding the representation of the embattled subjectivity of the (white, governing, patriarchal) coloniser.
36 The term is that of Fredric Jameson in his *The Political Unconscious: Narrative as a Socially Symbolic Act* (London: Methuen, 1983), *passim*. This represents the most profound attempt to assimilate psychoanalytic concepts into a materialist account of narrative production.

I would like to record my deepest thanks to the editors and to Peter Stallybrass, Ann Jones, Andrew Crozier, Alan Fair, Eric Woods and especially Barry Taylor for their enormous help in the preparation of this paper. My main debt, as ever, is to Lesly Brown.

Transgression and surveillance in *Measure for Measure*

In the Vienna of *Measure for Measure* unrestrained sexuality is ostensibly subverting social order; anarchy threatens to engulf the State unless sexuality is subjected to renewed and severe regulation. Such at least is the claim of those in power. Surprisingly critics have generally taken them at their word even while dissociating themselves from the punitive zeal of Angelo. There are those who have found in the play only a near tragic conflict between anarchy and order, averted in the end it is true, but unconvincingly so. Others, of a liberal persuasion and with a definite preference for humane rather than authoritarian restraint, have found at least in the play's 'vision' if not precisely its ending an ethical sense near enough to their own. But both kinds of critic have apparently accepted that sexual transgression in *Measure for Measure* – and in the world – represents a real force of social disorder intrinsic to human nature and that the play at least is about how this force is – must be – restrained.

J. W. Lever, in an analysis of the play noted for its reasonableness,[1] draws a comparison with Shakespeare's romantic comedies where disorders in both society and individual, especially those caused by 'the excesses of sentiment and desire' are resolved: 'not only the problems of lovers, but psychic tensions and social usurpations or abuses, found their resolution through the exercise of reason, often in the form of an adjudication by the representatives of authority'. In *Measure for Measure* the same process occurs but more extremely: 'Not only are the tensions and discords wrought up to an extreme pitch, threatening the dissolution of all human values, but a corresponding and extraordinary emphasis is laid upon the role of true authority, whose intervention alone supplies the equipoise needed to counter the forces of negation'. Lever draws a further contrast with *Troilus and Cressida* where 'no supreme authority exists; age and wisdom can only warn, without stemming the inevitable tide of war and lechery'. On this view then unruly desire is extremely subversive and has to be countered by 'true' and 'supreme authority', 'age and wisdom', all of which qualities are possessed by the Duke in *Measure for Measure* and used by him to redeem the State (pp. lx and lxxi). Only these virtues, this man, can retrieve the State from anarchy.[2]

But consider now a very different view of the problem. With the considerable attention recently devoted to Bakhtin and his truly important analysis of the subversive carnivalesque, the time is right for a radical reading of *Measure for Measure*, one which insists on the oppressiveness of the Viennese State and which interprets low-life transgression as *positively* anarchic, ludic, carnivalesque – a subversion from below of a repressive official ideology of order. What follows aims (if it is not too late) to forestall such a reading as scarcely less inappropriate than that which privileged 'true' authority over anarchic desire. Indeed, such a reading, if executed within the parameters of some recent appropriations of Bakhtin, would simply remain within the same problematic, only reversing the polarities of the binary opposition which structures it (order/chaos). I offer a different reading of the play, one which, perhaps paradoxically, seeks to identify its absent characters and the history which it contains yet does not represent.

Transgression

Whatever subversive identity the sexual offenders in this play possess is a construction put upon them by the authority which wants to control them; moreover control is exercised through that construction. Diverse and only loosely associated sexual offenders are brought into renewed surveillance by the State; identified in law as a category of offender (the lecherous, the iniquitous) they are thereby demonised as a threat to law. Like many apparent threats to authority this one in fact legitimates it: control of the threat becomes the rationale of authoritarian reaction in a time of apparent crisis. Prostitution and lechery are identified as the causes of crisis yet we learn increasingly of a corruption more political than sexual (see especially v.i.316ff). Arguably then the play discloses corruption to be an effect less of desire than authority itself. It also shows how corruption is downwardly identified – that is, focused and placed with reference to low-life 'licence'; in effect, and especially in the figure of Angelo, corruption is displaced from authority *to* desire and by implication from the rulers to the ruled. The Duke tells Pompey:

> Fie, sirrah, a bawd, a wicked bawd;
> The evil that thou causest to be done,
> That is thy means to live. Do thou but think
> What 'tis to cram a maw or clothe a back
> From such a filthy vice. Say to thyself,
> From their abominable and beastly touches
> I drink, I eat, array myself, and live.
> Canst thou believe thy living is a life,
> So stinkingly depending? (III.ii.18–26)

This is in response to Pompey's observation that such exploitation not only exists at other levels of society but is actually protected 'by order of law' (l. 8). This is just what the Duke's diatribe ignores – cannot acknowledge – fixating instead on the 'filthy vice' and its agents in a way which occludes the fact that it is Angelo, not Pompey, who, unchecked, and in virtue of his social position, will cause most 'evil ... to be done'. But, because Angelo's transgression is represented as growing from his desire rather than his authority, his is a crime which can be construed as a lapse into the corruption of a lower humanity, a descent of the ruler into the sins of the ruled. Provocatively, his crime is obscurely theirs.

If we can indeed discern in the demonising of sexuality a re-legitimation of authority we should not then conclude that this is due simply to an ideological conspiracy; or rather it may indeed be conspiratorial but it is also ideological in another, more complex sense: through a process of displacement an imaginary – and punitive – resolution of real social tension and conflict is attempted.

The authoritarian demonising of deviant behaviour was common in the period, and displacement and condensation – to and around low life – were crucial to this process (see also Paul Brown's analysis on these lines in the previous chapter). But what made displacement and condensation possible was a prior construction of deviancy itself. So, for example, diatribes against promiscuity, female self-assertion, cross-dressing and homosexuality construed these behaviours as symptomatic of an impending dissolution of social hierarchy and so, in effect, of civilisation.[3] This was partly because transgression was conceived in public and even cosmic terms; it would not then have made sense to see it in, say, psychological or subjective terms – a maladjustment of the individual who, with professional assistance, could be 'normalised'. On the one hand then homosexuality was not considered to be the 'defect' of a particular personality type since 'the temptation to debauchery, from which homosexuality was not clearly distinguished, was accepted as part of the common lot, be it never so abhorred. For the Puritan writer John

Rainolds homosexuality was a sin to which "men's natural corruption and viciousness is prone."' And this was because homosexuality 'was not a sexuality in its own right, but existed as a potential for confusion and disorder in one undivided sexuality' (Alan Bray, *Homosexuality in Renaissance England*, pp. 16–17, 25). On the other hand it was distinguished sufficiently to be associated with other cardinal sins like religious and political heresy and witchcraft. This association of sexual deviance with religious and political deviance – made of course in relation to Marlowe by the informer Richard Baines[4] and rather more recently by the British tabloid press in relation to Peter Tatchell[5] – facilitates the move from specific to general subversion: the individual transgressive act sent reverberations throughout the whole and maybe even brought down God's vengeance on the whole.

Stuart Clark has shown how the disorder which witches and other deviants symbolised, even as it was represented as a threat to order, was also a presupposition of it. Contrariety, he argues, was 'a universal principle of intelligibility as well as a statement about how the world was actually constituted' and 'the characterisation of disorder by inversion, even in relatively minor texts or on ephemeral occasions, may therefore be taken to exemplify an entire metaphysic' ('Inversion, Misrule and Witchraft', pp. 110–12). On this view then the attack on deviancy was not just a diversionary strategy of authority in times of crisis but an elementary and permanent principle of rule. Nevertheless, we might expect that it is in times of crisis that this principle is specially operative. The work of Lawrence Stone would seem to confirm this. He argues that in the early seventeenth century the family household becomes, at least in contemporary propaganda, 'responsible for, and the symbol of, the whole social system, which was thought to be based on the God-given principle of hierarchy, deference and obedience'. Such propaganda was stimulated in part by the experienced instability of rapid change, change which was interpreted by some as impending collapse. (For Stone's summary of this see above, p. 5). According to Stone then, 'the authoritarian family and the authoritarian nation-state were the solutions to an intolerable sense of anxiety, and a deep yearning for order' and the corollary was a ruthless persecution of dissidents and deviants. Sexuality became subject to intensified surveillance working in terms of both an enforced and an internalised discipline.[6] *Measure for Measure*, I want to argue, is about both kinds of discipline, the enforced and the internalised. Their co-existence made for a complex social moment as well as a complex play.

J. A. Sharpe's recent and scrupulous study of crime in seventeenth-century England confirms this discrepancy between the official depiction of moral collapse among the lower orders and their actual behaviour. Sharpe also confirms that the suppression of sexuality was only 'one aspect of a wider desire to achieve a disciplined society. Fornication, like idleness, pilfering, swearing and drunkenness, was one of the distinguishing activites of the disorderly'. Further, the Elizabethan and early Stuart period marked an historical highpoint in an authoritarian preoccupation with the disorderly and their efficient prosecution.[7] Nevertheless, many of those concerned with this prosecution really did believe standards were declining and the social fabric disintegrating. Puritan extremists like Stubbes saw prostitution as so abhorrent they advocated the death penalty for offenders (Lever, p. xlvi). But if, as Stone and others argue, this fervour is the result of insecurity in the face of change, then, even if that fervour was 'sincere', the immorality which incited it was not at all its real cause. This is one sense in which the discourse of blame involved displacement; but there was another: while the authorities who actually suppressed the brothels often exploited the language of moral revulsion it was not the sexual vice that worried them so much as the meeting together of those who used the brothels. George Whetstone was only warning the authorities of what they already feared when he told them to beware of 'haunts ... in Allies, gardens and other obscure corners out of the common walks of the Magistrate' whose guests are 'masterless men, needy shifters, thieves, cutpurses, unthrifty servants, both serving men and prentices'.[8] Suppression was an attempt to regulate not the vice, nor, apparently, even the spread of venereal disease, but the criminal underworld.[9] Similarly, in *Measure for Measure*, the more we attend to the supposed subversiveness of sexual licence, and the authoritarian response to it, the more we are led away from the vice itself towards social tensions which intersect with it – led also to retrace several distinct but related processes of displacement.

The play addresses several social problems which had their counterparts in Jacobean London. Mistress Overdone declares: 'Thus, what with the war, what with the sweat, what with the gallows, and what with poverty, I am custom shrunk' (I.ii.75–7). Lever points out that this passage links several issues in the winter of 1603–4: 'the continuance of the war with Spain; the plague in London; the treason trials and executions at Winchester in connection with the plots of Raleigh and others; the slackness of trade in the deserted capital' (p. xxxii). Significantly, all but the first of these, the war, are domestic problems. But even the war was in prospect of becoming such: if peace negotiations then under way (and also alluded to in the play – at I.ii.1–17) proved successful it would lead to a return home of 'the multitude of pretended gallants, banck-routs, and unruly youths who weare at this time settled in pyracie' (Lever, p. xxxii). In this political climate even peace could exacerbate domestic ills.

This play's plague references are especially revealing. Both here and at I.ii.85–9, where Pompey refers to a proclamation that 'All houses in the suburbs of Vienna must be plucked down' there is a probable allusion to the proclamation of 1603 which provided for the demolition of property in the London suburbs in order to control the plague. But the same proclamation also refers to the 'excessive numbers of idle, indigent, dissolute and dangerous persons, and the pestering of many of them in small and strait room'.[10] Here, as with the suppression of prostitution, plague control legitimates other kinds of political control. (Enemies of the theatre often used the plague threat as a reason to have them closed). As this proclamation indicates, there was a constant fear among those in charge of Elizabethan and Jacobean England that disaffection might escalate into organised resistance. This anxiety surfaces repeatedly in official discourse: any circumstance, institution or occasion which might unite the vagabonds and masterless men – for example famine, the theatres, congregations of the un-employed – was the object of almost paranoid surveillance. Yet, if anything, *Measure for Measure* emphasises the lack of any coherent opposition among the subordinate and the marginalised. Thus Pompey, 'Servant to Mistress Overdone' (list of characters), once imprisoned and with the promise of remission, becomes, with no sense of betrayal, servant to the State in no less a capacity than that of hangman.

Yet those in power are sincerely convinced there is a threat to order. At the very outset of the play Escalus, described in the list of characters as an 'ancient' Lord, is praised excessively by the Duke only to be subordinated to Angelo, the new man. The traditional political 'art and practice' (I.i.12) of Escalus is not able to cope with the crisis. Later, the Duke, speaking to the Friar, acknowledges that this crisis stems from a failure on the part of the rulers yet at the same time displaces responsibility on to the ruled: like disobedient children they have taken advantage of their 'fond fathers' (I.iii.23). Hence the need for a counter-subversive attack on the 'liberty' of the low-life. Yet even as we witness that attack we see also that the possibilities for actual subversion seem to come from quite another quarter. Thus when Angelo resorts to the claim that the State is being subverted (in order to discredit charges of corruption against himself) the way he renders that claim plausible is most revealing:

> These poor informal women are no more
> But instruments of some more mightier member
> That sets them on. Let me have way, my lord,
> To find this practice out. (V.i.235–7)

Earlier the Duke, pretending ignorance of Angelo's guilt, publicly denounces Isabella's charge against Angelo in similar terms:

> thou knowest not what thou speak'st
> Or else thou art suborn'd against his honour
> In hateful practice ...
> ... Someone hath set you on. (V.i.108–10; 115)

The predisposition of Escalus to credit all this gives us an insight into how the scapegoat mentality works: just as the low-life have hitherto been demonised as the destructive element at the heart (or rather bottom) of the State, now it is the apparently alien Friar (he who is 'Not of this country', III.ii.211) who is to blame. The kind old Escalus charges the Friar (the Duke in disguise) with 'Slander to th'state!' and cannot wait to torture him into confession (V.i.320, 309–10). That he is in fact accusing the Duke ironically underpins the point at issue: disorder generated by misrule and unjust law (III.ii.6–8) is ideologically displaced on to the ruled – 'ideologically' because Angelo's lying displacement is insignificant compared with the way that Escalus really believes it is the subordinate and the outsider who are to blame. Yet even as he believes this he is prepared to torture his way to 'the more mightier member' behind the plot; again there is the implication, and certainly the fear, that the origin of the problem is not intrinsic to the low-life but a hostile fraction of the ruling order.

Oddly the slander for which Escalus wants to have this outsider tortured, and behind which he perceives an insurrectionary plot, is only the same assessment of the situation which he, Angelo and the Duke made together at the outset. What does this suggest: is his violent reaction to slander paranoid, or rather a strategy of *realpolitik*? Perhaps the latter – after all, it is not only, as Isabella reminds Angelo (II.ii.135–7) that rulers have the power to efface their own corruption, but that they need to do this to remain in power. And within the terms of *realpolitik* the threat of exposure is justification enough for authoritarian reaction. But the problem with the concept of *realpolitik* is that it tends to discount the non-rational though still effective dimensions of power which make it difficult to determine whether crisis is due to paranoia generating an imaginary threat or whether a real threat is intensifying paranoia. And, of course, even if the threat is imaginary this can still act as the 'real' cause of ensuing conflict. Conversely, terms like paranoia applied to a ruling class or fraction, while useful in suggesting the extent to which that class's discourse produces its own truth and apprehends that truth through blame, can also mislead with regard to the class's power to rationalise its own position and displace responsibility for disorder. Put another way, *realpolitik* and paranoia, in so far as they are present, should be seen to coexist more at a social rather than an individual level. An interesting case in point is George Whetstone's *A Mirror for Magistrates* (1584), a possible source for Shakespeare's play. This work related the story of how the Roman emperor, Alexander Severus, re-establishes order in the State by setting up a system of sophisticated surveillance and social regulation which includes himself going disguised among his subjects and observing their transgressions at first hand. These are denounced with moral fervour and the implication of course is that they are condemned just because they are sinful. But as Whetstone's retelling of the story develops we can see a pragmatic underside to his blameful discourse. In fact, as so often in this period, political strategy and moral imperative openly coexist. The focus of Whetstone's reforming zeal are the 'Dicing-houses, taverns and common stews' – 'sanctuaries of iniquity'. But what gives him most cause for concern is not the behaviour of the low but that of the landed gentry who are attracted to them: 'Dice, Drunkenness and Harlots, had consumed the wealth of a great number of ancient Gentlemen, whose Purses were in the possession of vile persons, and their Lands at mortgage with the Merchants ... The Gentlemen had made this exchange with vile persons: they were attired with the Gentlemen's bravery, and the Gentlemen disgraced with their beastly manners' (Izard, *George Whetstone*, p. 135).

Here, apparently, hierarchy is subverted from above and those most culpable the gentlemen themselves. Yet in Whetstone's account the low are to blame; they are held responsible for the laxity of the high, much as a man might (then as now) blame a woman for tempting him sexually whereas in fact he has coerced her. The gentlemen are 'mildly' reproached and restored to that which they have transacted away while the low are disciplined. Whetstone believed that the survival of England depended on its landed gentry; in rescuing them from the low-life he is rescuing the State from chaos and restoring it to its 'ancient and most laudable orders' (Izard, *George Whetstone*, p. 136). A reactionary programme is accomplished at the expense of the low, while those who benefit are those

responsible for precipitating 'decline' in the first place. The same
process of displacement occurs throughout discourses of power in
this period. One further example: one of the many royal proclamations attempting to bring vagabonds under martial law asserts that
'there can grow no account of disturbance of our peace and quiet but
from such refuse and vagabond people' (*Tudor Royal Proclamations*, III, 233) – and this despite the fact that the proclamation
immediately preceeding this one (just six days before) announced the
abortive Essex rebellion. The failure of the rebellion is interpreted by
the second proclamation as proof of the loyalty of all other subjects
with the exception of that 'great multitude of base and loose people'
who 'lie privily in corners and bad houses, listening after news and
stirs, and spreading rumours and tales, being of likelihood ready to
lay hold of any occasion to enter into any tumult or disorder'
(p. 232). For the authoritarian perspective as articulated here, the
unregulated are by definition the ungoverned and always thereby
potentially subversive of government. At the same time it is a
perspective which confirms what has been inferred from *Measure for
Measure*: in so far as the socially deprived were a threat to government this was only when they were mobilised by powerful elements
much higher up the social scale. Moreover the low who were likely to
be so mobilised were only a small part of the 'base and loose people'
hounded by authority. In fact we need to distinguish, as Christopher
Hill does, between this mob element, little influenced by religious or
political ideology but up for hire, and the 'rogues, vagabonds and
beggars' who, although they 'caused considerable panic in ruling
circles ... were incapable of concerted revolt' (*The World Turned
Upside Down*, pp. 40–1). Of course there were real social problems
and 'naturally' the deprived were at the centre of them. Moreover, if
we recall that there *were* riots, that fornication *did* produce charity
dependent bastards, that drunkenness *did* lead to fecklessness, it
becomes apparent that, in their own terms there were also real
grounds for anxiety on the part of those who administered depriva-
tion. At the same time we can read in that anxiety – in its very
surplus, its imaginative intensity, its punitive ingenuity – an ideological displacement (and hence misrecognition) of much deeper fears of
the uncontrollable, of being out of control, themselves corresponding to more fundamental social problems.[11]

Surveillance

In II.i. we glimpse briefly the State's difficulties in ensuring the levels
of policing which the rulers think is required. Escalus discreetly

inquires of Elbow whether there are any more officers in his locality more competent than he. Elbow replies that even those others who have been chosen happily delegate their responsibility to him.

A similar anxiety about the ungovernability of his subjects leads the Duke to put those of them he encounters under a much more sophisticated and effective mode of surveillance; though remaining coercive, it seeks additionally to get subjects to reposition themselves. First though, a word about the Duke's use of disguise. The genre of the disguised ruler generally presented him in a favourable light. But in Jacobean England we might expect there to have been an ambivalent attitude towards it. In Jonson's *Sejanus*, contemporary with *Measure for Measure*, it is a strategy of tyrannical repression; Jonson himself was subjected to it while in jail, apparently with the intention of getting him to incriminate himself.[12] Next there is the question of the Duke's choice of *religious* disguise. As I've argued elsewhere, there was considerable debate at this time over the 'Machiavellian' proposition that religion was a form of ideological control which worked in terms of internalised submission.[13] Even as he opposes it, Richard Hooker cogently summarises this view; it represents religion as 'a mere politic devise' and whereas State law has 'power over our outward actions only' religion works upon men's 'inward cogitations ... the privy intents and motions of their heart'. Armed with this knowledge 'politic devisers' are 'able to create God in man by art'.[14]

The Duke, disguised as a friar, tries to reinstate this kind of subjection. Barnardine is the least amenable; 'He wants advice', remarks the Duke grimly (IV.ii.144) and is infuriated when the offer is refused. Barnardine is especially recalcitrant in that he admits guilt yet is unrepentant and even disinclined to escape; he thus offers no response on which the Duke might work to return him to a position of dutiful submission. But the Duke does not give up and resolves to 'Persuade this rude wretch willingly to die' (IV.iii.80; cf. II.i.35). A similar idea seems to be behind his determination to send Pompey to prison – not just to rot but for 'Correction and instruction' (III.ii.31). Earlier the Duke had been rather more successful with Claudio. His long 'Be absolute for death' speech (III.i.5ff) does initially return Claudio to a state of spiritual renunciation, but Claudio has not long been in conversation with Isabella before he desires to live again. Isabella, herself positioned in a state of intended renunciation, struggles to restore Claudio to his. She fails but the Duke intervenes again and Claudio capitulates.

The Duke makes of Mariana a model of dutiful subjection. Predictably, he is most successful with those who are least powerful and so most socially dependent. He tells Angelo to love Mariana, adding: 'I have confess'd her, and I know her virtue' (V.i.524). He has indeed, and earlier Mariana confirms his success in this confessional positioning of her as an acquiescent, even abject subject (IV.1.8–20); for her he is one 'whose advice / Hath often still'd my brawling discontent' (IV.i.8–9). His exploitation of her – 'The maid will I frame, and make fit for his attempt' (III.i.256–7) – is of course just what she as confessed subject must not know, and the Duke confirms that she does not by eliciting from her a testimony:

> *Duke*: Do you persuade yourself that I respect you?
> *Mariana*: Good friar, I know you do, and so have found it
> (IV.i.53–4)

Thus is her exploitation recast and indeed experienced by Mariana, as voluntary allegiance to disinterested virtue.

The Duke's strategy with Isabella is somewhat different. Some critics of the play, liking their women chaste, have praised Isabella for her integrity; others have reproached her for being too absolute for virtue.[15] Another assessment, ostensibly more sympathetic than either of these because psychological rather than overtly moralistic, is summarised by Lever. He finds Isabella ignorant, hysterical and suffering from 'psychic confusion', and he apparently approves the fact that 'through four ... acts' she undergoes 'a process of moral education designed to reshape her character' (pp. lxxx, lxxvii, lxxix, xci). Here, under the guise of normative categories of psychosexual development, whose objective is 'maturity', moralistic and patriarchal values are reinstated the more insidiously for being ostensibly 'caring' rather than openly coercive. But in the play the coercive thrust of such values suggests that perhaps Isabella has recourse to renunciation as a way of escaping them. When we first encounter her in the nunnery it is her impending separation from men that is stressed by the nun, Francisca. The same priority is registered by Isabella herself when she affirms the prayers from 'preserved souls, / From fasting maids, whose minds are dedicate / To nothing temporal' (II.ii.154–6). She seeks in fact to be preserved specifically from men:

> Women? – Help, heaven! Men their creation mar
> In profiting by them. Nay, call us ten times frail;
> For we are soft as our complexions are,
> And credulous to false prints. (II.iv.126–9)

If we remember that in the play the stamp metaphor signifies the formative and coercive power of authority, we see that Isabella speaks a vulnerability freed in part from its own ideological mis-recognition; she conceives her weakness half in terms of women's supposed intrinsic 'frailness', half in terms of exploitative male coercion. Further, we see in Isabella's subjection a conflict within the patriarchal order which subjects: the renunciation which the Church sanctions, secular authority refuses. The latter wins and it is Isabella's fate to be coerced back into her socially and sexually subordinate position – at first illicitly by Angelo, then legitimately by the Duke who 'takes' her in marriage.

His subjects' public recognition of his own integrity is important in the Duke's attempt to reposition them in obedience. Yet the play can be read to disclose integrity as a strategy of authority rather than the disinterested virtue of the leader. The Duke speaks frequently of the integrity of rulers but the very circumstances in which he does so disclose a pragmatic and ideological intent; public integrity legitimates authority, and authority takes sufficient priority to lie about integrity when the ends of propaganda and government require it (IV.ii.77–83). And the Duke knows that these same ends require that integrity should be publicly displayed in the form of reputation. Intriguingly then, perhaps the most subversive thing in the play is the most casual, namely Lucio's slurring of the Duke's reputation. Unawares and carelessly, Lucio strikes at the heart of the ideological legitimation of power. Along with Barnardine's equally careless refusal of subjection, this is what angers the Duke the most. Still disguised, he insists to Lucio that he, the Duke, *'be but testimonied in his own bringings-forth*, and he shall appear to the envious a scholar, a statesman, and a soldier' (III.ii.140–2, italics added). After Lucio has departed he laments his inability to ensure his subject's dutiful respect: 'What king so strong / Can tie the gall up in the slanderous tongue?' (ll. 181–2; cf. IV.i.60–5). If the severity of the law at this time is anything to go by, such slander was a cause of obsessive concern to Elizabethan and Jacobean rulers,[16] just as it is here with the Duke and, as we have already seen, with Escalus.

The ideological representation of integrity can perhaps be judged best at the play's close – itself ideological but not, it seems to me, forced or flawed in the way critics have often claimed. By means of the Duke's personal intervention and integrity, authoritarian reaction is put into abeyance but not discredited: the corrupt deputy is unmasked but no law is repealed and the mercy exercised remains the prerogative of the same ruler who initiated reaction. The Duke also embodies a public reconciliation of law and morality. An omniscience, inseparable from seeming integrity, permits him to close the gulf between the two, one which was opening wide enough to demystify the one (law) and enfeeble the other (morality). Again, this is not a cancelling of authoritarianism so much as a fantasy resolution of the very fears from which authoritarianism partly grows – a fear of escalating disorder among the ruled which in turn intensifies a fear of impotence in the rulers. If so it is a reactionary fantasy, neither radical nor liberating (as fantasy may indeed be) but rather conservative and constraining; the very disclosure of social realities which make progress seem imperative is recuperated in comedic closure, a redemptive wish-fulfilment of the status quo.

In conclusion then the transgressors in *Measure for Measure* signify neither the unregeneracy of the flesh, nor the ludic subversive carnivalesque. Rather, as the spectre of unregulated desire, they are exploited to legitimate an exercise in authoritarian repression. And of course it is a spectre: desire, culturally manifested, is never unregulated, perhaps least of all in Jacobean London. Apart from their own brutally exploitative sub-cultural codes, the stews were controlled from above. This took several forms, including one of the most subtly coercive of all: economic investment. Some time between 1599 and 1602 the Queen's Lord Chamberlain, Lord Hunsdon, appears to have leased property for the establishing of an especially notorious brothel in Paris Gardens, while Thomas Nashe declared in 1598 that 'whoredom (the next doore to the Magistrates)' was set up and maintained through bribery, and Gāmini Salgādo informs us that 'Most theatre owners ... were brothel owners too'.[17]

At the same time in this period, in its laws, statutes, proclamations and moralistic tracts, the marginalised and the deviant are, as it were, endlessly recast in a complex ideological process whereby authority is ever anxiously relegitimating itself. *Measure for Measure*, unlike the proclamation or the statute, gives the marginalised a voice, one which may confront authority directly but which more often speaks of and partially reveals the strategies of power which summon it into visibility. Even the mildly transgressive Claudio who, were it not for the law, was all set to become law-abiding, becomes briefly that 'warped slip of wilderness' (III.i.141). But if Claudio's desire to live is momentarily transgressive it becomes so only at the potential expense of his sister. The same is true of Pompey and Lucio who, once put under surveillance or interrogation by authority voice a critique of authority itself (III.ii.6–8; 89–175), yet remain willing to exploit others in their position by serving that same authority when the opportunity arises. Ironically though, it is Angelo's transgressive desire which is potentially the most subversive; he more than anyone else threatens to discredit authority. At the same time his transgression is also, potentially, the most brutally exploitative. This is an example of something which those who celebrate transgression often overlook: even as it offers a challenge to authority, transgression ever runs the risk of re-enacting elsewhere the very exploitation which it is resisting immediately.

What Foucault has said of sexuality in the nineteenth and twentieth centuries seems appropriate also to sexuality as a sub-category of sin in earlier periods: it *appears* to be that which power is afraid of but in actuality is that which power works through. Sin, especially when internalised as guilt, has produced the subjects of authority as surely as any ideology. At the same time it may be that not everyone, indeed not even the majority, has fallen for this. The 'sin' of promiscuity, for example, has always been defended from a naturalistic perspective as no sin at all – as indeed we find in *Measure for Measure*. But those like Lucio who cheerfully celebrate instinct-ual desire simultaneously reify as natural the (in fact) highly *social* relations of exploitation through which instinct finds its expression, social relations which, we might say, determine the nature of instinct far more than nature itself:

> *Lucio.* How doth my dear morsel, thy mistress? Procures she still, ha?
> *Pompey.* Troth sir, she hath eaten up all her beef, and she is herself in the tub.
> *Lucio.* Why, 'tis good: it is the right of it: it must be so. Ever your fresh whore, and your powdered bawd; an unshunned consequence; it must be so. (III.ii.52–8)

And Pompey, whom he refuses to bail, Lucio perceives as 'bawd born' (III.ii.66). Mistress Overdone, her plight as described here notwithstanding, was one of the lucky ones; after all, the life of most prostitutes outside the exclusive brothels was abject. Overdone is at least a procuress, a brothel keeper. For most of the rest poverty drove them to the brothels and after a relatively short stay in which they had to run the hazards of disease, violence and contempt, most were driven back to it.

In pursuing the authority–subversion question, this chapter has tried to exemplify two complementary modes of materialist criticism. Both are concerned to recover the text's history. The one looks directly for history in the text including the historical condi-tions of its production which, even if not addressed directly by the text can nevertheless still be said to be within it, informing it. Yet there is a limit to which the text can be said to incorporate those aspects of its historical moment of which it never speaks. At that limit, rather than constructing this history as the text's unconscious, we might instead address it directly. Then at any rate we have to recognise the obvious: the prostitutes, the most exploited group in the society which the play represents, are absent from it. Virtually everything that happens presupposes them yet they have no voice, no presence. And those who speak for them do so as exploitatively as those who want to eliminate them. Looking for evidence of resistance we find rather further evidence of exploitation. There comes a time of course when the demonising of deviant sexuality meets with cultural and political resistance. From the very terms of its oppression deviancy generates a challenging counter-discourse and eventually a far-reaching critique of exploitation. That is another and later story.

Notes

1 *Measure for Measure*, ed. J. W. Lever (London: Methuen, 1965).
2 For another kind of critic sexuality in *Measure for Measure* continues to be seen as something deeply disruptive though now it is the individual psyche rather than the social order which is under threat. Thus for Marilyn French this is a play which 'confronts directly Shakespeare's own most elemental fears' – hence its 'sexual obsessiveness, mixed guilt, abhorrence'. She writes further of 'the hideous and repellent quality sex has throughout the play. It is, it remains, evil, filthy, disgusting, diseased' (*Shakespeare's Division of Experience* (London: Jonathan Cape, 1982), pp. 195–7).
3 Alan Bray, *Homosexuality in Renaissance England* (London: Gay Men's Press, 1982); Stuart Clark, 'Inversion, Misrule and the Meaning of Witchcraft', *Past and Present*, 87 (1980), 98–127; Christopher Hill, *The World Turned Upside Down: Radical Ideas During the English Revolution* (Harmondsworth: Penguin, 1975).
4 For the Baines document see C. F. Tucker Brooke, *The Life of Marlowe and the Tragedy of Dido Queen of Carthage* (London: Methuen, 1930), pp. 98–100.
5 Peter Tatchell, *The Battle for Bermondsey*, preface by Tony Benn (London: Heretic Books, 1983).
6 Lawrence Stone, *The Family Sex and Marriage in England 1500–1800* (London: Weidenfeld and Nicolson, 1977), pp. 653, 217, 654, 623–4; and F. G. Emmison has estimated that in the county of Essex around 15,000 people were summoned on sexual charges in the forty-five years up to 1603 (*Elizabethan Life: Morals and the Church Courts* (Chelmsford: Essex County Council, 1973), p. 1). Commenting on these figures Stone remarks that 'in an adult lifespan of 30 years, an Elizabethan inhabitant of Essex ... had more than a one-in-four chance of being accused of fornication, adultery, buggery, incest, bestiality or bigamy' (*The Family*, p. 519).
7 J. A. Sharpe, *Crime in Seventeenth-Century England: a County Study* (Cambridge University Press, 1983), pp. 57, 70, 215–16.
8 *A Mirror for Magistrates* quoted from Thomas C. Izard's helpful study, *George Whetstone: Mid-Elizabethan Gentleman of Letters* (New York: Columbia University Press, 1942; reprinted New York: AMS Press, 1966), p. 140.
9 See the Proclamation of 1546 ordering London brothels to be closed, in *Tudor Royal Proclamations* (3 vols.), ed. Paul L. Hughes and James L. Larkin (New Haven: Yale University Press, 1964–9), I, 365–6; also Wallace Shugg, 'Prostitution in Shakespeare's London', *Shakespeare Studies* 10 (1977), 291–313, especially p. 306.
10 *Stuart Royal Proclamations* (vol.I), ed. James F. Larkin and Paul L. Hughes (Oxford: Clarendon, 1973), p. 47.

11 See especially Leonard Tennenhouse, 'Representing Power: *Measure for Measure* in its Time', in *The Power of Forms in the English Renaissance*, ed. Stephen Greenblatt (Norman: Pilgrim Books, 1982), pp. 139–56; David Sundelson, 'Misogyny and Rule in *Measure for Measure*', *Women's Studies*, vol. 9, no. 1 (1981), 83–91.

12 Ben Jonson, *Works*, ed. C. H. Herford and P. Simpson, 11 vols. (Oxford: Clarendon, 1922–52), I, 19, 139.

13 Jonathan Dollimore, *Radical Tragedy: Religion Ideology and Power in the Drama of Shakespeare and His Contemporaries* (Brighton: Harvester, 1984; University of Chicago Press, 1984), pp. 9–17.

14 Richard Hooker, *Of the Laws of Ecclesiastical Polity*, 2 vols., introduction by C. Morris (London: Dent, 1969), II, 19.

15 In the nineteenth century for example A. W. Schlegel praised 'the heavenly purity of her mind ... not even stained with one unholy thought' and Edward Dowden her 'pure zeal' and 'virgin sanctity'. By contrast Coleridge found her 'unamiable' and Hazlitt reproved her 'rigid chastity'. These other passages from earlier critics are conveniently collected in C. K. Stead, ed., *Shakespeare: Measure for Measure, a Casebook* (London: Macmillan, 1971); see especially pp. 43–5, 59–62, 45–7, 47–9.

16 See especially Joel Samaha, 'Gleanings from Local Criminal Court Records: Sedition among the inarticulate in Elizabethan Essex', *Journal of Social History*, 8 (1975), 61–79.

17 E. J. Burford, *Queen of the Bawds* (London: Neville Spearman, 1974); Thomas Nashe, *The Unfortunate Traveller and Other Works*, ed. J. B. Steane (Harmondsworth: Penguin, 1972), p. 483; Gāmini Salgādo, *The Elizabethan Underworld* (London: Dent, 1977), p. 58.

The patriarchal bard: feminist criticism and Shakespeare: *King Lear* and *Measure for Measure*

I

Every feminist critic has encountered the archly disingenuous question 'What exactly is feminist criticism?' The only effective response is 'I'll send you a booklist', for feminist criticism can only be defined by the multiplicity of critical practices engaged in by feminists. Owing its origins to a popular political movement, it reproduces the varied theoretical positions of that movement. Sociologists and theorists of culture have, for example, investigated the processes by which representations of women in advertising and film reproduce and reinforce dominant definitions of sexuality and sexual relations so as to perpetuate their ideological power.[1] Within English departments critical activity has been divided among those who revived and privileged the work of women writers and those who have focused critical attention on reinterpreting literary texts from the traditional canon. In the case of Shakespeare, feminist critics have contested the apparent misogyny of the plays and the resistance of their feminist students by directing attention to the 'world' of the plays, using conventional tools of interpretation to assess Shakespeare's attitude to the events within it.[2]

In a number of essays[3] the feminist concern with traditional evaluations of sexual identity has been used to explore the importance of ideals of violence in the psychological formation of Shakespeare's male characters.[4] Janet Adelman has analysed the importance of structures of psychological dependence in accounting for Coriolanus's phallic aggression[5] and Coppelia Kahn has described the feud in *Romeo and Juliet* as 'the deadly *rite de passage* that promotes masculinity at the price of life'.[6] These essays have built on and developed a feminist psychoanalysis[7] which places motherhood at the centre of psychological development, as Coppelia Kahn makes explicit in her book on *Masculine Identity in Shakespeare*: 'the critical threat to identity is not, as Freud maintains, castration, but engulfment by the mother ... men first know women as the matrix of all satisfaction from which they must struggle to differentiate themselves ... [Shakespeare] explores the unconscious attitudes behind cultural definitions of manliness and womanliness and behind the mores and institutions shaped by them.'[8]

Modern feminist psychoanalysis could be applied to Shakespearean characters for the texts were seen as unproblematically mimetic: 'Shakespeare and Freud deal with the same subject: the expressed and hidden feelings in the human heart. They are both psychologists.'[9] Shakespeare was thus constructed as an authoritative figure whose views about men and women could be co-opted to the liberal feminism of the critic. Within this critical practice, academic debate centred on conflicts over the authors' views rather than on the systems of representation or the literary traditions which informed the texts. Linda Bamber, for example, reminded her readers of the evident misogyny of Shakespeare's treatment of his tragic heroines and placed her own work 'in reaction against the tendency for feminist critics to interpret Shakespeare as if his work directly supports and develops feminist ideas'.[10] While noting the fundamental inconsistencies between Shakespeare's treatment of women in comedy and tragedy, she explicitly resists the temptation 'to revel in them offered by post-structuralism'. She finds instead a cohering principle in Shakespeare's recognition of women as 'other', which 'amounts to sexism only if the writer fails to attribute to opposite sex characters the privileges of the other'.[11] In tragedy his women are strong because they are coherent – 'certainly none of the women in the tragedies worries or changes her mind about who she is' – and the attacks which are made on them are the product of male resentment at this strength – 'misogyny and sex nausea are born of failure and self doubt'.[12] The comic feminine, on the other hand, is opposed not to men but to a reified 'society':'In comedy the feminine either rebels against the restraining social order or (more commonly) presides in alliance with the forces which challenge its hegemony: romantic love, physical nature, the love of pleasure in all its forms.'[13]

These assertions rest on a reductive application of feminist anthropological discussions of nature and culture but their primary effect is to construct an author whose views can be applied in moral terms to rally and exhort the women readers of today: 'the comic heroines show us how to regard ourselves as other ... the heroines laugh to see themselves absorbed into the ordinary human comedy; the heroes rage and weep at the difficulty of actually being as extraordinary as they feel themselves to be'.[14] These moral characteristics ascribed to men and women take no account of their particular circumstances within the texts, nor indeed of their material circumstances and the differential power relations which they support. Feminism thus involves defining certain characteristics as feminine and admiring them as a better way to survive in the world. In order to assert the moral connection between the mimetic world of Shakespeare's plays and the real world of the audience, the characters have to be seen as representative men and women and the categories male and female are essential, unchanging, definable in modern, commonsense terms.

The essentialism of this form of feminism is further developed in Marilyn French's *Shakespeare's Division of Experience*. Like Bamber, she constructs a god-like author who 'breathed life into his female characters and gave body to the principles they are supposed to represent'.[15] Although shored up by references to feminist philosophy and anthropology, this feminine principle amounts to little more than the power to nurture and give birth and is opposed to a masculine principle embodied in the ability to kill. These principles are not, however, located in specific men or women. When men are approved of they are seen as embracing feminine principles whereas women are denied access to the male and are denigrated when they aspire to male qualities. French suggests that Shakespeare divides experience into male (evil) and female (good) principles and his comedies and tragedies are interpreted as 'either a synthesis of the principles or an examination of the kinds of worlds that result when one or other principle is abused, neglected, devalued or exiled'.[16]

The essentialism which lies behind Marilyn French's and Linda Bamber's account of the men and women in Shakespeare is part of a trend in liberal feminism which sees the feminist struggle as concerned with reordering the values ascribed to men and women without fundamentally changing the material circumstances in which their relationships function. It presents feminism as a set of social attitudes rather than as a project for fundamental social change. As such it can equally easily be applied to an analysis of Shakespeare's plays which situates them in the ideological currents of his own time. In *Shakespeare and the Nature of Women*, for example, Juliet Dusinberre admires 'Shakespeare's concern ... to dissolve artificial distinctions between the sexes'[17] and can claim that concern as feminist in both twentieth-century and seventeenth-century terms. She examines Shakespeare's women characters – and those of some of his contemporaries – in the light of Renaissance debates over women conducted in puritan handbooks and advice literature. Building on the Hallers' essay on 'The puritan art of love',[18] she notes the shift from misogyny associated with Catholic asceticism to puritan assertions of the importance of women in the godly household as partners in holy and companionate marriage. The main portion of the book is an elaboration of themes – Chastity,

Equality, Gods and Devils – in both polemic and dramatic literature. The strength of her argument lies in its description of the literary shift from the discourses of love poetry and satire to those of drama. However her assertions about the feminism of Shakespeare and his contemporaries depend once again upon a mimetic model of the relationship between ideas and drama. Contemporary controversy about women is seen as a static body of ideas which can be used or rejected by dramatists whose primary concern is not with parallel fictions but simply to 'explore the real nature of women'. By focusing on the presentation of women in puritan advice literature, Dusinberre privileges one side of a contemporary debate, relegating expressions of misogyny to the fictional world of 'literary simplifica- tion' and arbitrarily asserting more progressive notions as the dramatists' true point of view.[19]

A more complex discussion of the case would acknowledge that the issues of sex, sexuality, sexual relations and sexual division were areas of conflict of which the contradictions of writing about women were only one manifestation alongside the complexity of legislation and other forms of social control of sex and the family. The debates in modern historiography on these questions indicate the difficulty of assigning monolithic economic or ideological models to the early modern family, while the work of regional historians has shown the importance of specific material conditions on both the ideology and practice of sexual relations.[20] Far from being an unproblematic concept, 'the nature of women' was under severe pressure from both ideological discourses and the real concomitants of inflation and demographic change.

The problem with the mimetic, essentialist model of feminist criticism is that it would require a more multi-faceted mirror than Shakespearean drama to reflect the full complexity of the nature of women in Shakespeare's time or our own. Moreover this model obscures the particular relationship between Shakespearean drama and its readers which feminist criticism implies. The demands of the academy insist that feminist critics reject 'a literary version of placard carrying',[21] but they cannot but reveal the extent to which their critical practice expresses new demands and a new focus of attention on the plays. Coppelia Kahn concedes that 'Today we are questioning the cultural definitions of sexual identity we have inherited. I believe Shakespeare questioned them too ...'[22] and, rather more frankly, Linda Bamber explains: 'As a heterosexual feminist ... I have found in Shakespeare what I want to imagine as a possibility in my own life'.[23] However, the alternative to this simple co-option of Shakespeare is not to assert some spurious notion of objectivity. Such a procedure usually implies a denigration of feminism[24] in favour of more conventional positions and draws the criticism back into the institutionalised competition over 'readings'.

A different procedure would involve theorising the relationship between feminism and the plays more explicitly, accepting that feminist criticism, like all criticism, is a reconstruction of the play's meaning and asserting the specificity of a feminist response. This procedure differs from claiming Shakespeare's views as feminist in refusing to construct an author behind the plays and paying attention instead to the narrative, poetic and theatrical strategies which construct the plays' meanings and position the audience to understand their events from a particular point of view. For Shakespeare's plays are not primarily explorations of 'the real nature of women' or even 'the hidden feelings in the human heart'. They were the products of an entertainment industry which, as far as we know, had no women shareholders, actors, writers, or stage hands. His women characters were played by boys and, far from his plays being an expression of his idiosyncratic views, they all built on and adapted earlier stories.

The witty comic heroines, the powerful tragic figures, the opposition between realism and romance were the commonplaces of the literary tradition from which these tests emerged. Sex and sexual relations within them are, in the first analysis, sources of comedy, narrative resolution and *coups de théâtre*. These textual strategies limit the range of meaning which the text allows and circumscribe the position which a feminist reader may adopt *vis-à-vis* the treatment of gender relations and sexual politics within the plays. The feminist reader may resist the position which the text offers but resistance involves more than simple attitudinising.

II

In traditional criticism Shakespeare's plays are seldom regarded as the sum of their dramatic devices. The social location of the action, their visual dimension and the frequent claims they make for their own authenticity, invite an audience's engagement at a level beyond the plot. The audience is invited to make some connection between the events of the action and the form and pressure of their own world. In the case of sex and gender, the concern of feminists, a potential connection is presented between sexual relations as an aspect of narrative — who will marry whom and how? — and sexual relations as an aspect of social relations — how is power distributed between men and women and how are their sexual relations conducted? The process of interpretative criticism is to construct a social meaning for the play out of its narrative and dramatic realisation. However this is no straightforward procedure: the positions offered by the texts are often contradictory and meaning can be produced by adopting one of the positions offered, using theatrical production or critical procedures to close off others. The critic can use historical knowledge to speculate about the possible creation of meaning in the light of past institutions and ideologies but the gap between textual meaning and social meaning can never be completely filled for meaning is constructed every time the text is reproduced in the changing ideological dynamic between text and audience.

An interesting case in point is *Measure for Measure*, in which the conflicting positions offered by the text have resulted in critical confusion among those who wish to fix its moral meaning as the authentic statement of a coherent author. The problems have centred in large part on the narrative resolution in which the restoration of order through marriages seems both an affront to liberal sensibilities and an unsatisfactory suppression of the powerful passions evoked throughout the action. There seems to be an irresolvable gap between the narrative strategies – the bed-trick, the prince in disguise plot – and the realism of the other scenes in which we see 'corruption boil and bubble till it o'errun the stew'.

The relevance of discussions of early modern sexuality and social control is evident in the play's treatment of public regulation of morality. Nevertheless such historically informed attention as the play has received[25] has been in the attempt to close off its meaning by invoking Jacobean marriage law or Christian theology in order to determine the rightness or wrongness of Angelo's judgements, the reason or lack of it in Isabella's defence of her chastity. These arguments fail to convince, not because history is irrelevant but because they cannot solve problems which arise in the first instance from the production of meaning by the text.

The confusion in the narrative meaning is created because it offers equal dramatic power to mutually exclusive positions. The comic vitality of the low-life characters and their anarchic resistance to the due processes of law dramatises the inadequacy of any system of control which stops short of an order to 'geld and splay all the youth of the city' (II.i.230). Nevertheless engagement with them is complicated by the equal dramatic impact of the Duke's disgust with their trade in flesh (III.ii.22–27). Similarly Isabella's single-minded protection of her sexual autonomy is placed first by the masochism of the sexual imagery in which it is expressed and then by its juxtaposition with her brother's equally vividly expressed terror at the thought of death. Moral absolutes are rendered platitudinous by the language and verse, particularly in the Duke's summary where the jingling rime of the couplet mocks the very morals it asserts.

This speech, at the mid point of the play, offers a summary of the tension between narrative and social meaning. The moral absolutes of the first part of the speech are set against the Duke's solution to the problem. But the terms of the solution are moral and pragmatic:

> Craft against vice I must apply.
> With Angelo tonight shall lie
> His old betrothed but despised.
> So disguise shall, by th'disguised
> Pay with falsehood false exacting
> And perform an old contracting. (III.ii.280–5)

Yet the ending of the play, for all its narrative manipulation, imposes not only a narrative solution but also a possible social resolution. Both the *coup de théâtre* of the Duke's reappearance and the language which accords his merciful authority the status of 'power divine' provide theatrical satisfaction for the finale which endorses the social implications of the Duke's judgement. Marriage is the solution to the puzzle of the bed-trick but it is also the solution to the disruptive power of Lucio who has offered troublesome alternatives to the main narrative line. The solution is imposed in this play by a figure from within the action, the all-powerful Duke, but it is no more inappropriate to the characters concerned than the finale of many another romantic comedy.

It is impossible to say how this resolution was regarded by Shakespeare's contemporaries. There is evidence to suggest that marriage was regarded as just such an instrument of effective social control and social harmony. However there is no reason why the elusive responses of past audiences need carry privileged status as the ultimate meaning of the text. The ideological struggle over sexuality and sexual relations which informs the text has emerged in different terms in the late twentieth century, and a liberal humanist reading of the text might present its social meaning as a despairing (or enthusiastic) recognition of the ineffectiveness of attempts at the control of such private, individual matters. A radical feminist production of the text could on the other hand, through acting, costume and style, deny the lively energy of the pimps and the bawds, foregrounding their exploitation of female sexuality. It might celebrate Isabella's chastity as a feminist resistance, making her plea for Angelo's life a gesture of solidarity to a heterosexual sister and a recognition of the difficulty of breaking the bonds of family relations and conventional sexual arrangements.

These different 'interpretations' are not, however, competing equals in the struggle for meaning. They each involve reordering the terms in which the text is produced, which of its conflicting positions are foregrounded, and how the audience response is controlled. In Jonathan Miller's production of the play, for example, Isabella literally refused the Duke's offer of marriage and walked off stage in the opposite direction. Miller has been a powerful advocate for the right of a director to reconstruct Shakespeare's plays in the light of modern preoccupations, creating for them an afterlife which is not determined by their original productions.[26] As a theatre director, he is aware of the extent to which the social meaning of a play depends upon the arrangements of theatrical meaning; which is different from simply asserting alternative 'interpretations'. The concept of interpretation suggests that the text presents a transparent view on to the real life of sexual relations whether of the sixteenth or the twentieth century. The notion of 'constructed meaning' on the other hand, foregrounds the theatrical devices by which an audience's perception of the action of the play is defined. The focus of critical attention, in other words, shifts from judging the action to analysing the process by which the action presents itself to be judged.

This shift in the critical process has important implications for feminist criticism: the theatrical strategies which present the action to be judged resist feminist manipulation by denying an autonomous position for the female viewer of the action. Laura Mulvey and others have explored through the notion of scopophilia the pleasures afforded by particular ways of perceiving men and women in classic film narrative. Mulvey argues that in classic Hollywood films the techniques of lighting, focus and narrative pattern create women as the object, men as the bearers of the look: 'A woman performs within the narrative, the gaze of the spectator and that of the male characters in the film are neatly combined without breaking narrative verisimilitude.'[27] Theatrical production, of course, effects less complete control on the spectators' gaze than Hollywood cinema. Nevertheless the techniques of soliloquy, language and the organisation of the scenes limit the extent to which women characters are 'seen' in the action. One of the most common strategies of liberal mimetic interpretation is to imagine a past life, a set of alternatives and motivation for the characters. Yet the text much more frequently denies this free play of character, defining women as sexualised, seen *vis-à-vis* men.

The effect of this process can be seen in *Measure for Measure* where the women characters define a spectrum of sexual relations from Mistress Overdone (Overdone by her last husband), the elderly bawd, through Juliet who is visibly pregnant, to Isabella whose denial of sexuality is contained in the visual definition of her nun's habit. Mariana's ambiguous position as 'neither maid, widow nor wife' affords her no autonomy but is seen as problematic: indeed the narrative organisation of the latter part of the play is directed to reinstating her within the parameters of permitted sexual relations.

Mariana's introduction into the play shows how the text focuses the spectator's attention and constructs it as male.[28] She is introduced in tableau, the visual accompaniment to the boy's song. Her role in the action is defined not by her own activity but by her physical presence, itself contextualised within the narrative by the song's words:

> Take, O, take those lips away
> That so sweetly were forsworn;
> And those eyes, the break of day,
> Lights that do mislead the morn;
> But my kisses bring again, bring again;
> Seals of love, but seal'd in vain, seal'd in vain. (IV.i.1–6)

Isabella, for all her importance in the play, is similarly defined theatrically by the men around her for the men in the audience. In the scene of her first plea to Angelo, for example, she is physically framed by Angelo, the object of her demand, and Lucio the initiator of her plea. When she gives up after Angelo's first refusal, Lucio urges her back with instructions on appropriate behaviour:

> Give't not o'er so. To him again! entreat him,
> Kneel down before him, hang upon his gown!
> You are too cold. (II.ii.43–5)

As her rhetoric becomes more impassioned, her speeches longer, our view of her action is still dramatically mediated through Lucio whose approving remarks and comic asides act as a filter both for her action and for the audience's view of it.

Through Lucio and the provost the text makes us want her to win. However, the terms of her victory are also defined by the rhetoric and structure of the scene. A woman pleading with a man introduces an element of sexual conflict which is made explicit in the bawdy innuendo of Lucio's remarks (II.ii.123–4). The passion of the conflict, the sexualising of the rhetoric, and the engagement of the onstage spectators create a theatrical excitement which is necessary to sustain the narrative: it also produces the kind of audience involvement which makes Angelo's response make sense. Like Angelo we are witnesses to Isabella's performance so that we understand, if we do not morally approve of, his reaction to it. It is, moreover, rendered theatrically valid in the heartsearching soliloquy which closes the scene. His rhetorical questions 'Is this her fault or mine ... Can it be that modesty may more betray the sense / Than woman's lightness?' define the sexually appealing paradox of the passionate nun, and the audience is intellectually engaged in his quandary by his dilemma being put in the questioning form.

A feminist reading of the scene may wish to refuse the power of Angelo's plea, may recognise in it the double bind which blames women for their own sexual oppression. However to take up that position involves refusing the pleasure of the drama and the text, which imply a coherent maleness in their point of view.[29]

Isabella's dilemma is, by contrast, a pale affair. Her one soliloquy deals only in the abstract opposition of chastity against her brother's life. Her resounding conclusion 'Then Isobel live chaste and brother die: / More than our brother is our chastity' (II.iv.184–5) offers no parallel intellectual pleasures; it does not arise out of the passion of the preceding scene which was a conflict between Angelo and Isabella not Isabella and Claudio; its lack of irony or paradox offers no scope for audience play. It is simply the apparently irresolvable problem which the ensuing action, under the Duke's control, must seek to resolve. Isabella's action is determined in the text by her sexuality and her space for manouevre is explicitly defined in Angelo's reminder of her circumscribed condition:

> Be that you are
> That is, a woman; if you be more, you're none;
> If you be one, as you are well expressed
> By all external warrants, show it now,
> By putting on the destined livery. (II.iv.134–7)

Angelo's definition of a woman 'by all external warrants' is shared by the theatrical devices of the text. Any criticism which argues whether Isabella is a vixen or a saint places itself comfortably in the limited opening that the text allows for it; it takes up the argument about whether Isabella is to be more than a woman in giving up her brother or less than one in submitting to Angelo's lust. The text allows her no other role. The radical feminist 'interpretation' floated earlier would require a radical rewriting both of the narrative and of the way the scenes are constructed.

Feminist criticism of this play is restricted to exposing its own exclusion from the text. It has no point of entry into it, for the dilemmas of the narrative and the sexuality under discussion are constructed in completely male terms – gelding and splaying hold no terror for women – and the women's role as the objects of exchange within that system of sexuality is not at issue, however much a

Kathleen McLuskie

feminist might want to draw attention to it. Thus when a feminist accepts the narrative, theatrical and intellectual pleasures of this text she does so in male terms and not as part of the locus of feminist critical activity.

III

In *Measure for Measure* the pleasure denied is the pleasure of comedy, a pleasure many feminists have learned to struggle with as they withhold their assent from the social approval of sexist humour. A much more difficult pleasure to deny is the emotional, moral and aesthetic satisfaction afforded by tragedy. Tragedy assumes the existence of 'a permanent, universal and essentially unchanging human nature'[30] but the human nature implied in the moral and aesthetic satisfactions of tragedy is most often explicitly male. In *King Lear* for example, the narrative and its dramatisation present a connection between sexual insubordination and anarchy, and the connection is given an explicitly misogynist emphasis.

The action of the play, the organisation of its point of view and the theatrical dynamic of its central scenes all depend upon an audience accepting an equation between 'human nature' and male power. In order to experience the proper pleasures of pity and fear, they must accept that fathers are owed particular duties by their daughters and be appalled by the chaos which ensues when those primal links are broken. Such a point of view is not a matter of consciously-held opinion but it is a position required and determined by the text in order for it to make sense. It is also the product of a set of meanings produced in a specific way by the Shakespearean text and is different from that produced in other versions of the story.

The representation of patriarchal misogyny is most obvious in the treatment of Goneril and Regan. In the chronicle play *King Leir*, the sisters' villainy is much more evidently a function of the plot. Their mocking pleasure at Cordella's downfall takes the form of a comic double act and Regan's evil provides the narrative with the exciting twist of an attempt on Lear's life.[31] In the Shakespearean text by contrast, the narrative, language and dramatic organisation all define the sisters' resistance to their father in terms of their gender, sexuality and position within the family. Family relations in this play are seen as fixed and determined, and any movement within them is portrayed as a destructive reversal of rightful order (see I.iv). Goneril's and Regan's treatment of their father merely reverses existing patterns of rule and is seen not simply as cruel and selfish but as a fundamental violation of human nature – as is made powerfully

Kathleen McLuskie

feminist might want to draw attention to it. Thus when a feminist accepts the narrative, theatrical and intellectual pleasures of this text she does so in male terms and not as part of the locus of feminist critical activity.

explicit in the speeches which condemn them (III.vii.101–3; IV.ii.32–50). Moreover when Lear in his madness fantasises about the collapse of law and the destruction of ordered social control, women's lust is vividly represented as the centre and source of the ensuing corruption (IV.vi.110–28). The generalised character of Lear's and Albany's vision of chaos, and the poetic force with which it is expressed, creates the appearance of truthful universality which is an important part of the play's claim to greatness. However, that generalised vision of chaos is present in gendered terms in which patriarchy, the institution of male power in the family and the State, is seen as the only form of social organisaion strong enough to hold chaos at bay.

The close links between misogyny and patriarchy define the women in the play more precisely. Goneril and Regan are not presented as archetypes of womanhood for the presence of Cordelia 'redeems nature from the general curse' (IV.vi.209). However Cordelia's saving love, so much admired by critics, works in the action less as a redemption for womankind than as an example of patriarchy restored. Hers, of course, is the first revolt against Lear's organising authority. The abruptness of her refusal to play her role in Lear's public drama dramatises the outrage of her denial of conformity and the fury of Lear's ensuing appeal to archetypal forces shows that a rupture of 'Propinquity and property of blood' is tantamount to the destruction of nature itself. Cordelia, however, is the central focus of emotion in the scene. Her resistance to her father gains audience assent through her two asides during her sisters' performances; moreover the limits of that resistance are clearly indicated. Her first defence is not a statement on her personal autonomy or the rights of her individual will: it is her right to retain a part of her love for 'that lord whose hand must take my plight'. Lear's rage thus seems unreasonable in that he recognises only his rights as a father; for the patriarchal family to continue, it must also recognise the rights of future fathers and accept the transfer of women from fathers to husbands. By the end of the scene, Cordelia is reabsorbed into the patriarchal family by marriage to which her resistance to Lear presents no barrier. As she reassures the king of France:

> It is no vicious blot, murder or foulness,
> No unchaste action or dishonoured step
> That hath deprived me of your grace and favour. (I.i.228–31)

Her right to be included in the ordered world of heterosexual relations depends upon her innocence of the ultimate human violation of

murder which is paralleled with the ultimate sexual violation of
unchastity.

However, any dispassionate analysis of the mystification of real
socio-sexual relations in *King Lear* is the antithesis of our response
to the tragedy in the theatre where the tragic power of the play
endorses its ideological position at every stage. One of the most
important and effective shifts in the action is the transfer of our
sympathy back to Lear in the middle of the action. The long sequence
of Act II, scene iv dramatises the process of Lear's decline from the
angry autocrat of Act I to the appealing figure of pathetic insanity.
The psychological realism of the dramatic writing and the manipulation of the point of view, forges the bonds between Lear as a complex
character and the sympathies of the audience.

The audience's sympathies are engaged by Lear's fury at the insult
offered by Kent's imprisonment and by the pathos of Lear's belated
attempt at self-control (II.iv.101–4). His view of the action is further
emotionally secured by his sarcastic enactment of the humility
which his daughters recommend:

> Do you but mark how this becomes the house:
> Dear daughter, I confess that I am old.
> Age is unnecessary. On my knees I beg
> That you'll vouchsafe me raiment, bed and food. (II.iv.53–6)

As Regan says, these are unsightly tricks. Their effect is to close off
the dramatic scene by offering the only alternative to Lear's
behaviour as we see it. The dramatic fact becomes the only fact and
the audience is thus positioned to accept the tragic as inevitable,
endorsing the terms of Lear's great poetic appeal:

> O reason not the need! Our basest beggars
> Are in the poorest things superfluous.
> Allow not nature more than nature needs,
> Man's life is cheap as beasts. (II.iv.263–6)

The ideological power of Lear's speech lies in his invocation of
nature to support his demands on his daughters; its dramatic power
lies in its movement from argument to desperate assertion of his
crumbling humanity as the abyss of madness approaches. However,
once again, that humanity is seen in gendered terms as Lear appeals
to the gods to

> touch me with noble anger,
> And let not women's weapons, water drops
> Stain my man's cheeks. (II.iv.275–7)

The theatrical devices which secure Lear at the centre of the audience's emotional attention operate even more powerfully in the play's denouement. The figure of Cordelia is used as a channel for the response to her suffering father. Her part in establishing the terms of the conflict is over by Act I; when she reappears it is as an emblem of dutiful pity. Before she appears on stage, she is described by a 'gentleman' whose speech reconstructs her as a static, almost inanimate daughter of sorrows. The poetic paradoxes of his speech construct Cordelia as one who resolves contradiction,[32] which is her potential role in the narrative and her crucial function in the ideological coherence of the text:

> patience and sorrow strove
> Who should express her goodliest. You have seen
> Sunshine and rain at once: her smiles and tears
> Were like a better way: those happy smilets
> That played on her ripe lip seemed not to know
> What guests were in her eyes, which parted thence
> As pearls from diamonds dropped. (IV.iii.15–23)

With Cordelia's reaction pre-empted by the gentleman, the scene where Lear and Cordelia meet substitutes the pleasure of pathos for suspense. The imagery gives Cordelia's forgiveness divine sanction, and the realism of Lear's struggle for sanity closes off any responses other than complete engagement with the characters' emotions. Yet in this encounter Cordelia denies the dynamic of the whole play. Lear fears that she cannot love him:

> for your sisters
> Have, as I do remember, done me wrong.
> You have some cause, they have not. (IV.vii.73–5)

But Cordelia demurs with 'No cause, no cause'.

Shakespeare's treatment of this moment contrasts with that of the earlier chronicle play from which he took a number of details, including Lear kneeling and being raised. In the old play the scene is almost comic as Leir and Cordella kneel and rise in counterpoint to their arguments about who most deserves blame.[33] The encounter is used to sum up the issues and the old play allows Cordella a much more active role in weighing her debt to Leir. In Shakespeare's text, however, the spectacle of suffering obliterates the past action so that audience with Cordelia will murmur 'No cause, no cause'. Rather than a resolution of the action, their reunion becomes an emblem of possible harmony, briefly glimpsed before the tragic debacle.

The deaths of Lear and Cordelia seem the more shocking for this moment of harmony but their tragic impact is also a function of thwarting the narrative expectation of harmony restored which is established by the text's folk-tale structure.[34] The folk-tale of the love test provides an underlying pattern in which harmony is broken by the honest daughter and restored by her display of forgiveness. The organisation of the Shakespearean text intensifies and then denies those expectations so as once more to insist on the connection between evil women and a chaotic world.

The penultimate scene opposes the ordered formality of the resolution of the Gloucester plot with the unseemly disorder of the women's involvement. The twice-repeated trumpet call, the arrival of a mysterious challenger in disguise, evoke the order of a chivalric age when conflict was resolved by men at arms. The women, however, act as disrupters of that order: Goneril attempts to deny the outcome of the tourney, grappling in an unseemly quarrel with Albany (V.iii.156–8) and their ugly deaths interrupt Edgar's efforts to close off the narrative with a formal account of his part in the story and Gloucester's death.

Thus the deaths of Lear and Cordelia are contrasted with and seem almost a result of the destructiveness of the wicked sisters. Albany says of them: 'This judgement of the heavens, that makes us tremble, / Touches us not with pity' (V.iii.233–4). The tragic vicitims, however, affect us quite differently. When Lear enters, bearing his dead daughter in his arms, we are presented with a contrasting emblem of the natural, animal assertion of family love, destroyed by the anarchic forces of lust and the 'indistinguished space of woman's will'. At this point in the play the most stony-hearted feminist could not withhold her pity even though it is called forth at the expense of her resistance to the patriarchal relations which it endorses.

The effect of these dramatic devices is to position the audience as a coherent whole, comfortably situated *vis-à-vis* the text. To attempt to shift that position by denying Lear's rights as a father and a man would be to deny the pity of Lear's suffering and the pleasurable reaffirmation of one's humanity through sympathetic fellow feeling. A feminist reading of the text cannot simply assert the countervailing rights of Goneril and Regan, for to do so would simply reverse the emotional structures of the play, associating feminist ideology with atavistic selfishness and the monstrous assertion of individual wills. Feminism cannot simply take 'the woman's part' when that part has been so morally loaded and theatrically circumscribed. Nor is any purpose served by merely denouncing the text's misogyny, for *King Lear's* position at the centre of the Shakespeare canon is assured by its continual reproduction in education and the theatre and is unlikely to be shifted by feminist sabre-rattling.

A more fruitful point of entry for feminism in is the process of the text's reproduction. As Elizabeth Cowie and others have pointed out,[35] sexist meanings are not fixed but depend upon constant reproduction by their audience. In the case of *King Lear* the text is tied to misogynist meaning only if it is reconstructed with its emotional power and its moral imperatives intact. Yet the text contains possibilities for subverting these meanings and the potential for reconstructing them in feminist terms.

The first of these lies in the text's historical otherness; for in spite of constant critical assertion of its transcendent universality, specific connections can be shown between Shakespeare's text and contemporary material and ideological conflict without presenting a merely reductive account of artistic production in terms of material circumstances.[36]

Discussing the 'gerontocratic ideal', for example, Keith Thomas has noted that 'The sixteenth and seventeenth centuries are conspicuous for a sustained desire to subordinate persons in their teens and twenties and to delay their equal participation in the adult world ... such devices were also a response to the mounting burden of population on an unflexible economy'.[37] This gerontocratic ideal was not without contradiction, for the very elderly were removed from economic and political power and 'essentially it was men in their forties or fifties who ruled'.[38] Moreover the existence of this ideal did not obviate the need for careful material provision for the elderly. There is a certain poignancy in the details of wills which specify the exact houseroom and the degree of access to the household fire which is to be left to aged parents.[39] However, this suggests that Lear's and his daughter's bargaining over the number of his knights need not be seen as an egregious insult and that the generational conflict within the nuclear family could not be resolved by recourse to a simply accepted ideal of filial piety.

As a corrective to prevailing gloomy assessments of the happiness of the early modern family, Keith Wrightson has produced evidence of individuals who show considerable concern to deal with family conflict in a humane and flexible fashion.[40] But it is equally clear from his evidence that family relations were the focus of a great deal of emotional energy and the primary source both of pleasure and pain. This is also borne out in Michael MacDonald's account of a seventeenth-century psychiatric practice in which, as today, women were more susceptible to mental illness than men:

> Not all the stress women suffered was caused by physical illness ... women were also more vulnerable than men to psychologically disturbing social situations. Their individual propensities to anxiety and

sadness were enhanced by patriarchal custom and values that limited
their ability to remedy disturbing situations ... Napier and his
troubled patients also believed that oppression made people miserable
and even mad, but the bondage they found most troubling subordinated daughters to parents, wives to husbands rather than peasants to
lords.[41]

This discussion of social history cannot propose an alternative
'interpretation' of the text or assert its true meaning in the light of
historical 'facts'. Rather it indicates that the text was produced
within the contradictions of contemporary ideology and practice
and suggests that similar contradictions exist within the play. These
contradictions could fruitfully be brought to bear in modern
criticism and productions. The dispute between Lear and his
daughters is in part concerned with love and filial gratitude but it also
dramatises the tense relationship between those bonds and the
material circumstances in which they function. Lear's decision to
publish his daughters' dowries is so 'that future strife / May be
prevented now': the connection between loving harmony and
economic justice is the accepted factor which underlies the formal
patterning of the opening scene and is disrupted only by Cordelia's
asides which introduce a notion of love as a more individual and
abstract concept, incompatible both with public declaration and
with computation of forests, champains, rivers and meads.
Cordelia's notion of love gained precedence in modern ideology but
it seriously disrupts Lear's discussion of property and inheritance.
When Lear responds with 'Nothing will come of nothing' his words
need not be delivered as an angry calling to account: they could
equally be presented as a puzzled reaction to an inappropriate idea.
Moreover Cordelia is not opposing hereditary duty to transcendent
love – she does not reply 'There's beggary in the love that can be
reckoned'. When she expands on her first assertion her legal
language suggests a preference for a limited, contractual relationship: 'I love your majesty / According to my bond, no more nor less'
(I.i.94–5). The conflict between the contractual model and the
patriarchal model of subjects' obligations to their king was at issue in
contemporary political theory[42] and Cordelia's words here introduce a similar conflict into the question of obligations within the
family.

When in Act II Lear again bargains with his daughters, a similar
confusion between affective relations and contractual obligations is
in play. Lear asserts the importance of the contractual agreement
made with his daughters, for it is his only remaining source of power.
Since they are now in control, Goneril and Regan can assert an

apparently benign notion of service which does not depend on contract or mathematical computation:

> What need you five and twenty? ten? or five?
> To follow in a house where twice so many
> Have a command to tend you? (II.iv.259–62)

The emotional impact of the scene, which is its principal power in modern productions, simply confuses the complex relations between personal autonomy, property and power which are acted out in this confrontation. The scene could be directed to indicate that the daughters' power over Lear is the obverse of his former power over them. His power over them is socially sanctioned but its arbitrary and tyrannical character is clear from his treatment of Cordelia. Lear kneeling to beg an insincere forgiveness of Regan is no more nor less 'unsightly' than Goneril's and Regan's formal protestations to their father. Both are the result of a family organisation which denies economic autonomy in the name of transcendent values of love and filial piety and which affords no rights to the powerless within it. Such a production of meaning offers the pleasure of understanding in place of the pleasure of emotional identification. In this context Lear's speeches about nature and culture are part of an argument, not a *cri de coeur*; the blustering of his threats is no longer evidence of the destruction of a man's self-esteem but the futile anger of a powerful man deprived of male power.

Further potential for comically undermining the focus on Lear is provided by the Fool, who disrupts the narrative movement of the action, subverting if not denying the emotional impact of the scenes in which he appears. In an important sense the Fool is less an *alter ego* for Lear than for his daughters: like them he reminds Lear and the audience of the material basis for the change in the balance of power. However, where they exploit Lear's powerlessness with cruelty and oppression he denies that necessity by his continued allegiance. In modern productions this important channel for an alternative view of events is closed off by holding the Fool within the narrative, using him as a means to heighten the emotional appeal of Lear's decline.[43]

The potential for subversive contradiction in the text is, however, restricted to the first part. Lear's madness and the extrusion of Gloucester's eyes heavily weight the action towards a simpler notion of a time when humanity must perforce prey upon itself like monsters of the deep, denying comic recognition of the material facts of existence. Yet even Cordelia's self-denying love or Gloucester's stoic resignation are denied the status of ideological absolutes. The grotesque comic lie of Gloucester's fall from Dover cliff is hardly a firm basis for a belief in the saving power of divine providence and Cordelia's acceptance of her father's claims on her is futile because it is unsupported by material power.

A production of the text which would restore the element of dialectic, removing the privilege both from the character of Lear and from the ideological positions which he dramatises, is crucial to a feminist critique. Feminist criticism need not restrict itself to privileging the woman's part or to special pleading on behalf of female characters. It can be equally well served by making a text reveal the conditions in which a particular ideology of femininity functions and by both revealing and subverting the hold which such an ideology has for readers both female and male.

The misogyny of King Lear, both the play and its hero, is constructed out of an ascetic tradition which presents women as the source of the primal sin of lust, combining with concerns about the threat to the family posed by female insubordination. However the text also dramatises the material conditions which lie behind assertions of power within the family, even as it expresses deep anxieties about the chaos which can ensue when that balance of power is altered.

An important part of the feminist project is to insist that the alternative to the patriarchal family and heterosexual love is not chaos but the possibility of new forms of social organisation and affective relationships. However, feminists also recognise that our socialisation within the family and, perhaps more importantly, our psychological development as gendered subjects make these changes no simple matter.[44] They involve deconstructing the sustaining comforts of love and the family as the only haven in a heartless world. Similarly a feminist critique of the dominant traditions in literature must recognise the sources of its power, not only in the institutions which reproduce them but also in the pleasures which they afford. But feminist criticism must also assert the power of resistance, subverting rather than co-opting the domination of the patriarchal Bard.

Notes

1 See Michele Barrett, *Ideology and Cultural Production* (London: Croom Helm, 1979), Judith Williamson, *Decoding Advertisements* (London: Marion Boyars 1978) and Annette Kuhn, *Women's Pictures: Feminism and Cinema* (London: Routledge, 1982).

2 See the preface to Carolyn Lenz, Gayle Greene and Carol Neely, eds., *The Woman's Part: Feminist Criticism of Shakespeare* (Urbana: Illinois Univ. Press, 1980).

3 See Lenz, Greene and Neely, 'Women and Men in Shakespeare: a selective bibliography', *ibid.*, pp. 314–36.
4 See especially Madelon Gohlke, '"I wooed thee with my sword": Shakespeare's Tragic Paradigms', *ibid.*, pp. 150–70.
5 Janet Adelman, '"Anger's my meat": Feeding, Dependency and Aggression in *Coriolanus*' in David Bevington and J. L. Halio eds., *Shakespeare's Pattern of Excelling Nature* (Newark, 1978), pp. 108–24.
6 Coppelia Kahn, 'Coming of Age in Verona', in Lenz, Greene and Neely, *op. cit.*, p. 171.
7 In particular Dorothy Dinnerstein, *The Mermaid and the Minotaur: Sexual Arrangements and Human Malaise* (New York: Harper and Row, 1977) and Nancy Chodorow, *The Reproduction of Mothering: Psychoanalysis and the Sociology of Gender* (Berkeley and Los Angeles: California Univ. Press, 1979).
8 Coppelia Kahn, 'Man's Estate', in *Masculine Identity in Shakespeare* (Berkeley and Los Angeles: California Univ. Press, 1981) p. 11.
9 *Ibid.*, p. 1.
10 Linda Bamber, *Comic Women, Tragic Men: a Study of Gender and Genre in Shakespeare* (Stanford: Stanford Univ. Press), p. 1.
11 *Ibid.*, p. 5.
12 *Ibid.*, p. 15.
13 *Ibid.*, p. 32.
14 *Ibid.*, p. 39.
15 Marilyn French, *Shakespeare's Division of Experience* (London: Cape, 1982).
16 *Ibid.*, p. 25.
17 Juliet Dusinberre, *Shakespeare and the Nature of Women* (London: Macmillan, 1975) p. 153. Dusinberre's understanding of feminism has been challenged by Martha Anderson-Thom, 'Thinking about Women and their Prosperous Art: a Reply to Juliet Dusinberre's *Shakespeare and the Nature of Women*', *Shakespeare Studies*, 11 (1978), 259–76.
18 William Haller and Malleville Haller, 'The Puritan Art of Love', *Huntington Library Quarterly*, 5, (1942) 235–72. Cf. K. Davies, '"The sacred condition of equality": how original were Puritan doctrines of marriage?' *Social History*, 5 (1977), 566–7.
19 Juliet Dusinberre, *op. cit.*, p. 183.
20 Chapter 4, 'Husbands and Wives, Parents and Children' of Keith Wrightson, *English Society 1580–1680* (London: Hutchinson, 1982) provides a comprehensively informed discussion of the controversy. See also Lawrence Stone, *The Family, Sex and Marriage in England, 1500–1800* (London: Weidenfeld and Nicolson, 1977); G. R. Quaife, *Wanton Wenches and Wayward Wives: Peasants and Illicit Sex in Early Seventeenth Century England* (London: Croom Helm, 1969); Margaret Spufford, *Contrasting Communities: English Villagers in the Sixteenth and Seventeenth Centuries* (Cambridge University Press, 1974).
21 Lenz, Greene and Neely, *op. cit.* preface, p. ix.
22 Coppelia Kahn, *op. cit.*, p. 20.
23 Linda Bamber, *op. cit.*, p. 43.
24 See for example Lisa Jardine's summary dismissal of feminist criticism in favour of historical criticism in *Still Harping on Daughters: Women and Drama in the Age of Shakespeare* (Brighton: Harvester, 1983), introduction, or Inga-Stina Ewbank reminding her audience at the bicentennial congress of the Shakespeare Association of America of Ibsen's distinction between 'feminism' and the truth about men and women: 'Shakespeare's Portrayal of Women: a 1970s View' in Bevington and Halio, eds. *op. cit.*, pp. 222–9.
25 See Ernest Schanzer, 'The Marriage Contracts in *Measure for Measure*' *Shakespeare Survey*, 13 (1960), 81–9, and replies by J. Birje-Patil, 'Marriage Contracts in *Measure for Measure*', *Shakespeare Studies*, 5 (1969), 106–11; S.

Kathleen McLuskie

Narajan, 'Measure for Measure and Elizabethan Betrothals', Shakespeare Quarterly 14, (1963), 115–19.
26 This idea was fully developed in Jonathan Miller's Eliot Lectures, 'The After Life of Plays' delivered at the University of Kent in 1978 (London: Faber and Faber, forthcoming).
27 Laura Mulvey, 'Visual Pleasure and Narrative Cinema', Screen 16, no. 3, p. 13. For a more extended discussion see Annette Kuhn, op. cit.
28 Cf. Laura Mulvey's account of the way songs and close-up are used in order to fetishise women characters in Hollywood cinema, op. cit., p. 13. The fact that Mariana was played by a boy does not alter the point: she is always played by a woman in modern representation.
29 Cf. the discussion of 'Reading as a Woman' in Jonathan Culler, Theory and Criticism after Structuralism (Ithaca: Cornell University Press, 1982), pp. 43–63. The implication there is that positioning the reader as a woman is a matter of free choice and the position adopted is coherent and determines clear cut readings.
30 Raymond Williams, Modern Tragedy (London: Chatto, 1966), p. 45.
31 See The True Chronicle History of King Leir, ed. Geoffrey Bullough, The Narrative and Dramatic Sources of Shakespeare, vol. VII (London: Routledge, 1973), 337–402.
32 The imagery of ll. 12–14 gives this resolution a political tinge; resolution is seen as subjection.
33 See The True Chronicle History of King Leir ed. Bullough, p. 393.
34 Freud in 'The Theme of the Three Caskets' accounts for the psychological power of the myth in terms of 'the three inevitable [sic] relations that a man has with a woman – the woman who bears him, the woman who is his mate and the woman who destroys him'. Lear's entrance with Cordelia dead in his arms is, for Freud, a wish-fulfilling inversion of the old man being carried away by death (The Collected Papers of Sigmund Freud, ed. Ernest Jones, vol. IV (London: Hogarth, 1925), pp. 244–56).
35 'The problem of stereotyping is not that it is true or false, distorting or manipulated, but that it closes off certain production of meaning in the image', Elizabeth Cowie, 'Images of Women', Screen Education, 23 (1977), 22.
36 Bullough (op. cit., p. 270) has drawn attention to 'the remarkable historical parallel' of the case of Sir Brian Annesley whose daughter Cordell took steps to prevent her sister declaring their father insane so that she could take over the management of his estate. Cordell Annesley's solution was that a family friend should be entrusted with the old man and his affairs.
37 Keith Thomas, 'Age and Authority in Early Modern England', Proceedings of the British Academy, 62 (1976), 214.
38 Ibid., p. 211.
39 Discussed in Margaret Spufford, op. cit., p. 113.
40 See note 20.
41 Michael MacDonald, Mystical Bedlam: Madness, Anxiety and Healing in Seventeenth Century England (Cambridge Univ. Press, 1981), pp. 39–40.
42 See Gordon Schochet, Patriarchalism in Political Thought (Oxford: Blackwell, 1975).
43 For example in the 1982–3 Royal Shakespeare Company production Antony Sher played the fool as a vaudeville clown but the theatrical inventiveness of his double act with Lear emphasised the closeness of their relationship with the fool as a ventriloquist's dummy on Lear's knee.
44 See Michele Barrett and Mary McIntosh, The Anti-Social Family (London: Verso, 1982).

Strategies of State and political plays: *A Midsummer Night's Dream, Henry IV, Henry V, Henry VIII*

I

For over fifty years traditional literary criticism has read Shakespeare's history plays in one of three ways: as overt political texts that can be interpreted by reference to the historical source material; as dramatic entertainments to be compared aesthetically with examples from the more familiar genres of comedy, tragedy or romance; or as part of a process of personal development which accompanied his youthful comedies and prepared him for the grand metaphysical tragedies and the mature vision of his lyrical romances.[1] Each of these positions testifies to a belief in the distinction between literature and politics and so serves the interests of modern society by imposing this belief on the past. Yet none of these can begin to explain why Shakespeare – whether alone or in collaboration – could not write a good chronicle history play at the close of his career.[2]

What if, on the other hand, we were to show that a play such as *Henry VIII* uses non-dramatic material much more the way such material was used in dramatic romance and tragicomedy than as it was used in the chronicle histories of the 1590s? And what if the histories written under Elizabeth represented political problems and resolved them in terms resembling the romantic comedies and the Petrarchan lyrics of the same period? Would we not have to rethink our notion of artistic genre, if these Elizabethan and Jacobean literary forms were found to resemble contemporaneous strategies of political argumentation more than they resembled each other? This, even when the texts compared were written by the same author over the length of his career? Were such a relationship among various forms of Renaissance writing discovered, it would indicate that the opposition between a literary use of language and a political use of the same linguistic materials is largely a modern invention. We would have to conclude that what we now call Renaissance literature displayed its politics as it idealised or demystified specific forms of power, that such a display rather than a work's transcendence or referentiality, was what made it aesthetically successful.

During the Tudor and Stuart periods the monarchy confronted different forms of political opposition over which it had to display authority by means of quite different strategies. We cannot describe this change in the exercise and representation of power as a matter of choice or whimsy on the part of the individual occupying the throne, as if James simply decided to modify Elizabeth's most characteristic policies. With the ascension of James we are not entering new semiotic territory even though there appears to be a widespread attempt on the part of the literate classes to revise the problematics of power. While the problems confronting the monarchy were taking on a recognisably modern form, James's own practice of political authority was clearly archaic in comparison with Elizabeth's. Given the abrupt shift in the strategies necessary for maintaining monarchical power between the Reformation and the Interregnum, we cannot expect the literature which idealised that power to develop according to either its own logic or that of an individual author. Quite the contrary: as the inherited prerogatives of the monarch were challenged, first by a contending faction within the aristocracy, but then later by dissenting voices outside the oligarchy, literature had to employ radically discontinuous political strategies for idealising political authority. Indeed, we find a whole set of literary genres fell out of favour with the accession of James I and a new set provided the appropriate means of setting oneself in proximity to political power. Along with such forms as romantic comedy, Petrarchan poetry and prose romance, the chronicle history play enjoyed a period of unprecedented popularity during the 1590s. And, like so many other literary forms that had been popular in the last two decades of the sixteenth century, chronicle history plays with few exceptions simply ceased to be written after 1599, the year *Henry V* was produced. The most notable exception to this widespread shift in literary tastes was, of course, *Henry VIII*.

II

To understand how political conditions made history plays virtually unwritable, one might consider exactly what the history play shared with romantic comedy and Petrarchan poetry that enabled these genres to address the interests of the same audience successfully and then hasten into obsolescence together. For all their differences, romantic comedy and chronicle history use the same rhetorical strategy to produce political order out of sexual and political relations respectively. That is, they transform patriarchal hierarchies into a state of disorder for the purpose of creating two bases for authority, and thus two competing hierarchies of power, which only the monarch can hold together in harmonious discord. To this end, Shakespeare uses his drama to authorise political authority, and political authority as he represents it, in turn authorises art.

If we take the example of *Midsummer Night's Dream*, a play surely characteristic of Shakespeare's romantic comedies, we can see that the problem which authority has to master is a problem with authority itself, authority grown archaic. At the outset, the law seems to serve only the will of the father. A comedic resolution obviously requires either the independence of the law or the generosity of the father. It requires, in other words, a more inclusive order. Given that romantic comedy invariably poses this problem, only one form of resolution will do, the formation of an authority figure who overrules the existing law of the father. Oberon represents the traditional alternative to patriarchal law. He is the figure of carnival, and the introduction of this principle into the play triggers a series of inversions.[3] As if Titania's playing the role of an unruly woman were not enough to tell what this is all about, Puck reproduces similar forms of inversion among the Athenians – both lovers and mechanicals – who have wandered into the woods.[4] Such inversions – of gender, age, status, even of species – violate all the categories organising Elizabethan reality itself. This Renaissance nightmare can occur precisely because patriarchal law is initially so closely identified with political authority that to violate the will of the father is to return to what Hobbes would later represent as the horrors of a state of nature.

The figures of festival operate to break down the hierarchical distinctions organising Elizabethan society, only – in the end – to be taken within the social order where they authorise a new form of political authority.[5] This mutually transforming exchange places disorder within the framework of festival and displaces it on to art, as illustrated by 'the story of the night told o'er', Bottom's 'dream', as well as the mechanicals' production of the tragedy of Pyramus and Thisbe. When Theseus and his party come upon the sleeping couples lying intermingled on the ground, the Duke surmises, 'No doubt they rose up early to observe / The rite of May ...' (IV.i.132–3).[6] By

[111]

identifying the lovers as revellers, Theseus does more than decriminalise their transgression of the law; he identifies their state of disarray with the order of art. 'I know you two for rival enemies,' he says to the young men, 'How came this gentle concord in the world ...?' (IV.i.142–3). At the same time, however, the inclusion of filial disobedience within a field of permissible illegalities, changes the construction of political authority. What had been a violation of the father's law, in other words, thus becomes a scene of harmony. Indeed, when Egeus presses Theseus to punish the youthful offenders, the Duke overrules the father.

But if Theseus authorises certain inversions of power relations by situating them within the framework of festival and art, then it is also true that the introduction of disorder into the play ultimately authorises political authority. Once Theseus includes the rites of May within the domain of the permissible, the revellers in turn fall on their knees before him. Thus brought together, revellers and Duke can comprise a harmonious political body where the juridical power of the monarch exists independently from that of the patriarch. When Theseus overrules the angry father, juridical power can no longer be identified with patriarchal power. A new set of political conditions appears where competing bases for authority are held in equipoise by the Duke. That is, his ideal role is an improvement, in terms of the play, over the punitive power he threatened to exercise at its opening. The entire last act of the play consequently theorises the process of inversion whereby art and politics end up in this mutually authorising relationship. This process is then reproduced on the stage in the form of an Elizabethan tragedy which has been converted into comedy as rude mechanicals play a range of parts from those of noble lovers to the creatures and objects of the natural world.

The popularity of such inversions becomes clear when we see how Elizabeth herself used various forms of authority against one another. It is not enough to say that the transfiguration of authority in romantic comedy resembles Elizabeth's actual style of exercising power. To be sure, she used her power as a patron to affect the power of the ruling families and thus set economically-based political authority in opposition to that based on blood. Yet this strategy was more than personal ingenuity on her part, for her characteristic strategies for expressing power were just as dependent upon the political conditions of the time as the form of a comedy such as *Midsummer Night's Dream*.

The Acts of Parliament of 1536 and 1543 had given Henry VIII the power to determine succession. His will not only specified that the crown would pass to Edward, Mary, and Elizabeth in that order, it also specified that if his children should die without issue, the crown would pass to his younger sister's children in the Suffolk line and not to her older sister's children in the superior hereditary Stuart line.[7] Henry thus treated the crown as property, governed by the same common-law rules against alien inheritance as any other piece of English property. By exploiting his legal prerogative to authorise this line of descent, Henry used the civil authority of a property owner to define the monarchy in such terms. Thus he set the principle of inheritance against that of primogeniture which would be invoked later by supporters of Mary Queen of Scots and her line. During Elizabeth's reign both Catholic and Stuart spokesmen insisted on the traditional view of the monarch as two bodies, a body natural and a body mystical, in the same body.[8] Theirs was a monolithic view of power that saw the body politic as the corporate body of the crown in perpetuity. The mystical body purged the body natural of attainder; it joined the king with his royal predecessors so that they were one and the same corporate person; and it was joined to the king, they argued, like an affair of the heart in a marital pre-contract of the blood royal.

A similar logic operates in *Midsummer Night's Dream* as the law and the father temporarily come into contradiction in the last act of the play. In this instance, however, the splitting of one form of power into two competing voices is hardly the dramatic problem. It is rather the comedic resolution to a problem created when authority assumed an absolute and monolithic form. Since Elizabeth's ascendancy could be justified according to her father's will and primogeniture both, her very person temporarily reconciled the competing viewpoints formulated during the debates concerning her succession. Because these arguments had spoken for competing interest groups during the succession debates, however, the monarch could no longer be understood as the mediatory figure of an earlier tradition, for such a figure maintained the distinction between inheriting the crown and inheriting property as it drew authority from blood and bestowed that authority upon the law. Elizabeth was a paradox, in other words, by virtue of the contradictory definitions of monarchal authority her succession had occasioned. Correspondingly to produce the comic resolution of dramatic conflict one had to produce a political contradiction such as that which is created between Theseus and Egeus. Indeed, in turning from drama to courtly poetry, we find the same strategy for idealising power obtains as the patron is endowed with the attributes of the reluctant lover. The puns characterising the Petrarchan mode of poetry effectively create a gulf between the power of property (in the form of economic favours) and that of blood (through marriage into the aristocracy), even as the two modes for representing power are brought together in one figure of speech. It is little wonder that Petrarchan poetry came into favour at the very time when power seemed to be exercised through the giving or the withholding of love in the form of economic favours.⁹ This poetry translated patronage relationships into sexual terms only to relegate such an ideal form of gratification to the status of pure fantasy. It is as if figures of contradiction were necessary for imagining one's relation to political authority. Such figures provided a form of self-definition for the prospective client that was inherently at odds with that figure of authority with whom the client sought to identify.

Her use of her sexuality – which includes her refusal to marry – indicates the degree to which Elizabeth maintained her political identity as the source of economic benefits, the patron of patrons, over and above that which descended upon her as legitimate bearer of blood. Her first two Parliaments frequently pressed her to resolve the succession question either by marrying and having issue or by naming her sucessor, but she refused to do either. It better served her interests to maintain a situation which frustrated all competing factions and alienated none of them. After 1571 the debate moved from Parliament to the Inns of Court and into polemical tracts as well where it split predictably along religious and nationalist lines.¹⁰ The dominant Protestant and English view tended to support the legality of Henry's will and so emphasised the contractual nature of the kingship, in contrast with Catholic and with Scottish views which continued to mystify the crown. When in her last hours Elizabeth finally named her successor, James VI of Scotland seemed the obvious choice particularly since he had been reared a Protestant. By naming her successor, the Queen acted in accordance with a view of the crown as an object of property, which was therefore dispensed according to the will of its owner. By naming James rather than an English claimant, however, she also acted according to the law of primogeniture.

III

Jonson's masque of *Oberon* (1611) written for the investiture of Henry as Prince of Wales, provides a useful comparison between the Elizabethan and Jacobean strategies for idealising political authority. Jonson evidently found it advantageous to revise the Elizabethan figure of misrule and thus the artistic authority associated with him. One purpose of the masque was the undoing of the opposition between the carnivalesque and the law of the father, an opposition, as we have seen, upon which such a comedy as *Midsummer Night's Dream* depends for its comic resolution. Various forms of carnival, particularly those associated with mayday festivities, became increasingly controversial during Elizabeth's reign. These were evidently viewed as recalcitrant practices that persisted despite the Reformation and, as such, were considered to be sacrilegious by certain radical Protestant factions. These reformers bolstered their theological arguments with economic and political ones, claiming that festival pastimes and maygames interrupted the work week, distracted apprentices, interfered with economic productivity, and mocked established forms of order. Certainly, Elizabeth's government felt some threat in the figures of inversion and boundary dissolution, and yet the government's response was mixed. On the one hand, as Stallybrass has argued, when Elizabeth's accession day, 17 November, became a national holiday it was clearly an attempt on the part of the State 'to harness and appropriate the forces of misrule'.[11] On the other hand, Elizabeth was careful not to arouse opposition to the central administration either by actively supporting traditional festival celebrations or by enforcing rules that would suppress them. Also her government frustrated attempts to make into law the practice of sabbatarianism despite the growing support this movement enjoyed in the industrial areas and urban centres.[12] These very same towns were also enacting legislation against theatrical performances and entertainments, and it is this legislation that reveals the political motivation most germane to my project.

Margot Heinemann summarises the letters from the Lord Mayor and Aldermen of London to the Privy Council in 1597 listing their objections to the theatre. Not only did they condemn plays for drawing people away from sermons on Sunday, she notes, but the city fathers also felt such entertainments were a source of social disruption: 'they encouraged apprentices to absent themselves from work ... they caused traffic jams and spread infection in time of plague: and they gave an opportunity for the unemployed and idle to meet in riotous assemblies. Indeed, unruly apprentices and servants had admitted that they foregathered at stage plays to organize their "mutinous attempts", "being also the ordinary places for masterless men to come together".'[13] Yet even as they condemned the popular theatre, 'the Aldermen themselves freely staged shows, plays, and masques privately in their own houses. They lavished thousands of pounds on Lord Mayors' pageants to impress Londoners with the wealth and glory of their city, and to preach, through allegorical tableaux, the virtues of industry and thrift'

Leonard Tennenhouse

(p. 31). It was not theatre *per se* that disturbed the town fathers. What was at stake was not the nature of the performance, not a moral issue, but a political one: who had control of the means for representing power. Only those performances could be authorised in London which in turn authorised the governing powers of that city.

In contrast to Elizabeth, James made it a matter of royal policy not only to seek control of the theatre but also to advocate the celebration of festivals and the practice of various maytime sports. In the *Basilikon Doron* he approves of the practices of the traditional festivities, and in the infamous *Book of Sports* (1618) he argues that participating in sports and festivities did more than improve the health of the labouring poor and make them fit for the army. It actually prevented the populace from engaging in subversive political activities. In declaring his position openly, he necessarily defined his authority in opposition to radical Protestantism where Elizabeth had successfully avoided such confrontation. Maygames and misrule thus became a highly charged political language and '... to advocate such pastimes became tantamount to a declaration of loyalty to the king and conservative Anglicanism ...'.[14]

What more effective way, then, of revising the figures of Elizabethan literature than using revels to represent the investiture of the heir to the English throne? What better way to dramatise the new concept of political power than by using Oberon to portray the future monarch of England and thus to symbolise a rebirth of the powers of blood? In this masque he thus inhabits a palace along with the noblest knights of history now 'Quickened with a second birth'.[15] As a figure for the prince, Oberon's costume incorporates the signs of Roman, Arthurian, and Jacobean nobility, and two white bears draw his chariot toward the centre of power to the accompaniment, significantly, of this song:[16]

> Melt earth to sea, sea flow to air,
> And air fly into fire,
> Whilst we in tunes to Arthur's chair
> Bear Oberon's desire,
> Than which there nothing can be higher
> Save James, to whom it flies:
> But he the wonder is of tongues of ears, of eyes.

(ll. 220–6)

As the father of Prince Henry, James is the origin of his son's power. In the guise of Oberon the son acknowledges the principle of genealogy as he places all the powers traditionally opposing the patriarch – those of youth, nature, and the tradition of romance – in

[116]

the king's service.[17] Thus we learn Oberon and his knights pay homage to James, 'To whose sole power and magic they do give / The honour of their being ...' (ll. 49–50). Moreover the costume which Inigo Jones designed for the faery king in this masque alludes to the three monarchies James claimed to unite within himself. It was as if the masque brought all the traditional signs of authority under the governance of the contemporary monarch for the sole purpose of identifying that monarch as an historically earlier, more monolithic, and mythical form of political authority.

It was particularly appropriate for the royal masque to present the monarch in the grandly hierarchical terms we find in *Oberon*, furthermore, for throughout the previous year the king had been locked in debate with Parliament over precisely this issue of whether there were two competing basis for political power or, indeed, only one. The year before Jonson's *Oberon* was produced at Court, the king and Parliament were negotiating the Great Contract.[18] This proposal would have had the crown give up certain traditional sources of income in exchange for a large subsidy and a yearly grant of money. After six weeks of debate it was clear that James's use of royal prerogatives, his notion of an absolute monarchy, and his notorious liberality all contributed to Parliament's unwillingness to accept Cecil's proposals on behalf of the king. Parliament's refusal to co-operate readily in relieving his debts infuriated James, making him less willing to compromise on crucial issues. In his speech to Parliament on 21 March 1610 James tried to force Parliament into helping him solve his financial dilemma by redefining their refusal to do so as a violation of divine law. He would have the political hierarchy understood in terms of the same mystical notion of patriarchy that shapes Jonson's *Oberon*, for his speech identifies the monarch's power with that of God and with that of the father: 'The State of MONARCHIE is the supremest vpon earth: For Kings are not only GODS Lieutenants vpon earth, and sit vpon GODS throne, but euen by GOD himselfe they are called GODS ... In the Scriptures Kings are called GODS, and their power after a certaine relation compared to the Diuine power. Kings are also compared to Fathers of families: for a King is trewly *Parens Patriae* ...'.[19] The monolithic figure of State power is not simply how authors imagined the king wanted his authority represented; these are the very terms in which the king imagined political power.[20] His logic ('but', 'for') is overwhelmed by his use of repetition, which at first allegorically links secular power with divine power but ultimately makes 'King', 'God', and 'father' into interchangeable concepts. James elaborated these points by drawing further analogies between the king's power and God's: like God and like the father (according to the law of nature), kings have the power to raise up, to reward, to make low and to punish. The king's authority in this system of belief is not only a metaphysical fact (he is called God) but a social fact (he is a father), as well as a fact of nature (he is the descendent of kings). Such political rhetoric allows for no legitimate form of authority other than his.

Establishing this view of monarchical authority would certainly serve James's interests in dealing with Parliament, for in the three previous sessions the king's finances had been the major point of contention. When James came to the throne he inherited a sizeable debt from Elizabeth, a soaring inflation rate, diminished land capital of the crown, and decreasing supplies of revenue to meet the rapidly increasing costs of government. The economy had become quite complex, and the system of patronage which managed the crown's sources of income was grossly inefficient. To hear many in Parliament tell of it, however, James's most serious liability was his extravagance. To maintain his household, which performed many government functions, cost more that double Elizabeth's expenses during her last years. Worse still, the grants of honours and annuities he made were five times those of the late Queen.[21] While Parliament was unwilling to turn against the very power that authorised it to sit, its relations with the monarch took a turn under James that would eventually make his preferred model of authority into a figure of misrule. When, by the end of the year 1610, the king had refused to give up his feudal rights of wardship and purveyance, fearing his exercise of hereditary authority would become subject to the control of Parliament, Parliament refused to yield the king £600,000 in subsidy and the yearly grant of £200,000, fearing in turn that the king would grow financially independent of Parliament and never feel pressed to call them to sit, or worse, that he might grow still more extravagant. The debates over the Great Contract reached a stalemate as parliament granted James a small subsidy of £100,006, and James dismissed Parliament, preferring to rely chiefly on his hereditary prerogatives for financing both the royal household and the government.

As he attempted to suppress the contradictions Elizabeth incorporated within her very person and acted out through political policies, however, James seems to have reawakened the conceptual dualism informing the succession debate and, what is more, to have shot this dualism through with new political meaning. James's first year and a half as King of England saw numerous complaints about the inefficiency of his bureaucracy and his misuse of what remained of feudal sources of revenue.[22] Throughout his first parliament there were serious disagreements over who constituted the law, James claiming for himself the power to be the *lex loquens* while the Commons countered that he could only be the law speaking with the aid of a sitting Parliament.[23] To justify their rejection of the king's requests, ironically enough, Parliament did not contest the hereditary prerogatives of the king. Indeed, they accepted those prerogatives as the basis of their own authority but then claimed for Parliament a separate history of rights and privileges which arose with – but often contested – that of the king. While they granted that James was the source of authority, even their own, and thus had a right to request funds of them, Parliament did in fact distinguish those of his needs which were needs of the political body from those which were illicit forms of display, thus driving a wedge in the figurative logic of a tradition that identified the display of wealth and title with the proper exercise of aristocratic authority. Speaking for many in Parliament, Sir Henry Neville told the king, 'Where your Majesty's expense groweth by Commonwealth, we are bound to maintain it, otherwise not'.[24] To challenge the mystical identification of the political body with the inherited power of blood was to pave the way, semiotically, for the day when, as Jacques Donzelot puts it, 'the state was no longer the end of production, but its means: it was the responsibility of the state to govern social relations, in such a manner as to intensify this production to a maximum by restricting consumption'.[25]

At least until the Interregnum England could hardly see extravagant displays of State authority as a form of misrule; the traditional opposition between licit and illicit displays of power held. But as the State came to be seen more as the means than as the end of production, what had been the legitimate – if not primary – function of the monarch, his extravagant displays of State authority, would be equated with misrule. Throughout the Renaissance, of course, this counter-argument had a voice. The anti-theatrical propaganda and the sabbatarian tracts and sermons commonly represented the figures of carnival as something that corrupted the social order from within. The government's position, on the other hand, seems to have been that such transgressions of civil and religious law were ultimately the less threatening for being incorporated in the official rituals, pageants, and games of the State.[26] A conflation of opposing political figures – the display of legitimate power and the illicit practices of popular festival – would eventually become the libertine figure of the *ancien régime* early on in the process of making a modern society, the process which Williams so aptly named 'the long revolution'.[27] As Harry Payne has convincingly demonstrated, the formulation of this libertine figure succeeded in identifying the qualities of 'blood, magic, belief, and tradition', all signs of aristocratic privilege, with the gross sensuality of the populace, thus authorising a new aristocracy of fiscally responsible, rational intellectuals as the proper agents of moral reform.[28]

IV

Though they may seem to have little to do with politics, such forms as Petrarchan lyrics or romantic comedy are openly and expressly political in the strategies by which they idealise State authority. We must assume the chronicle history play can hardly be less so. But what makes it difficult to perceive these strategies operating in the material of chronicle history is not quite the same as the obstacle we confront in attempting to historicise romantic comedy. Shakespeare's use of political rather than psycho-sexual subject matter in his history plays entices many to make that material allude to contemporary events, which is to prevent us from seeing his work as a symbolic activity of a piece with and giving shape to those events. In fact, it is fair to say that the form of the history play is so completely that of the Elizabethan controversies, that the materials of chronicle history cannot be so assembled once the official strategies for mastering those controversies have changed.

In certain respects, *Henry V* can be called a piece of political hagiography. Henry discovers domestic conspirators as if by omniscience and punishes them. He secures his borders against Scottish invaders, unifies the dispirited and heterogeneous body under his authority, and wins the battle of Agincourt, thus taking control of territory which had been claimed by French inheritance law and contested by English laws of succession. The hagiographical theme of this play understands power as the inevitable unfolding of order. But to idealise political authority Shakespeare evidently found it necessary to catch this theme up in a contrary one.

Here history is nothing else but the history of forms of disorder, over which Henry can temporarily triumph because he alone embodies the contradictions that can bring disruption into the service of the State and make a discontinuous political process appear as a coherent moment. Thus the Epilogue continues on past a comedic resolution to remind the Elizabethan audience that the very marriage which secured the peace with France and established the line of succession eventually led to the War of the Roses:

Henry the Sixt, in infant bands crown'd King
Of France and England, did this king succeed;
Whose state so many had the managing,
That they lost France, and made his England bleed ...

(ll. 9–12)

Providence temporarily comes under the control of the monarch. Working against political order, however, it provides a tide that one can ride into power but against which one must struggle vainly in order to remain there. This seems to be the point of Richard III's rise, of Henry Richmond's victory over Richard, of Bolingbroke's successful challenge to Richard II, but particularly of Hal's defeat of Hotspur and his subsequent victory as king over the French. In each case, State authority does not descend directly through blood. Rather, it pursues a disrupted and discontinuous course through history, arising out of conflicts within the reigning oligarchy as to which bloodline shall legitimately rule. Together these chronicle history plays demonstrate, then, that authority goes to that contender who can seize hold of the symbols and signs legitimising authority and wrest them from his rivals, thus making them serve his own interests. What else is accomplished, however perversely, by Richard III's incarceration of the young princes? Or Bolingbroke's public ceremony in which Richard is forced to hand over the crown? And surely Hal's self-coronation, pre-emptive though it may be, dramatises the same principle, that power is an inversion of legitimate authority which gains possession, as such, of the means of self-legitimisation.

Such a rhetorical strategy guarantees that figures of carnival will play a particularly instrumental role in the idealising process that proves so crucial in legitimising the State. It cannot be accidental that the *Henriad*, which produces Shakespeare's most accomplished Elizabethan monarch, should also produce his most memorable figure of misrule. The complete king was by birth entitled to the throne, but a youth misspent in low-life activities, at the same time, lends him the demonic features of the contender, a potential regicide, whose power has yet to be legitimised. The various conflicts comprising *Henry IV*, Parts I and II, by virtue of resembling the vicissitudes of fate, in actuality cohere as a single strategy of idealisation. In opposition to legitimate authority, Hal takes on a populist energy. At the same time, the law of the father seems to have atrophied and grown rigid to the degree that it can be inverted by the likes of Falstaff, whose abuses of legitimate authority, like those of Oberon, take on a menacing quality when unconstrained by the forest glade or tavern. Thus Shakespeare uses the figures of carnival to represent a source of power which poses a contradiction to that power inhering in genealogy. However, the various confrontations between licit and illicit authority in the *Henriad* more firmly draw the distinction between aristocracy and populace even as they overturn this primary categorical distinction. The figures of carnival ultimately authorise the State as the State appears to take on the vigour of festival. We see this, for example, in Vernon's account of Hal and his men preparing to do battle with Hotspur:

> Glittering in golden coats like images,
> As full of spirit as the month of May,
> And gorgeous as the sun at midsummer;
> Wanton as youthful goats, wild as young bulls. (IV.i.100–3)

The same process transfers what is weak and corrupt on to the tavern folk where it is contained and finally driven even from that debased world. Legitimate order can come into being only through disruption according to this principle, and it can maintain itself only through discontinuous and self-contradictory policies.

If Henry V appears to be Shakespeare's ultimate monarch, it is because in this king historical sources provided the author with material that met the Elizabethan conditions for idealisation. Yet these semiotic conditions for producing the ideal political figure are precisely what make Henry V so resistant to modern criticism's attempts at recuperating him for a post-Enlightenment humanism. The king's identity coalesces and his power intensifies as he unifies those territories that are his by hereditary law under his authority. But as this occurs, one finds that the figure of the monarch breaks apart and disappears into many different roles and dialects. He uses the strategies of disguise and inversion to occupy a range of positions from humble soldier to courtly lover and several in between. As a consequence, the king is virtually everywhere. He occupies the centre of every theatre of social action and in this way constitutes a State that to modern readers appears to have no centre at all, neither a continuous political policy nor an internally coherent self. To make sense to an Elizabethan audience, we must therefore assume, the king's body did not have to behave as if it were that of the modern individual in either his self-enclosed or his abstract totalising form. That body had to behave, semiotically speaking, as if blood had conspired with the disruptive operations of Providence to produce it. In becoming so many functions and dialects of a single political body, he makes the various social groups he thus contains lose their autonomy but he gives them their ideal identity. In other words, he instates a political hierarchy by practising forms of inversion.

In *Henry VIII*, on the other hand, Shakespeare uses quite different means to idealise political authority. This work of the mature playwright suppresses the discontinuities and contradictions which give Elizabethan history plays, as well as the monarchs which came to dominance in them, their distinctive form. Shakespeare's belated history play consequently resembles more the dramatic romances and masques that come into favour under James than it does the chronicle history play.[29] Operating in violation of the very strategy he so perfectly realised right through the end of the Epilogue of *Henry V*, Shakespeare makes genealogy one and the same thing as Providence in *Henry VIII*. The events which constitute this model of history are those which reproduce Henry VIII and thus perpetuate the power of blood; Henry's divorce from Katherine, for example, and the union with Anne from which Elizabeth is subsequently born. Operating under this imperative, the playwright has no cause to engender sympathy for Katherine or endow his monarch with it. He may in fact equate the unproductive mate with Wolsey and Buckingham – as being opposed to legitimate political authority – because they obstruct genealogy. Buckingham represents a contending line of succession and Wolsey's populist energy serves only his own ambitions. These, we must remember, were the very figures that lent the Elizabethan hero power and enabled him to seize the throne. As these figures came to define the forces conspiring against the Tudor and Stuart lines, Shakespeare rather obviously used them to revise the politics of his Elizabethan plays.

Shakespeare's Jacobean strategy for idealising power is no less tautological than the Elizabethan strategy it effectively revises. It should be noted that, unlike the political heroes of an earlier stage, Henry VIII does not have to overpower those who possess the symbols of authority in order to make his line legitimate. Quite the contrary: in possessing the blood, his body is in fact a living icon in relation to which all other signs and symbols acquire meaning and value. This is acknowledged when the king removes his mask after he and his revellers, disguised as shepherds and dressed in gold costumes, intrude upon Wolsey's banquet. Not only is Henry's presence felt by Wolsey and his guests before the king removes his mask to appear in his own guise, but once he does reveal himself the festivities reorganise around him. Wolsey simply cedes his position to one 'More worthy this place than myself, to whom / (If I but knew him) with my love and duty / I would surrender it' (I.iv.79–81). Henry need not struggle with his opponents because they possess no

power except that which he confers on them. It is as if they exist
only to demonstrate the absolute supremacy of his blood by their
utter subjection to it. Wolsey's famous advice to Cromwell just
before the deposed Cardinal goes off echoes Katherine's and Buckingham's last words by acknowledging Henry as the source of all
earthly power:

> Serve the King, and – prithee lead me in.
> There take an inventory of all I have,
> To the last penny, 'tis the King's. My robe
> And my integrity to heaven, is all
> I dare now call my own. (III.ii.450–4)

This is the triumph of the hagiographical theme: to locate the
essence of the fully realised figure in the original. In perfectly
realising this political strategy, however, history gives way to a slow
procession of tableaux which convert all metonymy into the same
static and hierarchical figure of political power.

Shakespeare's use of the carnivalesque in this play provides us
with a useful means of comparing this idealising strategy with
that giving the materials of chronicle history their Elizabethan form.
As his identity makes itself known, the King instantly assumes
Wolsey's role as the king of misrule. The illicit practices of this
'keech', or lump of suet, as Buckingham calls him become the
legitimate prerogatives of the State:

> Let's be merry,
> Good my Lord Cardinal: I have half a dozen healths
> To drink to these fair ladies, and a measure
> To lead 'em once again, and then let's dream
> Who's best in favour. Let the music knock it. (I.iv.104–8)

In this play the disruptive power associated with the erotic, the
demonic, and the folk never constitutes a field of contention.
Indeed, we find all that is politically threatening caught up,
sexualised and aestheticised in the official ceremony of Anne's
coronation:

> Such joy
> I never saw before. Great-bellied women,
> That had not half a week to go, like rams
> In the old time of war, would shake the press
> And make 'em reel before 'em. No man living
> Could say, 'This is my wife' there, all were woven
> So strangely in one piece. (IV.i.75–81)

Such a strategy for harnessing populist energy clearly maintains the absolute identification of power and genealogy.

It is no mere accident of history, then, that the ending of *Henry VIII* presents such a striking contrast to the Epilogue of *Henry V*. The blessing of the infant Elizabeth heralds the fulfilment of divine prophecy and guarantees the corporate nature of the Crown in perpetuity. It does not usher in a period of controversy and misrule over which a new contender will triumph. The poetics of Jacobean politics aim at transforming all such change into continuity. The fulfilment of this prophecy is none other than King James, whom Cranmer's speech unites with both Elizabeth and Henry VIII in the corporate identity of the crown.

V

If nothing else, Shakespeare's inability to write an Elizabethan chronicle history play for a Jacobean audience indicates the degree to which Renaissance drama was a political activity. I have not even attempted to show – as well one might in describing the political Shakespeare – how the individual writer immersed in this milieu sought to question political authority. By examining how he includes recalcitrant cultural materials and dramatises their suppression under the pressure of official strategies of idealisation, we could identify such a subversive Shakespeare.[30] My point is rather to suggest that during the Renaissance political imperatives were also aesthetic imperatives. As political circumstances changed and presented the monarch with new forms of opposition, then the strategies for legitimising that authority changed. In the Elizabethan history play, art authorises genealogy. That is, to legitimise blood one must acquire the signs and symbols of authorisation, which is to question the iconicity of the king's body and entertain the possibility of its arbitrary relation to the laws and ceremonies of State. Shakespeare's only Jacobean history play declares itself a contradiction in terms by emphatically cancelling out this notion of power. Genealogy authorises art in this play, and the production of art consequently comes under the political imperative to display wealth and title. Shakespearian drama could not hold up a constant mirror to political events any more than it could display the unfolding of a formalist logic or point to the development of a single personality; circumstances called forth discontinuous strategies for idealising power.

If art and politics defined the same domain of truth when Shakespeare wrote, we must assume his art was always political and that

Leonard Tennenhouse

it is our modern situation and not his world of meaning which prevents our finding his politics on the surface and seeing his strategies of displacement as political strategies. In contrast with the Renaissance, the modern brand of humanism opposes the literary use of language to its use as political discourse. Such a definition of literature obviously sets our tradition of reading apart from that of the Renaissance and makes the political Shakespeare invisible. Yet this explanation for the elusiveness of the political Shakespeare, however accurate, cannot remain unquestioned. To leave my argument at such a point would be to conclude that our critical tradition of reading does not let us see the politics of Renaissance writing because ours is not a political discourse. I must insist, to the contrary, that modern literature's attempt to produce transcendent truth is a terribly effective strategy for idealising political authority. Given the panoptical nature of authority in a modern society, however, we must conceal that authority in order to idealise it. Thus art makes power invisible as it makes the political operations of language itself invisible and locates that power both in the individual's subjectivity and in the object world which such language constitutes. It seems to me nothing else but this imperative to conceal the fact that language continues to idealise power can explain why the most obvious political features of Shakespeare's texts have gone largely unnoticed in Anglo-American literary criticism.

Notes

1 This tendency for criticism of the history plays to divide along such predictable lines was first noted by Harold Jenkins, 'Shakespeare's History Plays: 1900–1951', *Shakespeare Survey*, 6 (1953), 1–25. His categories still hold, as recent criticism of the history play shows.

2 R. A. Foakes, in his Introduction to the Arden edition of *King Henry VIII* (London: Methuen, 1957; rpt. 1968) offers the argument for Shakespeare's sole authorship. Cyrus Hoy, who has argued for Fletcher's share in the play, holds the work is nevertheless largely Shakespeare's, 'The Shares of Fletcher and his Collaborators in the Beaumont and Fletcher Canon (VII)', *Studies in Bibliography*, 15 (1962), 76. For the purposes of this paper, however, it does not matter whether the play is in part or in whole by Shakespeare, but rather why this Jacobean text took a different form from that of Elizabethan chronicle histories.

3 My discussion of the rhetorical figures of carnival and misrule owes a debt to Mikhail Bakhtin's *Rabelais and His World*, trans. Helene Iswolsky (Cambridge: MIT Press, 1968) and Michel Foucault's *Surveiller et Punir: Naissance de la prison* (Paris: Gallimard, 1975). For Bakhtin in particular, carnival represents those cultural practices which oppose the norm enforcing ceremonies and institutions of the State. In this critical tradition, then, carnival is neither a literary phenomenon nor an archetypal one. It is a means of describing certain

material practices of the body as they underwent literary displacement – or resisted it – in the making of modern society. Throughout this essay I am indebted to the work of Peter Stallybrass and Allon White who have traced this process of the displacement of carnival from the Renaissance to the modern period in their forthcoming *The Politics and Poetics of Trangression*. The authors very generously allowed me to consult portions of their book in manuscript and to cite their research.

4 For a discussion of the 'unruly woman' as a feature of carnival, see Natalie Zemon Davis, 'Women on Top', in *Society and Culture in Early Modern France* (Stanford University Press, 1975), pp. 124–51.

5 The many references to festival and misrule in this play have been discussed in a different fashion by C. L. Barber, *Shakespeare's Festive Comedy: a Study of Dramatic Form and its Relation to Social Custom* (Princeton University Press, 1959), pp. 155–62.

6 *The Riverside Shakespeare* (Boston: Houghton Mifflin, 1974). All citations of the plays are to this edition.

7 The problems with Henry VIII's will and the succession have been discussed by Mortimer Levine, *The Early Elizabethan Succession Question: 1558–1568* (Stanford University Press, 1966); see especially pp. 99–162.

8 This summary draws upon Marie Axton's admirable study *The Queen's Two bodies: Drama and the Elizabethan Succession* (London: Royal Historical Society, 1977). Ernst H. Kantorowicz, *The King's Two Bodies: a Study in Medieval Political Theology* (Princeton University Press, 1957) traces the origin of this controversy.

9 On this point see Leonard Tennenhouse, 'Sir Walter Ralegh and the Literature of Clientage', in *Patronage in the Renaissance*, eds. Guy Fitch Lytle and Stephen Orgel (Princeton University Press, 1981), pp. 235–58 and Arthur F. Marotti, '"Love is not Love": Elizabethan Sonnet Sequences and the Social Order,' *ELH*, 49 (1982), 396–428.

10 See Axton, pp. 18–37.

11 In the paper, 'Carnival Contained', delivered at MLA, New York, December, 1983.

12 Christopher Hill, *Society and Puritanism in Pre-Revolutionary England* (London: Secker and Warburg, 1964; rpt. New York: Schocken, 1967), p. 160.

13 *Puritanism and Theatre: Thomas Middleton and Opposition Drama under the Early Stuarts* (Cambridge University Press, 1980), p. 32.

14 Leah Sinanoglou Marcus, 'Herrick's *Hesperides* and the "Proclamation made for May"', *Studies in Philology*, 76 (1979), 52. Throughout this section, my discussion has drawn upon Marcus's argument.

15 *Ben Jonson: the Complete Masques*, ed. Stephen Orgel (New Haven: Yale University Press, 1969), l. 105. Citations of the text are to this edition.

16 For a discussion of the implications of Prince Henry's costume see Stephen Orgel, *The Illusion of Power: Political Theater in the English Renaissance* (Berkeley: University of California Press, 1975), pp. 66–70.

17 Jonathan Goldberg has discussed the many ironies in Jonson's presentation of this act of homage, *James I and the Politics of Literature: Jonson, Shakespeare, Donne, and Their Contemporaries* (Baltimore: Johns Hopkins University Press, 1983), pp. 123–6.

18 Alan G. R. Smith has analysed the contending positions during the debate on the Great Contract in 'Crown, Parliament and Finance: The Great Contract of 1610', *The English Commonwealth 1547–1640: Essays on Politics and Society*, eds. Peter Clark, Alan G.R. Smith and Nicholas Tyacke (New York: Barnes and Noble, 1979), pp. 111–27. See also Wallace Notestein, *The House of Commons, 1604–1610* (New Haven: Yale University Press, 1971), pp. 225–434.

19 *The Political Works of James I*, ed. Charles H. McIlwain (Cambridge, Mass.: Harvard University Press, 1918), p. 307. Citations in the text are to this edition.

20 See Goldberg, pp. 85–112 and Gordon J. Schochet, *Patriarchalism in Political Thought: the Authoritarian Family and Political Speculation and Attitudes Especially in Seventeenth Century England* (Oxford: Basil Blackwell, 1975).

21 Lawrence Stone, *The Crisis of the Aristocracy: 1558–1640* (Oxford University Press, 1965), pp. 403–49.

22 R. C. Munden, 'James I and the "growth of mutual distrust": King, Commons, and Reform, 1603–1604', *Faction and Parliament*, ed. Kevin Sharpe (Oxford: Clarendon Press, 1978), pp. 43–72.

23 *The Political Works of James I*, pp. 310–16 and Notestein, pp. 278–327.

24 Notestein, p. 421.

25 Jacques Donzelot, *The Policing of Families*, trans. Robert Hurley (New York: Pantheon, 1979), p. 13.

26 Jonas Barish, *The Anti-theatrical Prejudice* (Berkeley: University of California Press, 1981), pp. 80–131.

27 Raymond Williams, *The Long Revolution* (London: Chatto, 1961).

28 'Elite *versus* Popular Mentality in the Eighteenth Century', *Studies in Eighteenth Century Culture*, 8 (1979), 21.

29 For discussions of the features of masque and romance *Henry VIII* exhibits, see Ronald Berman, '*Henry VIII*: History and Romance', *English Studies*, 47 (1967), 112–27; H. M. Richmond, 'Shakespeare's *Henry VIII*: Romance Redeemed by History', *Shakespeare Studies*, 4 (1968), 334–49; Lee Bliss, 'The Wheel of Fortune and the Maiden Phoenix of Shakespeare's *King Henry the Eighth*', *ELH*, 42 (1975), 1–25; Edward I. Berry, '*Henry VIII* and the Dynamics of Spectacle', *Shakespeare Studies*, 12 (1979), 229–46.

30 For an important study of Jacobean drama from just such a perspective, see Jonathan Dollimore, *Radical Tragedy: Religion, Ideology and Power in the Drama of Shakespeare and his Contemporaries* (Brighton: Harvester, 1984; University of Chicago Press, 1984).

Part II
Reproductions, interventions

Introduction: Reproductions, interventions

It is often said that a play only really exists when it is given life in a performance; the text, the argument runs, is a mere shadow of any realisation. But, of course, performances differ greatly from each other; so what, then, is 'the play'? The question bulks especially large in the instance of 'Shakespeare's plays' where, on the one hand, there are so many and so diverse performances and, on the other hand, so much editorial effort is expended on establishing the text nearest to Shakespeare's presumed intentions. A comparably potent issue is whether 'the play' is really what it meant to its original audiences or a supposed 'timeless' meaning, for the historical context of 'Shakespeare's plays' has been intensively reconstructed, but the idea that he is 'not for an age but for all time' can be traced to Ben Jonson.

The sensible move with such apparently endless disputes is usually to get round behind them, to investigate the premises on which they are constructed. Claims that this or that version is 'Shakespeare's play' cannot be adjudicated because there is no common ground between them: the textual scholar and the theatre enthusiast are arguing in different terms and so are the historicist and the believer in 'what it means for us today'. There is no determinate entity called Shakespeare's play (having made the point the quotation marks may perhaps be abandoned), and we should consider the implications, which are inescapably political, of rival claims to have the privileged perspective.

Diverse groups insist that they have the true Shakespeare because, almost like a religious relic, he constitutes a powerful cultural token. Shakespeare's plays are one site of cultural production in our society – they are one of the places where our understanding of ourselves is worked out and, indeed, fought out. A culture is 'a *signifying system* through which ... a social order is communicated, reproduced, experienced and explored'.[1] This signifying system has continually to be produced – 'social orders and cultural orders must be seen as being actively made: actively and continuously, or they may quite quickly break down' (*Culture*, p. 199). Cultural production occurs all the time and at every point where meaning is communicated – in modes of speech and dress as well as through 'the media' and 'the arts'. Shakespeare's plays constitute an influential medium through which certain ways of thinking about the world may be promoted and others impeded, they are a site of cultural struggle and change.

The main effect of cultural production will generally be the *reproduction* of the existing order. But this is no simple process, with a dominant ideology reproducing its structures as if with a rubber stamp (there must be an image more appropriate to the age of the micro-chip); a complex interplay of the dominant with residual, emergent, subordinate and oppositional forces affords space for socialist *intervention*. As several of the essays in Part I showed, such intervention (or subversion) is immediately liable to be contained and made to contribute, in turn to the reproduction of the existing order. The same issue arises in respect of the present volume: is not its oppositional impetus contained, from the start, by its implication with established institutions (universities and their presses, reviewing journals, booksellers, syllabuses)? Perhaps so – but contradictions in the system do allow positions from which interventions can be made, and part of the reason for drawing attention to structures of containment (in Shakespeare's time and in our own) is to facilitate evasions of them.

A comparison between two critics may illustrate how Shakespeare is appropriated in the making of meaning. Both E. M. W. Tillyard and Jan Kott make reference to the mid-twentieth-century experience of war, tyranny and suffering in Europe when they describe Shakespeare's ideology. Tillyard concludes that Shakespeare and other Elizabethan writers should be valued for 'the earnestness and the passion and the assurance with which they surveyed the range of the universe':[2] he finds a Shakespeare who is fundamentally confident about a hierarchical view of the universe and about the political order which that seems to legitimate. Kott on the other hand believes that in Shakespeare's plays 'The order of history and the order of nature are both cruel; terrifying are the passions that breed in the human heart':[3] Kott is sceptical and pessimistic, apparently seeing the opposite Shakespeare from Tillyard. That these two accounts are really two sides of the same conservative coin – both predicated on the ideas of an essential human nature and the desirability of 'order' and both hostile to positive political action – is argued by Jonathan Dollimore and myself elsewhere.[4] The point here is that we have two responses not just to Shakespeare but, explicitly, to the European political situation. Shakespeare is read through a perception of that situation and the reading seems to add Shakespeare's authority to the critic's political standpoint. Tillyard, writing during the Second World War, thought that 'the Elizabethan habit of mind' would help to secure peace – that its neglect 'by our scientifically minded intellectuals has helped not a little to bring the world into its present conflicts and distresses' (*Elizabethan World Picture*, p. 132). Kott, writing as a Pole for whom Nazi occupation was succeeded by Stalinism and then by emigration across the 'iron curtain' to the United States, believed: 'Like our world, Shakespeare's world did not regain its balance after the earthquake. Like our world, it remained incoherent' (*Shakespeare Our Contemporary*, p. 99). Each of these positions appears repeatedly in criticism and the theatre, often under the guise of academic neutrality or dramatic effectiveness, but nevertheless with the kind of general political implications that they had for Tillyard and Kott. Shakespeare is one of the places where ideology is made.

If Shakespeare can be appropriated by these conservative standpoints, there is scope for intervention also for an oppositional politics, and that is the project of this book. The essays in the first part show how the plays may be discussed in terms of a materialist analysis: the second part considers how they are being handled in the principal institutions through which they are produced in modern times – education, theatre, film and television. We assess both the tendencies towards conservative reproduction and the conditions and modes of radical intervention.

The issues are complex and specific to each institution, depending upon the position of Shakespeare within each and the social formations with which each is involved. For instance, there are limits to 'how far' one can 'go' in interpreting Shakespeare, but they are far more elastic for theatre, film and television than they are in education. Often it is difficult to say who is using whom: Shakespeare's plays both confer and receive significance. Scholarly editing contributes to the status of a text, so Shakespeare is more edited than other texts; at the same time, some of Shakespeare's status seeps down into the editorial apparatus at the foot of the page and so helps to sanction the academic system. Again, the presentation of Shakespeare gives television companies a varnish of high culture whilst, at the same time, confirming Shakespeare's reputation as the author who speaks to all conditions, even through the most popular medium. Even an attempt at a radical stage production funded by the Arts Council may be said to be helping established institutions to present a liberal stance; a similar question might be raised about the present volume, but yet one must take the opportunities that arise.

It may be that we must see the continuous centring of Shakespeare as the cultural token which must be appropriated as itself tending to reproduce the existing order: that however the plays are presented they will exercise a relatively conservative drag, that any radical influence can hardly extend beyond the educated middle class, that in practice conservative institutions are bound to dominate the production of such a national symbol, and that for one cultural phenomenon to have so much authority must be a hindrance to radical innovation. The essays which follow contemplate those possibilities but try to be constructive; at the least, it must be granted that cultural intervention can be conducted through significant cultural symbols and institutions. We conclude on a positive note, for Margot Heinemann's account of Brecht's explicitly Marxist work with Shakespeare shows some of the possibilities of a creative political engagement with the plays, in theory and in the theatre.

Notes

1 Raymond Williams, *Culture* (Glasgow: Fontana, 1981), p. 13. See also Williams, *Marxism and Literature* (Oxford University Press, 1977) and Janet Wolff, *The Social Production of Art* (London: Macmillan, 1981).
2 E. M. W. Tillyard, *The Elizabethan World Picture* (Harmondsworth: Penguin, 1963), p. 130.
3 Jan Kott, *Shakespeare Our Contemporary*, 2nd edn. (London: Methuen, 1967), p. 40.
4 Jonathan Dollimore and Alan Sinfield, 'History and Ideology: the Instance of *Henry V*', in John Drakakis, ed., *Alternative Shakespeares* (London: Methuen, 1985).

8 Alan Sinfield

Give an account of Shakespeare and Education, showing why you think they are effective and what you have appreciated about them. Support your comments with precise references

Any social order has to include the conditions for its own continuance, and capitalism and patriarchy do this partly through the education system. The positions in the productive process which people are to occupy are an effect of the relations of production, but the preparing of people to occupy those positions is accomplished by the family, the media and education, and the State finances schools, requires attendance at them, trains and employs teachers. This preparation is only in small part a matter of specific training and qualifications: in the main, it is achieved through the whole regime of the school, from classroom practices to the hierarchy of decision-making, and through the mapping of knowledges by the curriculum and examinations.[1] Above all, education sustains 'the extended division between mental and manual labour that characterises the capitalist mode of production in general';[2] and, within that and overlapping unevenly with it, education sustains the subordination of women and ethnic minorities.

At the same time, the system is not monolithic. First, because the official ideology is democratic, the reproduction of an unjust society cannot be straightforward, it has to appear that education is for the good of all the pupils; second, in order to function educational institutions must have a certain relative autonomy, and within this teachers and administrators will have particular professional purposes and needs. These considerations allow space for divergent attitudes and practices; and, in fact, modern English education has developed around a dispute between traditional and progressive approaches, with varying relations between these approaches and government. As we will see, the debate has been vitiated by a reluctance to inspect economic and political determinants, and in consequence progressive approaches have often amounted to little more than a subtle mode of securing assent to the relations of production. Nevertheless, this element of play in the system indicates the scope for radical intervention: 'The many contradictions which confront teachers and pupils can also provide the "space" for practical action for change'.[3]

In education Shakespeare has been made to speak mainly for the right; that is the tendency which this book seeks to alter. His construction in English culture generally as the great National Poet whose plays embody universal truths has led to his being used to underwrite established practices in literary criticism and, consequently, in examinations. For literary criticism, Shakespeare is the keystone which guarantees the ultimate stability and rightness of the category 'Literature'. The status of other authors may be disputed – indeed, one of the ways criticism offers itself as serious and discriminating is by engaging in such disputes, policing its boundaries. But Shakespeare is always there as the final instance of the validity of Literature. Then, because it is such a profound and universal experience, Literature must be taught to school pupils, whereupon it becomes an instrument within the whole apparatus of filtering whereby schools adjust young people to an unjust social order. And when in 1983 the Secretary of State required the nine GCE boards to devise a common core for A level the English working party could agree only one thing that is not vague and general: that at least one play by Shakespeare must be studied.[4] (See note 10 for an explanation of the British examination system.)

'All pupils, including those of very limited attainments, need the civilizing experience of contact with great literature, and can respond to its universality', declared the Newsom Report of 1963, but it added anxiously: 'They will depend heavily on the skill of the teacher as an interpreter'.[5] In practice it is found that not all pupils 'respond': as empirical studies have demonstrated repeatedly, educational 'attainment' in England is vitally influenced by class and gender.[6] Literature becomes a mark of differential 'attainment', preparing pupils for the differential opportunities and rewards in society at large. 'But then again, I read Shakespeare, and they all thought I was pretty mad for reading it. You see, I was interested in things, really, that I shouldn't have been interested in .... thinking back, what they said was, well look, we've told you what you can be, you've got this marvellous opportunity. You can be a shorthand typist, or you can be a nursery nurse'.[7] A crucial ideological manoeuvre in education is this: that the allegedly universal culture to which equal access is apparently offered is, at the same time, a marker of 'attainment' and hence of privilege. Thus those who are discriminated against on the grounds of gender, class and ethnic origins come to believe that it is their own fault (it serves them right).[8] So pupils are persuaded to accept appropriate attitudes to Literature as a criterion of general capacity. The Bullock Report of 1975 complacently observes: 'In a very real sense a pupil is himself being judged each time he responds in class to a piece of literature ... is the value-judgement he forms the one the teacher finds acceptable? Is he betraying himself, he may well ask, as one who lacks discrimination?'[9] He may well; but discrimination is certainly what she or he is getting. The Report thinks the answer is for the teacher to handle the occasion with sensitivity: it does not observe that the pupil is being persuaded to internalise success or failure with particular and relative cultural codes as an absolute judgement on her or his potential as a human being.

The system works most plainly through examinations. For a start, as many as twenty-five per cent of pupils take no public examination, not even English Language (they are 'no good' at English, not good English). Then, Literature is the ground of a further discrimination. At CSE and O level the candidate can study English in terms of basic reading and writing skills and must make a positive choice to study Literature. One CSE board warns teachers: 'Candidates, particularly the less able, should be steered away from "The Works of William Shakespeare" (all of them!)'.[10] About fourteen per cent of the pupils taking O level English Language 'go on' to take A level English, but this is not just a growth in competence: this examination consists mainly of literary appreciation (with one of the three papers devoted to Shakespeare's plays). To advance is to move into Literature.[11]

Whilst Literature is made to operate as a mode of exclusion in respect of class, it disadvantages girls by including them (this seems a paradox, but it only shows Literature's flexibility as a cultural form). Of those taking A level English with the London board in 1982 three-quarters were girls (the figures were precisely the reverse for Physics); between a fifth and a quarter of all girls taking A level took English. We see here both an internalisation of dominant notions of the kinds of things girls should do, and also the outcome of all kinds of subtle pressures within schools.[12] The consequences are twofold. First, most of the texts studied reinforce the gender stereotyping which leads girls to these texts – 'women are portrayed as being passive and ineffectual, and taking action only for personal or destructive reasons' (Sharpe, *Just Like a Girl*, p. 150); Irene Payne recalls: 'One teacher gave us the following lines from *King Lear* to write out because we had been noisy: "Her voice was ever soft, / Gentle and low – an excellent thing in woman"'.[13] Second, girls are condemned to a relatively low position in the job market. Official reports assume that women will be essentially housewives or unskilled,[14] though in fact in 1975 they were 41 per cent of the labour force, and their failure to take technical subjects keeps them in relatively unskilled work and reduces their chances of further and higher education.

Of course, it should not be assumed that the process of ideological reproduction in schools is invariably successful. A survey of 1000 pupils taking O and A level English Literature in selective schools in 1968 found that although most of them expressed a commitment to Literature, their actual private reading was 'light'. 'It is as though many of these pupils have two sets of cultural values – one for school and the outside investigator, another for home and their leisure reading.'[15] Of the 800 O level pupils only one in eight showed any wish to go on reading poetry or plays after leaving school. This is little cause for satisfaction: it is likely that most of the disaffected had found that they were not 'good' at literature; and look at the waste of time, effort and money. However, it serves to indicate that hegemony is not easily, or in any straightforward way, achieved. Although the dominant class or class fraction controls the terms and conditions within which cultural production is carried on, 'Groups or classes which do not stand at the apex of power, nevertheless find ways of expressing and realising in their culture their subordinate position and experiences'.[16] I will show how the institutional construction of Shakespeare in education has had to struggle with subordinate cultures and with rival movements within the dominant.

Above all, Shakespeare does not have to work in a conservative manner. His plays do not have to signify in the ways they have customarily been made to (it will be the project of the next section to analyse how GCE constructs them in certain ways). It is partly a matter of reading them differently – drawing attention to their historical insertion, their political implications, and the activity of criticism in reproducing them. Such readings are exemplified in the first part of this book. And it is also a matter of changing the way Shakespeare signifies in society: he does not have to be a crucial stage in the justification of elitism in education and culture. He has been appropriated for certain practices and attitudes, and can be reappropriated for others.

Alan Sinfield

* * *

An analysis of the reading of a sample of children aged 10, 12 and 14 in maintained and direct-grant schools produced 7557 book titles of which 54 were 'adult quality narrative', but Shakespeare figures not at all.[17] The reading of Shakespeare begins with and overwhelmingly takes its character from the examination questions set at O and A level (see note 10). These are controlled entirely by certain universities; teachers, whether they like it or not, must in fairness prepare their pupils for them. A whole apparatus of school editions and cramming aids has sprung up around them. I will point out in the question papers the two fundamental mystifications of bourgeois ideology. All the questions specified were set in 1983.

The main move is the projection of local conditions on to the eternal. As Rachel Sharp puts it, 'The power relations which are peculiar to market society are seen as how things have always been and ought to be. They acquire a timelessness which is powerfully legitimised by a theory of human nature. ... Political struggles to alter present-day social arrangements are seen as futile for "things are as they are" because of man's basic attributes and nothing could ever be very different.'[18] This move is built in to the structure of the whole exercise, through the notion that Shakespeare is the great National Poet who speaks universal truths and whose plays are the ultimate instance of Literature. It is made also through the ways the questions invite the candidates to handle the plays. Almost invariably it is assumed that the plays reveal universal 'human' values and qualities and that they are self-contained and coherent entities; and the activity of criticism in producing these assumptions is effaced.

The appeal to absolute values and qualities is ubiquitous: 'At the centre of *King Lear* lies the question, "What is a man?" Discuss' (Oxford and Cambridge, A level); 'Beginning with a consideration of the following passage, discuss Shakespeare's presentation of Goodness in *Macbeth*' (Welsh, A level). Women, of course, are a special category within the universal (there are fewer questions about female than male characters): '"*The Winter's Tale* is much more concerned with the qualities of womanhood, its virtue, its insight, and its endurance". Discuss' (Southern, A level). If women seem not to be manifesting the expected qualities then that is a matter for comment: '"The men in *Twelfth Night* are ridiculous in what they say and do: it is the women who are full of common sense". Show how far you agree ...' (Welsh, O level).

The alleged coherence and self-containedness of the text re-enacts at the level of the particular reading the coherence and self-containedness claimed by ideology. In the examination questions almost no reference is made to the diverse forms which the play has taken and may take – to scholarly discussions about provenance, to the conditions under which it has been transmitted, to the different forms it takes today, from school editions to stage, film and TV productions.[19] Even the occasional question about staging is liable to involve the assumption that there is a true reading behind the diverse possibilities: 'How, as a young actor, would you try to cope with the difficulties of playing the part of John of Gaunt' (Southern, O level – bad luck if you're an actress). The text is *there*; the most common form of question at O level begins 'Give an account of ...' and 'precise reference' is repeatedly demanded. That the text is to be regarded as coherent, either in terms of action or of dramatic effect, is frequently insisted upon. ' "While we may hope for a happy ending to *King Lear*, Shakespeare's conclusion is entirely fitting". Discuss' (Associated, O level); 'Write about the dramatic effectiveness of the last act of *Twelfth Night*, and show how the ending is connected to earlier episodes of the play' (London, O level). Everything comes out the way it always had to, every incident is justified by its 'effectiveness' (one of the commonest terms on the papers).

The effacing of the activity of criticism works mainly through the assumption that the candidate will discover the true response or meaning in the manner established by literary criticism as appropriate to the text. Not only are these assumptions not exposed for inspection, they are drawn forth naturally, as it appears, from the interaction between the candidate and the text. The fact that between those two comes the learnt procedures of literary criticism is obscured. Of course, the questions often invite discussion, agreement or disagreement, but normally that is within a prescribed range of possibilities and to infringe these requires a repudiation of the authority of Shakespeare or the examiners, often both. A whole range of issues and positions is simply not allowed to reach visibility. 'Compare Shakespeare's treatment of the problem of evil in any *two* plays' (Oxford and Cambridge, A level): the candidate who sees that 'the problem of evil' is a mystified concept must force a space for such an analysis, knowing that she or he is out of accord with the examiners and will have little time to show the expected 'knowledge' of the plays. Questions which appear to invite a personal response are often all the more tyrannical: 'Give an account of the scene in Capulet's orchard where Romeo sees Juliet on the balcony, showing what you have enjoyed about the words spoken by the lovers' (Welsh, O level). Candidates are invited to interrogate their experience to discover a response which has in actuality been learnt. As Perry Anderson showed, this Leavisite strategy demands (whilst lamenting the absence of) 'one crucial precondition: a shared, stable system of beliefs and values';[20] what actually happens is that candidates are required to take up a certain system of values – those we have been identifying – in order satisfactorily to answer the question.

The second fundamental mystification of bourgeois ideology is the construction of individual subjectivity as a given which is undetermined and unconstituted and hence a ground of meaning and coherence: 'In effect the individual is understood in terms of a pre-social essence, nature, or identity and on that basis s/he is invested with a quasi-spiritual autonomy. The individual becomes the origin and focus of meaning – an individuated essence which precedes and – in idealist philosophy – transcends history and society.'[21] Eternal values can no longer be ratified securely by religion, but now they are grounded in their perception through authentic subjectivity. This relationship is figured precisely in the question: 'There are moments in *King Lear* when the insights of individual characters seem to provide a key to the play's deepest themes and preoccupations. Consider this claim in relation to *one* of the following "insights" ..' (Oxford and Cambridge, A level). The individual and the universal are constituted in a mutually supportive polarity.

The examination papers construct Shakespeare and the candidate in terms of individuated subjectivity through their stress upon Shakespeare's free-standing genius, their emphasis on characterisation, and their demand for the candidate's personal response. At no point do the GCE papers of 1983 invite candidates to consider the ways in which a play relates to its social context in Shakespeare's time or subsequently (the whole project of the present book). It seems to have been born, immaculately, into the classroom. Indeed, some questions actively encourage a notion of creation ex nihilo: 'By careful reference to appropriate scenes show how Shakespeare has created a dream-like world' (JMB, O level).

The call for commentary on individual characters is the staple fare, especially at O level. 'Do you think Falstaff is ever sincere in *Henry IV Part 1*?'; 'What sort of person is Henry IV? Do you think he always acts wisely?' – these are two of the three Associated O level questions on the play. Individuals are the unproblematic source of action and meaning, despite intermittent assertions, from diverse critical points of view, that this is not an appropriate framework for Elizabethan and Jacobean drama (consider E. E. Stoll, L.C. Knights, Muriel Bradbrook, Catherine Belsey). Even questions which seem to bear upon the issue nudge the candidate into assuming a realist convention: '"In *All's Well that Ends Well* Shakespeare is concerned to make Helena good rather than plausible". Discuss the role and character of Helena in the play to show to what extent you agree with this statement' (Northern Ireland, A level); notice how Shakespeare's autonomous decision seems to be the only determinant.

Subjectivity and authenticity are the programme also in the customary appeal to the candidate's judgement and, often, personal response. We have seen that the candidate is supposed to discover in herself or himself the necessary procedures and judgements of literary criticism; at the same time, contradictorily, a personal response is required. This demand for individual assessment is often more coercive than the 'neutral' question. The determination of the Cambridge board to get the candidate to reveal the required response is apparent in this novel kind of question: 'This short scene is really doing three things: advancing the "story", adding to our knowledge of the characters, and expanding some of the ideas (about relationships and about the condition of the world) that are going to be important in the play as a whole. Show how much of this a close reading of the scene helps you to discover' (Cambridge, O levels).

Peter Widdowson, looking at GCE questions on Hardy, found the same ideological construction: Hardy 'is reproduced within very limited parameters of intelligibility: "Hardy" as the tragic novelist of character struggling heroically with Nature, Fate, or other, preeminently non-social forces'.[22] Widdowson observed the total effacement of the fact that the critic, as much as the historian, is 'a "social phenomenon" who selects and organizes the facts/texts according to his/her positioning in history: ... who, in effect, "writes" Literature from the perspective of a historical and ideological present' (p. 4). It is this ideological construction that the present book is striving to overturn.

The twin manoeuvres of bourgeois ideology construct two dichotomies: universal versus historical and individual versus social. In each case the first term is privileged, and so meaning is sucked into the universal/individual polarity, draining it away from the historical and the social – which is where meaning is made by people together in determinate conditions, and where it might be contested. 'How far do you think that the fates of Antony and Cleopatra are inevitable rather than voluntary?' (Oxford and Cambridge, A level): that which is not universal is individual, any other level of explanation disappears down the yawning gulf between the two. The universal is unchangeable and the individual lives, quintessentially, in 'his' inner subjectivity; shared purpose to change the world is not just disqualified, it is not allowed into visibility. One question in 1983 promoted such an issue: '"In the realm of politics Shakespeare sees any hope for progress in human society as profoundly futile".

Discuss with reference to *two* plays' (Cambridge, A level). Of course, agreement with the proposition is expected – 'profoundly' and 'the realm' (suggesting a narrow range of operation for politics) work to secure this. The 'discussion' is hardly open.

We may envisage, then, the intellectual cast of the successfully socialised GCE candidate. She or he will be respectful of Shakespeare and high culture and accustomed to being appreciative of the cultural production which is offered through established institutions. She or he will be trained at giving opinions – within certain prescribed limits; at collecting evidence – though without questioning its status or the construction of the problem; at saying what is going on – though not whether that is what ought to happen; at seeing effectiveness, coherence, purposes fulfilled – but not conflict. And because the purposeful individual is perceived as the autonomous origin and ground of meaning and event, success in these exercises will be accepted as just reason for certain economic and social privileges.

It all seems perfectly adapted for the fastest-growing class fraction, the new petty bourgeoisie working in finance, advertising, the civil service, teaching, the health service, the social services and clerical occupations. The new petty bourgeoisie (unlike the old, of artisans and small shopkeepers) is constituted not by family but through education: 'The various petty bourgeois agents each possess, in relation to those subordinate to them, a fragment of the fantastic secret of knowledge that legitimises the delegated authority that they exercise ... Hence the belief in the 'neutrality of culture', and in the educational apparatus as a corridor of circulation by the promotion and accession of the "best" to the bourgeois state, or in any case to a higher state in the specific hierarchy of mental labour'.[23] The combination of cultural deference and cautious questioning promoted around Shakespeare in GCE seems designed to construct a petty bourgeoisie which will strive within limits allocated to it without seeking to disturb the system – 'it does not want to break the ladder by which it imagines it can climb' (Poulantzas, p. 292).

I will now look more closely and with a historical perspective at the theory, such as it is, which underpins modern literary education. The weakness of the dominant constructions of Shakespeare will be exposed. I will consider the historical conditions in which literary criticism has been endeavouring to maintain its position, finding that the practices imposed so vigorously upon pupils rest not on confident and coherent dogma, but on confused, anxious and pragmatic responses to pressures which continually defy containment. As I

have said, we may not assume that the ideology of GCE is successfully inculcated: it is undermined both by conflicting tendencies in
English society and by its own contradictions. These afford
numerous points at which it may be interrogated and challenged.

In 1944, when the Butler Act was passed, making secondary
education compulsory for all children and free for those who cannot
afford to buy their way into the private system and its network of
privileges, the dominant idea of education was the 'classical
humanist'. In this approach it is 'the task of the guardian class,
including the teachers, to initiate the young into the mysteries of
knowledge and the ways in which knowledge confers various kinds
of social power on those who possess it ... classical humanism has
been associated with clear and firm discipline, high attainment in
examinations, continuity between past and present, the cohesiveness
and orderly development of institutions.'[24] This is evidently an
approach designed to train an elite, and in fact it grew out of the
training which was given to the children of the upper and middle
classes in the late nineteenth century.

In English Literature classical humanism is exemplified in its
original form by Quiller-Couch. He was Professor of English
Literature at Cambridge and in a lecture delivered in 1917 he
declared that the best kind of education is reading aloud by the
teacher and pupils: 'it just lets the author – Chaucer or Shakespeare
or Milton or Coleridge – have his own way with the young plant –
just lets them drop "like the gentle rain from heaven", and soak in'.[25]
Children, at least if they are of the right class, will take naturally to
Shakespeare. Actually, of course, it is being drilled into them, and we
see here the origin of classical humanist ideas in the nineteenth-
century practice of mechanically construing classical texts – Quiller-
Couch says the reading should move round the class, 'just as in a
construing class'. This is the root of the most mechanical part of the
GCE examinations, the compulsory question one designed to show
whether the candidate has 'done' the text in detail.

However, a notion of education designed for the offspring of the
gentry and aspiring commercial bougeoisie could hardly survive
without adaptation in a society which proclaims equality of
opportunity. The necessary adjustment was made by Leavis and his
followers, and hence their importance. The Leavisite reader is in a
more complex relationship with authority. The great works are there
to be discovered, but they are not identical with the established
canon, they have to be reappropriated, won back from the upper-
class dilettantes who have abused them. And the reader does not
make this discovery without apparent effort but through a strenuous

engagement, a serious and deliberate process of discrimination which both tests and develops a personal sensibility. At the same time, the distance from lower-class culture cannot now be assumed. The true literary experience is threatened also from below, by commercialised 'mass' culture, and this too has to be repudiated. It is by such a repudiation that the student recognises the special culture which she or he has entered. In other words, this was an approach for the class-mobile – either those moving from the lower middle class (occasionally working class) towards professional and managerial occupations, or those moving from the established middle class towards professions like education and social work which justify themselves partly in terms of superior acquired knowledge and personal sensibility. The Leavisite does not receive Shakespeare as part of a natural heritage, she or he wins him and fights off the challenge of 'mass' culture (and passes the examination).

The spread of Leavisism through the education system – not through Cambridge, of course, there they were still educating gentlemen, but through schools, colleges of education and redbrick universities – coincided with the post-war extension of secondary education. The study of English Literature was extended vastly and the contradiction between its universalist and meritocratic pretensions became apparent (in 1951 13,000 students entered for A level English, by 1976 it was 66,000).[26] In 1963 G. H. Bantock declared, 'the number who benefit from this sort of task seems to me to be more limited than we commonly admit' and deplored the acquisition of 'a series of analytic tricks which enable a "right" judgement to be arrived at'.[27] In 1964, in a volume entitled *Crisis in the Humanities*, Graham Hough observed that 'much of English literature up to the threshold of modern times is now as remote as the ancient classics' and that literary criticism on Leavisite lines had become 'a set of special tricks'.[28] This latter complaint is just what we might expect, for the whole idea of personal judgement which has to approximate to received opinion invites exactly that learning of 'tricks'.

During the 1960s, four factors particularly were drawing attention to the curriculum: government pressure for more and better scientists, the anticipated raising of the school-leaving age to 16, the amalgamation of grammar and secondary modern schools into comprehensives and the demand for student participation.[29] They all served to problematise Literature. The first factor seemed initially to require the most strenuous Leavisite address,[30] but the others proved the real threat because they promoted rival student cultures. The strength and pretensions of literary institutions demanded that such benefits be more widely distributed, but how could it be made to work? The Newsom Report of 1963, dealing with 'average and below average pupils', betrays an understandable nervousness: 'It is of course within poetry and drama that the use of language goes deepest. Nobody should have to teach poetry against his will, but without it English will never be complete; poetry is not a minor amenity but a major channel of experience. ... How far the great poetry of earlier ages can be introduced with advantage only the teacher can say' (p. 156).

Usually, the problem was said to be that of the young people: they could not appreciate good culture. But it became apparent to sociologists that they had their own, preferred culture: 'Being highly committed to the *teenager* role tends to go with being an underachiever (relative to one's I.Q.). ... It also tends quite strongly to go with having a bad conduct record' – notice here the glimmering recognition of subcultural resistance alongside the terminology of hegemonic incorporation.[31] Youth culture was attributed to mass society and the mass media, to earning power and the disturbance of World War II, but it was also a product *of* the education system which it was perceived as undermining. Education created a hiatus between childhood and work, and organised young people into age-specific institutions where interaction within the institution was bound to be at least as important as the outward purposes of it. The teenage subculture was partly the product of young people's attempts to adjust to the conditions they were required to experience; whilst in many ways this involved a negotiated response which amounted to the incorporation of many of the values of school, it represented in other ways a resistance to it. Because this was manifested in the main culturally, through styles of speech, dress and demeanour, it seemed to confront especially English teaching.

It was possible for educators simply to deplore the influence of youth culture so long as this was the form, mainly, of the lower classes and of those who did not succeed in school (this, of course, was a circular construction). But the spread, from the mid-1960s, of an alternative culture in universities and colleges infiltrated an adversary to high culture into the main fortress where it survives. Even Shakespeare could be appropriated – as in Barbara Garson's play *MacBird!*, a rock opera of *Othello*, phrases in Beatles' songs, Hamlet's 'What a piece of work is a man' speech in *Hair*, Charles Marowitz's 'fringe' adaptations. The typical student now negotiates contradictory worlds – the rock concert and the tutorial – and whatever the outcome high culture does not retain the centrality which was its original justification. If it is one culture among others then what is it?

Alan Sinfield

The response from the right was immediate and clear: it had all been a mistake, most people are not educable beyond the acquisition of the basic skills necessary to keep the economy going. Classical humanism was reasserted in the *Black Papers* of 1969–70 and by Rhodes Boyson, who was to become a Tory education minister – he wanted 'a sense of purpose, continuity and authority' with schools giving 'order, values and guidance, while teaching skills and knowledge', and felt this would be best achieved by the state 'helping parents to buy the education they want'.[32] This movement gathered strength through the 1970s and issued, as part of a general collapse of consensus on the welfare state, in the education cuts of the Thatcher governments.

The left was more disorientated by the problematisation of education and culture, since for many decades the Labour Party and the Communist Party alike had accepted that education in roughly its present guise was a good thing and that what was required was 'reform' to equalise opportunities for individuals to benefit from it (see Jones, *Beyond Progressive Education*, chapters 3,5). This idea was the quintessence of welfare capitalism: the State provides the conditions whereby the individuals can maximise their personal advancement, and thus the economy will grow and everyone will be happy. From the late 1960s, initiatives on the left opened up new kinds of analysis and practice. There was trade-union militancy among teachers. The possibilities of subcultural resistance were theorised, moving on from Basil Bernstein's distinction between elaborated and restricted codes to an analysis of the scope for resistance and negotiation available to subordinate groups;[33] the *Language in Use* project identified literature as a particular impediment: 'habitual notions about the value and function of all varieties of written English are derived from notions about the language of literature'.[34] New publications, and especially the journal *Teaching London Kids*, discussed ways of developing in the classroom the *critical response* of working-class children to their social situation: they are encouraged to 'know their place' – not in the customary sense of accepting their subservience, but in terms of understanding their allocated place in the system, what the material determinants of that positioning are and how it might be otherwise.

But despite, and even within, these socialist initiatives, the principal resistance to rightist ideology among left-liberal educationists has been defensive and recuperative. It has sought to enhance the claims for school experience and tended to keep the system going while making sufficient gestures towards the complex and potentially disruptive cultural position of so many pupils. I shall discuss three major institutional developments of the 1960s and 1970s: the progressive movement, the Certificate of Secondary Education (CSE), and non-disciplinary humanities programmes. All three were in many ways recuperative, but they admitted oppositional possibilities as well. Literature featured in them because its failure to command the natural universal respect claimed for it seemed to manifest the impasse into which current theory and practice had worked themselves. Often it was invoked to add weight and legitimacy to these developments and, conversely, it seemed that they were ways of sustaining Literature. But the outcome was rather, in effect, the further problematising of it as a concept and of criticism as a practice. And Shakespeare was used increasingly as the supreme token of the viability of Literature, the one unchallengeable instance.

The progressivist movement is usually traced to Rousseau and his *Émile*, but it has been gathering strength since the late nineteenth century. It stresses not the acquisition of a given set of standards and body of knowledge but the personal fulfilment of the individual; not training for an established slot in society but the discovery and maturation of an authentic self. It is sometimes called 'romantic' because it values creativity and freedom; and it is called 'child-centred' because it assumes that the most valuable experiences can be drawn from the child her- or himself, rather than imposed by the teacher or a curriculum.[35] It advanced rapidly during the 1960s and 1970s, and seemed to offer a way of recuperating Literature, though eventually it calls it into question.

The most important figure in progressivism at the start of this period was David Holbrook, but his work now appears contradictory, recuperative and mystifying. He takes Shakespeare as the ultimate literary experience and argues that what the child will discover in her or his authentic self is a positive response to the play. In Holbrook's *English for Maturity*, first published in 1961, Shakespeare 'is the touchstone when we discuss literature – we may dispute the value, say, of Pope or Milton, but we can all agree that Shakespeare is a great poet'.[36] But now what we get from Shakespeare is not a disciplined training in traditional values but poems 'about the essentials of being': 'by experiencing his work we may come to have a renewed grasp on life, to understand how to live in this post-Renaissance era, fully recognizing our own feeble natures, and accepting the conditions of our lives which are dominated by Time and Death' (*English for Maturity*, p. 43). The guarantor of the link between Shakespeare and the self is none other than Leavis: his idea of responses to Literature as personal maturation could be used by Holbrook even while others were using his elitism to sustain the classical-humanist approach. 'We must experience Wordsworth's depression before we can experience his triumph over it. Leavis will encourage us to do this'[37] (compare Pope's reconciliation of nature and the ancients: 'To copy nature is to copy them'). Such determined accommodating of authority with personal freedom obviously masks a theoretical instability (the reader will have noticed the coercive strategies in the quotations above – 'we can all agree that'; 'fully recognizing'; 'we must experience'). Holbrook is actually promoting Literature by indirect means and persuading the students to accept his reading as deriving from their experience.

In Holbrook's approach a failure of students to find in themselves Shakespeare as he would have them – as seeing 'the reality of love and creativity in man' – is interpreted not as evidence of a problem with some part of the theory but as the result of interference: 'Answers by students to questions of Shakespeare's attitudes to human nature and love show how the destructive attitudes of the prevalent literary ethos prevent them from being able to respond to the greatest literature' (*Exploring Word*, p. 212). Latterly progressivists have acknowledged that the appeal to personal relevance cannot be so conveniently manipulated. Albert Rowe declares, 'The attempt to impose a minority taste upon the majority was doomed from the start ... literary culture is as relative as other forms of culture'.[38] The compromise with the canon is abandoned and even Shakespeare drops out of visibility. Peter Abbs, in a slashing attack on a GCE examiner who was unwise enough to visit his teacher-training course, insists: 'In the first place it is, surely, the process we value, *the process* of children responding in a personal way to literature. *It does not have to be Shakespeare*'.[39] None the less, Abbs himself, as one student complained, presents 'a literary heritage that supports your own philosophy' (*English within the Arts*, p. 134): Abbs tends to promote a canon and a syllabus while insisting that he is essentially addressing human values as they offer themselves to the individual subjectivity. This continual collapsing of values back into their alleged source in the mind of the student makes it very difficult for her or him to inspect the ideological construction of such education.

Progressivist questions have begun to appear on GCE papers, but they tend to smuggle in diverse discriminatory assumptions and the personal invitation may place only the thinnest mask over coercion: 'Give an account of the scene where Caliban first meets Trinculo and Stephano, making it clear in what ways you find it amusing, and what other feelings you have about it' (Cambridge, O level). Initially, the demand for an 'account' suggests that the text is there for reasoned paraphrase – the traditional wish to ensure that the candidate has read the play 'properly' is still there. At the other end of the question the appeal is to 'what other feelings you have' – an open-ended appeal to personal impressions. In the middle one must make 'clear in what ways you find it amusing': the response which the examiners have predetermined to be the right one must be discovered. This exerts a pressure on the invitation to express 'feelings' – the possibility that the scene might relate to colonial exploitation (see Chapter 3 above) is not encouraged. That would not be 'amusing'.

Progressivism also underlies invitations to consider Shakespeare's plays in terms of realisation in the theatre – it is part of the appeal to experience and creativity (such questions were set in 1983 by three boards). But theatre questions also may exert a drag back towards the classical-humanist position. Notice how this question starts off with excitement but moves back to precise recollection and the implication that 'the events and characters' are quantities that may be simply known: 'Select what you consider to be the most exciting scene from *Romeo and Juliet* and show how you would produce it to make the greatest impact on an audience. A close knowledge of the events and characters should be apparent in your production ideas' (Southern, O level). Most boards remain hostile to 'imaginative interpretations' (see below, p. 183).

There is radical impetus in the progressivists' position – in their attack on examinations, on the competitive hierarchy in schools and on the pressure exerted on schools by universities; and in their insistence that children's writing has a validity which challenges that of established Literature. However, from a materialist standpoint the drawbacks of the position are manifest. It reproduces in a particularly potent form the bourgeois ideology of individualism, effacing the historical construction both of the text and the moment in which it is read – not to mention the historical construction of individualism itself. The student is offered no political analysis or direction, but is exhorted to regard as her or his authentic response what can in actuality be only a combination of pressures from society at large and from the teacher in particular. The former will be largely conservative, the latter may be radical in some of its emphases, but its refusal to invite inspection of its own historical and political location must be mystifying. At the same time, progressivism has provided a starting point and a strategy of intervention for socialist teaching. The principle of appealing to the pupil's experience is transformed if that experience is placed in its political context – 'bringing them to an awareness of their social situation in a class-based society through the spoken and written word, and affirming the collective strength of their class'.[40]

CSE examinations (the second institutional development which has tended recently to rehandle Literature) began in the mid-1960s, and because they are designed for less 'able' pupils than those taking O level and not involved in the university selection sequence they could cut free from the academic/high-cultural conception of Literature. Almost invariably, a list of twenty or more books is proposed and the candidate answers on the ones he or she has studied; overwhelmingly, the texts are modern and chosen for their supposed appeal to young people; only Shakespeare persists from the traditional canon, and study of his work is not compulsory.

Often CSE questions are open-ended and do little to encourage the customary manoeuvres of literary criticism – 'Write about a book, play, or collection of poems that you really enjoyed reading as part of your C.S.E. English Course. Explain what it was that pleased you, and how your experience of people and/or places was enlarged by your reading' (East Anglia, South). This approximates to the way non-professional adult readers think about books (except, of course, that they don't write examination essays about them). Sometimes candidates are invited to rework the books in their own terms – the following question might be applied to *Macbeth*, *The Merchant of Venice* or *Romeo and Juliet*: 'Put yourself in the place of a character, in one of the works you have studied, faced with dangerous situations. (i) Describe the situations, (ii) show how you dealt with them, and (iii) explain the effect(s) of your action(s) or decision(s)' (North West). Such invitations to reconstruct the text undermine its stability and status as the one essential embodiment of the writer's genius; for the reverent 'neutrality' of literary criticism they substitute the manifest appropriation of the candidate. Such questions have spread from CSE to one O level board, the Oxford and Cambridge: 'Imagine that you are the nurse being interviewed by a reporter. Explain your part in the events of the play' (*Romeo and Juliet*); 'Write an editorial for the *Arden Gazette* on the recent outbreak of marriage in the district' (in *As You Like It*; the note of facetiousness is particularly bold and must have found many responses).

I have stressed the subversiveness of CSE, the extent to which it tends to undermine the canon and procedures of Literature. Actually, many of the examination questions are like those usually set at O level and pronouncements of the boards indicate conservative leanings. 'The use of extremely lightweight, modern, romantic authors should not be encouraged or allowed for examination purposes', the North West board declared in its *Reports on the 1983*

Examinations; and the South-East paper warned bluntly in its rubric: 'Questions refer to the books you have read, NOT to any radio, television, musical or film versions of them'. The idea of Literature lives on. Nevertheless, for radical teachers the more adventurous lists of texts and open-ended questions have permitted discussions of issues like racism, gender relations and peace, and the development in the students of a critical consciousness capable of analysing the ideological frameworks they encounter – including that of the examination system. Once more we see educational institutions manifesting a confusion of purpose which admits oppositional intervention.

The third institutional development which has been used to help Literature live up to its claims for general relevance is the subsuming of it into 'humanities' programmes. This tendency has made serious inroads into the status and pretensions of Literature, and has proved amenable to politicised teaching (it is related to the radical contextualising of Shakespeare's plays in Part I of the present study). It was given focus by a Schools Council/Nuffield study, *The Humanities Project* (Heinemann, 1970), which was produced to coincide with the raising of the school-leaving age (by one year to 16). 'The aim of the Project is: to develop an understanding of social situations and human acts and of the controversial issues which they raise' (p. 1); so the courses consist of a series of themes and issues. Visual material is emphasised; printed material may include 'poems and songs; extracts from drama, novels and biography; letters, reports and articles; readings from the social sciences; maps, cartoons, questionnaires, graphs and tables; and advertisements' (p. 11). Not much of the traditional or the progressivist exaltation of the literary text will survive such a process. In *Themes in Life and Literature*, edited by Robert S. Fowler and published by the Oxford University Press (1967) chapter four begins with two- to six-line snippets from 'The Lady of Shalott', 'I know where I'm going' (folk song), Shakespeare's sonnet 18, 'The Wife of Bath's Prologue', *The Girl with Green Eyes* (Edna O'Brien), *A Midsummer Night's Dream*, 'Tintern Abbey' and 'Under the Bridges of Paris' (pop song); then there are diverse prose passages. The Bullock Report (1975) was anxious: 'An obvious danger in humanities lessons is for the literature to be selected solely on the ground that it matches the theme, however inappropriate it may be in other ways. Moreover, when a poem or story is enlisted to serve a theme it can become the property of that theme to the extent that its richness is oversimplified, its more rewarding complexities ignored' (p. 132). Thus Bullock would have liked to

Alan Sinfield

reincorporate those 'literary' aspects which humanities programmes were devised to cover the failure of. It was able to conclude, however, that 'a permanent relationship with the great
classics ... is traditionally thought appropriate for pupils preparing
for examinations' (p. 130). So at least the GCE streams can be kept
uncontaminated.

Bullock did not say, though it certainly thought, that the traditional approach is politically safer. *The Humanities Project* envisaged that the teacher would be 'neutral' in the presentation of
themes (p. 1) but this was of course a chimera, and the opportunity
for radical intervention is manifest. The extent of politicised teaching
in humanities programmes cannot be estimated, but its presence is
indicated by the hostility shown both by classical humanists and
conservative progressivists. Roger Scruton writes in the *Daily Mail*
against Peace Studies and other 'relevant' courses as 'a continuous
stream of rubbish' (he moves easily into the idiom of the *Mail*),
preferring what he calls 'the "irrelevant" subjects – the great dead
languages, higher mathematics, literary criticism' – because they
force 'the pupil to understand something which has no immediate
bearing on his experience' (3 February 1984). For the progressivists,
Peter Abbs exposes his own politics when he complains that with
anthologies about strikes, women's liberation, prostitution, homosexuality and another dozen social issues the approach has become
'sordidly nihilistic. ... We politicize literature at the cost of authenticity' (*English within the Arts*, p. 22). Strikers, feminists, prostitutes,
gays and so on seem to be excluded from the authentic – or is it only
when they draw attention to their oppression?

The attempts of these rival theories and practices to cope in problematic historical conditions with the intractability of Literature in the
classroom have steadily eroded such coherence and status as it once
had. The 'crisis in English' which has recently been noticed in
universities is much more advanced and more far-reaching in
schools. There the high-cultural idea, the alleged universal appeal,
and the practices of literary criticism are questioned continuously,
and over large areas Literature is slipping out of visibility altogether.
This we can observe even in O level and sixth-form work. As this
book goes to press it has been decided, after years of hesitation, to
amalgamate O level and GCE into one examination with a single
scale of grades from 1988. There will be more and less 'difficult'
papers, aimed at preserving the 'academic' character of the top
grades; whether this will lead to current O level characteristics
intruding on the work of more pupils, or to further erosion of

traditional literary criticism, remains to be seen. Already there are A level rivals to English – Theatre Studies, and Communications. The Schools' Council has endorsed one-year sixth-form English courses which 'propose a direct interest in people in action, in the community and at work, as well as in documentary and poetic presentations of human experience'.[41] And the Associated Examining Board has introduced a new format of A level English assessment, including an open-book examination and a course-work folder, and involving the study of texts chosen in schools for their appropriateness in developing pupils' reading experiences; the aims include an extension of 'the range of English studies' and 'opportunity for more varied work' (Dixon, *Education 16–19*, pp. 66–70).

In the new Associated A level, for all that has been said, the study of one Shakespeare play is compulsory. The importance of Shakespeare is perhaps greater than ever, for he is becoming the *sole vehicle* of high-cultural ideology and establishment literary criticism in schools. This is true even in conventional GCE examinations: 'other former rivals in the English literary pantheon – Milton, Wordsworth, Tennyson – have faded almost without trace' from O level (Barnes and Seed, *Seals of Approval*, p. 18), and the tendency is similar at A level. Goulden and Hartley's 'league table' of set texts show Literature to be dispersed over a most eclectic range ('"Nor should such Topics"', p. 6). Shakespeare remains as the great witness to the universality of literary experience, but his position is absurd, for he is representative of a category, of a theory, of which he is the only undoubted instance.

The left-liberal consensus which, I have tried to show, has undermined Literature while seeming to recuperate it is itself now under attack from the right. Not only are resources being cut, but the Department of Education and Science is insisting upon traditional disciplines and elitist 'standards'; the Schools' Council, which has been a principal agency of reformist thought, is being abolished and more emphasis is being placed on the Assessment and Performance Unit. The courses provided by the Manpower Services Commission for people leaving school at 16 without jobs force them into practical studies intended to prepare them directly for the labour market (such as it is); there is very little scope there for Literature.[42]

Yet it is unlikely that Shakespeare's significance as a cultural token will diminish – it is too firmly established outside education as well as inside. His name has been the watchword for reactionaries and conservative progressivists alike. For Sir Cyril Burt, who was so determined to demonstrate a hierarchy of innate ability in children that he faked his evidence, Shakespeare's transcendent status is the first move in his *Black Paper* argument: 'No one, not even the most convinced egalitarian, would deny that a few outstanding person-alities, like Shakespeare or Newton, are born geniuses';[43] recently the Chancellor of the Exchequer has invoked Shakespeare in the same cause (see below, p. 203). David Holbrook appears to present a significant alternative, but his case for the creativity of the 'low IQ' child reincorporates the elitism and essentialism which it might seem to challenge: the child's writing 'was doing for the human mind that produced it, what Shakespeare's *Sonnets* did for his very great mind at a very different level'.[44] Socialists may challenge these appropria-tions of Shakespeare. The plays may be taught so as to foreground their historical construction in Renaissance England and in the institutions of criticism, dismantling the metaphysical concepts in which they seem at present to be entangled, and especially the construction of gender and sexuality. Teaching Shakespeare's plays and writing books about them is unlikely to bring down capitalism, but it is a point for intervention.

Notes

1 On the 'hidden curriculum' see Rachel Sharp, *Knowledge, Ideology and the Politics of Schooling* (London: Routledge, 1980), pp. 123–31; Sue Sharpe, *Just Like a Girl* (Harmondsworth: Penguin, 1976), ch. 4; Michelle Stanworth, *Gender and Schooling* (London: Hutchinson, 1983).

2 Nicos Poulantzas, *Classes in Contemporary Capitalism* (London: New Left Books, 1975), p. 252. See further Samuel Bowles and Herbert Gintis, *Schooling in Capitalist America* (New York: Basic Books, 1976; London: Routledge, 1976); Roger Dale, Geoff Esland and Madeleine MacDonald, eds., *Schooling and Capitalism* (London: Routledge and the Open University, 1976).

3 Michael Young and Geoff Whitty, 'Perspectives on Education and Society', in *Society, State and Schooling*, ed. Young and Whitty (Ringmer: Falmer Press, 1977), p. 12. See also in this book Simon Frith and Paul Corrigan, 'The Politics of Education' and Michael Erben and Denis Gleeson, 'Education as Reproduction'. And see further Education Group, Centre for Contemporary Cultural Studies, *Unpopular Education* (London: Hutchinson and Centre for Contemporary Cultural Studies, 1981), ch. 1.

4 *Common Cores at A level*, prepared by GCE Boards of England, Wales and Northern Ireland (London, 1983). On Shakespeare as National Poet see Derek Longhurst, '"Not for all time, but for an Age"; an Approach to Shakespeare Studies', in *Re-Reading English*, ed. Peter Widdowson (London: Methuen, 1982).

5 Ministry of Education, *Half Our Future* (the Newsom Report) (London: HMSO, 1963), p. 155.

6 See Noëlle Bisseret, *Education, Class, Language and Ideology* (London: Rout-ledge, 1979), ch. 2; J. W. B. Douglas, J. M. Ross and H. R. Simpson, *All Our Future* (London: Panther, 1971), pp. 36–41; A. H. Halsey, 'Towards Merit-ocracy? The Case of Britain', in *Power and Ideology in Education*, eds. Jerome Karabel and A. H. Halsey (New York: Oxford University Press, 1977).

7 Linda Peffer in *Dutiful Daughters*, ed. Jean McCrindle and Sheila Rowbotham (Harmondsworth: Penguin, 1979), p. 364. See also pp. 336–7.

8 See Pierre Bourdieu, 'Cultural Reproduction and Social Reproduction', in *Know-ledge, Education and Cultural Change*, ed. Richard Brown (London: Tavistock, 1973); and also Bourdieu's papers in Dale, Esland and MacDonald, eds., *Schooling and Capitalism*. Bourdieu's approach has been criticised by Bisseret in *Education, Class, Language and Ideology*, ch. 5; and by Sharp in *Knowledge, Ideology and the Politics of Schooling*, pp. 66–76.

9 Department of Education and Science, *A Language for Life* (the Bullock Report) (London: HMSO, 1975), p. 131.

10 North West Regional Examination Board: Certificate of Secondary Education, *Reports on the 1983 Examinations*. For those unfamiliar with the British system: CSE examinations are taken mainly as a leaving qualification at age 16 by pupils thought relatively less 'able'; they are set by twelve regional boards. The top grade of CSE is regarded as equivalent to a pass in GCE Ordinary (O) level, which is typically taken at 16. Pupils who 'stay on' may then take Advanced (A) level at 18 or 19. Two A level (and five O level) subjects are normally required for university entrance, but in many subjects and especially English three A levels are now necessary. GCE papers are set by nine boards: three are controlled by single universities: Cambridge, London and Oxford; six by combinations of universities or colleges: Associated (AEB), Joint (JMB), Northern Ireland, Oxford and Cambridge (not the same as the two separate boards already mentioned), Southern, and Welsh. The Scottish system is different, and points made in the present paper should not be assumed to be applicable to Scotland.

11 Universities of London, *General Certificate of Education Examination: Statistics* (1982). See further Pierre Macherey and Étienne Balibar, 'Literature as an Ideological Form', *Oxford Literary Review*, 3 (1978), 4–12; and Madan Sarup, *Marxism / Structuralism / Education* (London and New York: The Falmer Press, 1983), pp. 41–3, 117–22.

12 See Sharpe, *Just Like a Girl*; Eileen M. Byrne, *Women and Education* (London: Tavistock 1978); Rosemary Deem, *Women and Schooling* (London: Routledge, 1978); Jenny Shaw, 'Finishing School', in *Sexual Divisions and Society*, ed. Diana Leonard Parker and Sheila Allen (London: Tavistock, 1976); Margaret Sandra, 'She's good at English – is English good for her?', *Teaching London Kids*, 19 (1983), 8–11. On the early development of the relationship between women and English, see Brian Doyle, 'The Hidden History of English Studies', in Widdowson, *Re-Reading English*, pp. 22–5.

13 Irene Payne, 'A Working-Class Girl in a Grammar School', in *Learning to Lose*, eds. Dale Spender and Elizabeth Sarah (London: Women's Press, 1980), p. 16. See also in the same book Marion Scott, 'Teach Her a Lesson'.

14 See Ann Marie Wolpe, 'The Official Ideology of Education for Girls', in *Educability, Schools and Ideology*, ed. Michael Flude and John Ahier (London: Croom Helm, 1974).

15 G. Yarlott and W. S. Harpin, '1000 Responses to English Literature', *Educational Research*, 13 (1970–1), 3–11, 87–97; p. 6.

16 Stuart Hall and Tony Jefferson, eds., *Resistance Through Rituals* (London: Hutchinson and the Centre for Contemporary Cultural Studies, 1976), p. 12.

17 Frank Whitehead, A. C. Capey, Wendy Maddron, Alan Wellings, *Children and Their Books* (London: Schools Council and Macmillan, 1977), pp. 125–9.

18 Sharp, *Knowledge, Ideology and the Politics of Schooling*, p. 109. On GCE English questions, see further Derek Longhurst, ' "Not for all time, but for an Age" ', in Widdowson, *Re-Reading English*; Holly Goulden and John Hartley, ' "Nor should such Topics as Homosexuality, Masturbation, Frigidity..." ', *LTP: Journal of Literature Teaching Politics*, 1 (1982), 4–20; Douglas Barnes and John Seed, *Seals of Approval* (University of Leeds School of Education, 1981).

19 See Renée Balibar, 'An Example of Literary Work in France', in *1848: The Sociology of Literature*, ed. Francis Barker *et al.* (Colchester: University of Essex,

Alan Sinfield

1978); and Tony Bennett's identification of a 'metaphysic of the text' in his *Formalism and Marxism* (London: Methuen, 1979), pp. 146–8, 162–8.

20 Perry Anderson, 'Components of the National Culture', in *Student Power*, eds. Alexander Cockburn and Robin Blackburn (Harmondsworth: Penguin, 1969), p. 271. See also Catherine Belsey, 'Re-Reading the Great Tradition', in Widdowson, *Re-Reading English*.

21 Jonathan Dollimore, *Radical Tragedy* (Brighton: Harvester, 1984; University of Chicago Press, 1984), p. 250.

22 Peter Widdowson, 'Hardy in History: a Case Study in the Sociology of Literature', *Literature and History*, 9 (1983), 3–16; p. 13.

23 Poulantzas, *Classes In Contemporary Capitalism*, pp. 275, 292. See also Margaret Mathieson, *The Preachers of Culture* (London: Allen and Unwin, 1975), ch. 12: 'Social and Academic Background of Teachers'.

24 Malcolm Skilbeck and Alan Harris, eds., *Culture, Ideology and Knowledge* (Milton Keynes: Open University, 1976), pp. 26, 28. See also Denis Lawton, *Social Change, Educational Theory and Curriculum Planning* (University of London Press, 1973), ch. 2,3,5,6.

25 Sir Arthur Quiller-Couch, *On the Art of Reading* (London: British Publishers Guild, 1947), p. 56. For a full account of the development of English literary criticism in its historical context, see Chris Baldick, *The Social Mission of English Criticism* (Oxford University Press, 1983).

26 See John Dixon, *Education 16–19* (London: Macmillan and Schools' Council, 1979), p. 2.

27 G. H. Bantock, *Education in an Industrial Society*, 2nd edn. (London: Faber, 1973), p. 167.

28 In J. H. Plumb, ed., *Crisis in the Humanities* (Harmondsworth: Penguin, 1964), pp. 103, 99.

29 See Michael F. D. Young, 'An Approach to the Study of Curricula as Socially Organized Knowledge', in *Knowledge and Control*, ed. Michael F. D. Young (London: Collier Macmillan, 1971), pp. 20–2. For a general account of education in the period see Education Group, *Unpopular Education*; and for an account of literary institutions see Stuart Laing, 'The Production of Literature', in *Society and Literature 1945–1970*, ed. Alan Sinfield (London: Methuen, 1983).

30 See F. R. Leavis, *Two Cultures? The Significance of C. P. Snow* (London: Chatto, 1962), and Bantock, *Education in an Industrial Society*, pp. 145–77.

31 Barry Sugarman, in *Introduction to Moral Education*, by John Wilson, Norman Williams and Barry Sugarman (Harmondsworth: Penguin, 1967), p. 335. On subcultural resistance see note 33.

32 Rhodes Boyson, *The Crisis in Education* (London: Woburn Press, 1975), pp. 137, 139–40, 148. On Boyson and the *Black Papers* see Education Group, *Unpopular Education*, pp. 200–7; and Ken Jones, *Beyond Progressive Education* (London: Macmillan, 1983), pp. 74–86.

33 Bernstein's work goes back to 1958 and is collected in *Class, Codes and Control*, 3 vols., 2nd edn. (London: Routledge, 1977): see vol. I. For criticism of Bernstein see Harold Rosen, *Language and Class* (Bristol: Falling Wall Press, 1972); and W. Labov, 'The Logic of Nonstandard English', in P. P. Gigliogli, ed., *Language and Social Context* (Harmondsworth: Penguin, 1972). For more recent work on subcultures, see Hall and Jefferson, *Resistance Through Rituals*; Stuart Hall *et al.*, *Policing the Crisis* (London: Macmillan 1978); Dick Hebdige, *Subculture: the Meaning of Style* (London: Methuen, 1979); Richard Jenkins, *Lads, Citizens and Ordinary Kids* (London: Routledge, 1983); Robert B. Everhart, *Reading, Writing and Resistance* (London: Routledge, 1983).

34 Peter Doughty, *Programme in Linguistics and English Teaching* (London: University College and Longman, 1968), paper 1, p. 42. See further M. A. K.

Halliday, A. McIntosh and P. Strevens, *The Linguistic Sciences and Language Teaching* (London: Longman, 1964); Harold Rosen, *Language, the Learner and the School* (Harmondsworth: Penguin, 1969).

35 See Skilbeck and Harris, *Culture, Ideology and Knowledge*, pp. 28–34; Lawton, *Social Change, Educational Theory and Curriculum Planning*, ch. 2; Mathieson, *The Preachers of Culture*, chs. 7, 8; Jones, *Beyond Progressive Education*, ch. 2.

36 David Holbrook, *English For Maturity*, 2nd edn. (Cambridge University Press, 1967), pp. 40–1.

37 David Holbrook, *The Exploring Word* (Cambridge University Press, 1967), p. 186.

38 Albert Rowe, *English Teaching* (St Albans: Hart-Davis, 1975), p. 127.

39 Peter Abbs, *English within the Arts* (London: Hodder and Stoughton, 1982), p. 112.

40 Chris Searle, *This New Season* (London: Calder and Boyars, 1973), p. 52. For criticism of progressivism see Jones, *Beyond Progressive Education*; Sarup, *Marxism / Structuralism / Education*, pp. 123–7; Nigel Hand, 'What *is* English?', in *Explorations in the Politics of School Knowledge*, ed. Geoff Whitty and Michael Young (Driffield: Nafferton Books, 1976).

41 Dixon, *Education 16–19*, p. 128; see also pp. 29, 35–6, 121–8 and, on Communications A level, pp. 70–88. In Theatre Studies a third of the examination is practical; Shakespeare plays are set texts but not compulsory study. Dixon's analysis is limited by his belief that Literature 'is least in need of definition' (p. 43). On the general disarray in Literature teaching, see Mathieson, *The Preachers of Culture*, chs. 13 and 14.

42 See Jones, *Beyond Progressive Education*, pp. 68–72, 132–8; Education Group, *Unpopular Education*, ch. 11.

43 *The Black Papers on Education*, ed. C. B. Cox and A. E. Dyson (London: Davis Poynter, 1971), p. 47.

44 David Holbrook, *English for the Rejected* (Cambridge University Press, 1964), p. 31; see also p. 208.

Note. This paper has benefited immensely from the comments and suggestions of Keith Kimberley, Brian Street, Geoffrey Hemstedt, Michael Butcher, Linda Fitzsimmons and Mark Sinfield. From the errors and clumsinesses which remain not even they could save me.

9 Alan Sinfield

Royal Shakespeare: theatre and the making of ideology

a theatrical backwater, an adjunct to the tourist industry which was largely ignored by critics and stars ... (Richard Findlater)[1]

every conceivable value was buried in deadly sentimentality and complacent worthiness – a traditionalism approved largely by town, scholar and Press ... (Peter Brook)[2]

Certainty of financial support from the tourist public would have been every excuse for a *laissez faire* policy of artistic standard – and, indeed, this was the policy ... (Charles Landstone)[3]

A critic, a director and an officer of the Arts Council agree that what we now call the Royal Shakespeare Company was, at the end of the Second World War, artistically, culturally and politically insignificant. Since that time this has become one of the most prestigious companies in the world, the repeated winner of major international awards. In the 1950s the company broke even or made a small profit from box office receipts; in 1984–5 its Arts Council grant will total nearly five million pounds. We argued in the Introduction to Part II that 'Shakespeare' is not a fixed entity but a concept produced in specific political conditions, a powerful cultural token, a site of struggle and change. The rapid and convincing development of the RSC has been both a cause and an effect of the construction of Shakespeare which has become dominant in modern British society. It intersects fundamentally with our ways of thinking about the plays and about 'the arts' and political change within welfare capitalism.

The crucial structural changes in the RSC were made by Peter Hall when he became director in 1960 at the age of 29. He leased a London theatre, the Aldwych, thus making it possible to keep a permanent company together and to perform modern plays, and he pressured the Arts Council into subsidising the consequent deficit. The prevailing Stratford image was conservative – 'It was acknowledged that each year there should be some celebration of the bard,

[158]

and audiences arrived in Stratford very much as if they were on a pilgrimage'.[4] Hall's innovations signalled a new direction, they seemed politically progressive. The idea of a permanent company was egalitarian and was associated with Brecht's Berliner Ensemble; modern playwrighting meant the new wave which was challenging the establishment at the Royal Court and Theatre Workshop (and, indeed, it led the RSC into disagreements with the censor and a dispute in the press in 1964 about dirty plays); and State subsidy was widely regarded as necessary to protect innovative work from commercial pressures.

'I am a radical, and I could not work in the theatre if I were not. The theatre must question everything and disturb its audience' – so said Peter Hall in 1966.[5] This became the image of the RSC: 'The company was developing a radical identity which could be seen in every aspect of its existence'; 'While there was no question of the theatre promulgating an ideology, it was generally understood that the beliefs and ideals of the RSC were left of centre'.[6] And this image has persisted, broadly, through the replacement of Hall by Trevor Nunn in 1968 to the present; in 1974 Nunn declared, 'I want a socially concerned theatre. A politically aware theatre' (Addenbrooke, p. 182). This radical RSC identity is so well known that it may be taken for granted, but it is composed, surely, of paradoxes and surprises which suggest a more complicated and confused relationship between innovation and establishment. 'The Royal Shakespeare Company': as someone remarked, 'It's got everything in it except God' (Addenbrooke, p. 63). National subsidy for the company devoted to Shakespeare seems obvious and the royal epithet goes with that. But how did it get mixed in with radicalism? – to the point, apparently, where the chairman of the Arts Council 'questioned whether it was the duty of the state actually to subsidise those who were working to overthrow it' (Beauman, p. 284). And given this anxiety, why did the Arts Council maintain and increase its support?

Trevor Nunn reports that Hall 'insisted upon one simple rule: that whenever the Company did a play by Shakespeare, they should do it because the play was relevant, because the play made some demand upon our current attention' (Berry, *Directing Shakespeare*, p. 56); Nunn said that he himself produced the Roman plays in 1972 because they seemed 'to me to have the most meaning and the most point and the most relevance' (Addenbrooke, p. 174). Shakespeare-plus-relevance: this is the combination of traditional authority and urgent contemporaneity which proved so effective. We shall consider, in the changing political context of the time, what kind of authority this has been, what kinds of relevance and radicalism have been developed, and why the combination has been so necessary and powerful.

The Wars of the Roses (1963) was important in establishing the radical image of the RSC, and the conception was certainly adventurous. The three Henry VI plays and Richard III were rewritten by John Barton as three plays, titled Henry VI, Edward IV and Richard III. The playing text contained just over half the lines of the original four plays, and to those were added 1400 lines written by Barton, so that he was responsible for almost a tenth of what was said; also, many lines and scenes were moved around. One reason was that the company could not sustain, in box-office terms, three lesser-known plays in one season. Also, the rewriting was designed to substantiate a particular view of the political relevance of the plays.

Hall said that his direction of The Wars of the Roses was guided by two convictions about Shakespeare. One is that he believed in the 'Elizabethan World Picture' as described by Tillyard (see above, pp. 5-6): 'All Shakespeare's thinking, whether religious, political or moral, is based on a complete acceptance of this concept of order. There is a just proportion in all things: man is above beast, king is above man, and God above king'.[7] This, of course, is an extremely conservative idea (it was even conservative in theatrical terms, for Anthony Quayle had drawn upon Tillyard for his conception of Richard II, Henry IV and Henry V at Stratford in 1951). An ordered and harmonious society may be a good thing, but to base it upon such hierarchisation is to build in all the oppression which liberals, let alone socialists, have resisted. Hall, like Tillyard, seemed to justify such a vision with an extreme and partial idea of the alternative: 'Revolution, whether in the individual's temperament, in the family, or in the state or the heavens, destroys the order and leads to destructive anarchy' (p. x). In a classic conservative move, every possibility which is not the status quo is stigmatised as 'anarchy' – no other idea of order and harmony is admitted. Moreover, the hierarchy is reinforced, Hall said, by the claim that it is both natural and the concern of a retributive deity: 'punishment will follow the violation of natural laws. Bolingbroke ... and his family, suffer retribution for generations' (p. x). Such a threat is plainly designed to induce docility, and moreover, by projecting violent retribution on to a deity it legitimates punitive institutions and habits of mind in society. Hall said, amazingly, that he saw all this as 'humanitarian in its philosophy and modern and liberal in its application' (p. x).

Most of the rewriting of the text was in the service of this conservatve viewpoint. In particular, the death of the Bishop of Winchester (2 *Henry VI*, III.iii) was moved to follow the death of Suffolk (IV.i) and made to conclude the first play. The idea was that Winchester's 'death-bed confession' of responsibility for the death of Gloucester would make 'the main moral point that self-seeking and wickedness breed guilt in the doer, and rejection by other people' (*Wars of the Roses*, p. xix). But Winchester does not, in the received text, make such a confession: Hall and Barton therefore added a question from Warwick about it and a response in which Winchester implicitly admits the murder. It was also thought a good idea, to enforce the same moral in this concluding scene, to 'make Henry guiltily aware that his weakness has been responsible for the death of Gloucester' (p. xix). For this purpose, King Henry was given a speech made up of three lines from another character in *3 Henry VI*, an invented line, and six lines spoken by Henry elsewhere. Thus the scene was adjusted in three ways (including its move to a climactic position) to yield a coherence of event and ideology which, it might be thought, the received text assiduously eschews.

The radical reputation of the RSC did not derive from a commitment to the propaganda of the Elizabethan State, however, but from Hall's other conviction: that the rhetoric of the plays' characters was 'really' 'an ironic revelation of the time-honoured practices of politicians. I realised that the mechanism of power had not changed in centuries. We also were in the middle of a blood-soaked century. I was convinced that a presentation of one of the bloodiest and most hypocritical periods in history would teach many lessons about the present' (*Wars of the Roses*, p. xi). Hall found support for this in Jan Kott's book *Shakespeare Our Contemporary*, which he had read in proof. Kott argues that twentieth-century history has re-equipped us for the political violence of Shakespeare – he invites us to see in Gloucester's seduction of the Lady Anne 'the night of nazi occupation, concentration camps, mass-murders. One must see in it the cruel time when all moral standards are broken, when the victim becomes the executioner, and vice versa'.[8] This analogy (or perhaps continuity) is presented by Kott partly in political terms, as 'a cruel social order in which the vassals and superiors are in conflict with each other, the kingdom is ruled like a farm, and falls prey to the strongest' (p. 25); but also as something like the human condition, an unalterable given which political action cannot affect, offered as a pessimistic revision of the Marxist emphasis on history – 'The implacable roller of history crushes everybody and everything' (p. 39).

Kott's scepticism about any positive possibilities in politics is comprehensible enough, especially in relation to his native Poland, but whether it was constructive in England in 1963 is doubtful. However this is the aspect which Hall seized upon: 'Shakespeare always knew that man in action is basically an animal. Before man developed religion or philosophy, he had an instinctive will to dominate. This lust may be excused as self-defence, or the need to obtain food – but it is as basic to an animal as the desire to eat, to sleep or to procreate' (*Wars of the Roses*, p. xii). The combination of this notion that people are 'basically' animals (a common motif in the post-war period[9]) with the World Picture idea of divinely instituted order is most powerfully conservative. It offers no hope for humanity and no analysis of the sources and structures of injustice, whilst siphoning any residual idealism into deference towards the magnates who perpetrate oppression and reverence for the social system which sustains them. Kott at least repudiated the World Picture (*Shakespeare Our Contemporary*, p. 40); he finds satisfaction in the idea that the kings also (and Hitler and Stalin) are the ridiculous victims of history. This is applied even to Richmond at the end of *Richard III*: Kott says he 'suddenly gives a crowing sound like Richard's, and, for a second, the same sort of grimace twists his face. The bars are being lowered. The face of the new king is radiant again' (p. 46). This is, of course, an interpretation not explicitly suggested by the text; Kott represents the accession of the king who in Tillyard's view is the divinely appointed answer to political violence as just another cruel trick of history. Hall and Barton, contrariwise, were eager to exempt Richmond from the discredit attaching generally to politicians. Therefore they elaborated upon the received text by writing in a part for the Princess Elizabeth so as to 'bring out the historical and thematic point that her marriage with Richmond defined the reconciliation of York and Lancaster, and brought the Wars of the Roses to an end' (*Wars of the Roses*, p. xxii). Thus the arrival (in Elizabethan terms) at the status quo is made to seem even more satisfying than in the received text – the one miraculous exception to the otherwise universal human bestiality.

Such, then, is the conservative slant of *The Wars of the Roses*; how it appeared to be and perhaps was radical in the social context of 1963 will be considered later on. The other great influence on the RSC was Peter Brook. From the beginning, Brook's orientation was Modernist – in 1960 he asked: 'is there nothing in the revolution that took place in painting fifty years ago that applies to our own crisis today? Do we know where we stand in relation to the real and the unreal, the face of life and its hidden streams, the abstract and the concrete, the story and the ritual?'[10] This kind of concern, though a challenge to the complacency of west-end theatre in 1960 – a challenge cognate with attention to Beckett, Ionesco, Pinter and Artaud – neglects as external and trivial the realities of political power and political action. In 1963 Brook explained his opposition to a Shakespeare of 'outer splendour' – of romance, fantasy and decoration, declaring; 'on the inside lie themes and issues, rituals and conflicts which are as valid as ever'.[11] He allowed no space for a historical reality which is neither superficial nor subjective. In 1977 his basic position had not changed: 'I don't have any sense of or interest in history as a reality. . . . What interests me is that there are channels through which we can come into contact for a limited time with a more intense reality, with heightened perceptions' (Berry, *Directing Shakespeare*, p. 129).

Brook's *King Lear* (1962) was perceived, with *The Wars of the Roses*, as setting the tone and policy of the company. The production was a determined realisation of Kott's chapter '*King Lear*, or Endgame' – the idea that Shakespeare's vision in this play is like Beckett's. Charles Marowitz said of the rehearsals: 'our frame of reference was always Beckettian. The world of this Lear, like Beckett's, is in a constant state of decomposition. The set consists of geometrical sheets of metal which are ginger with rust and corrosion. The costumes, dominantly leather, have been textured to suggest long and hard wear. . . . Apart from the rust, the leather and the old wood, there is nothing but space – giant white flats opening on to a blank cyclorama.'[12] The politics of this is nihilist; Brook made sure that his *Lear* could not be construed as offering any positive possibilities for humanity by making the servants hostile instead of sympathetic to the blinded Gloucester, deleting Edmund's final repentance, and introducing as a last gesture a renewed rumbling of thunder, suggesting the storm still to come.

Brook's work on modern plays for the RSC in the 1960s developed the radical image of the company, though its political imprecision was gradually perceived.[13] His presentation of *A Midsummer Night's Dream* in 1970 was praised in England and the United States as an astonishing vision of the play. 'Tittuping fairies and fat jolly avuncular actors wearing loveable asses' heads' were replaced by

the rougher magic of the circus, of the puppet theatre and of the music hall. Thus Bottom sports a clown's nose when under the influence of the potion, love in idleness; thus we have Titania floating down from the flies in a crimson bower of ostrich feathers straight out of a folies bergères revue; thus we have Puck in yellow pantaloons trailing with him memories of the sturdy accomplishments of the *commedia dell'arte* troupers; thus we have Oberon nonchalantly spinning a saucer on the end of a stick whilst airborne on a trapeze. To say all this proved exhilarating would be the understatement of the year.[14]

Few people asked what it all meant; Brook said it was 'a work of pure celebration ... a celebration of the arts of the theatre' and that 'The play is about something very mysterious, and only to be understood by the complexity of human love'.[15]

Brook's distrust of political relevance set him in principle at odds with Hall, but in effect Brook's anguished Modernist disdain for history, politics and material reality approximated to Hall's despondent argument that nothing can be done because we are animals and unable to live up to the Elizabethan World Picture. Between them they implied a sense of general violent destruction, proceeding both from uncontrollable political systems and from mysterious inner compulsions. This Hall–Brook convergence amounted to the political stance of the RSC in the 1960s. That it helped to channel initially at least a certain radical impetus may be attributed to Kott, whose criticism was certainly more political than the main western academic tradition (though not in the Lear-Beckett chapter); to the intermittent invocation and influence of Brecht; and above all to the confused political awareness of the time.

The purposes and success of the RSC in the 1960s, and the imprecision of its radical gesture, should be perceived in terms of its situation at the focus of diverse cultural assumptions: the ineluctable status of Shakespeare, the feeling that the main impetus in English society demanded radicalism and relevance, and the idea that the State had a responsibility to support such work. This conjuncture must be analysed in its wider significance. The ruling concept I shall call *culturism*: the belief that a wider distribution of high culture through society is desirable and that it is to be secured through public expenditure. Culturism is an aspect of the theory of welfare capitalism, within which the market is accepted as the necessary agency for the production of wealth, and its tendency to produce unacceptable inequality is to be tempered by State intervention. Anthony Crosland in his seminal book *The Future of Socialism* (1956) envisaged this happening in two ways: 'first, by removing the greater handicap which poorer families suffer as compared with richer, during sickness, old age and the period of heaviest family responsibility, and secondly by creating standards of public health, education and housing which are comparable in scope and quality with the best available for private purchase'.[16]

The subsidisation of high culture fits precisely into this wider pattern of social policy: there is the same assumption that the market, left to itself, will produce inadequacies of quality and distribution, the same insistence upon State responsibility to extend to all classes the kind of provision which the middle classes have historically made for themselves. And from the vantage point of the present the outcome of culturism is unsurprising: the subsidised product has been appreciated and used overwhelmingly by middle-class audiences – one study suggests that in 1976 the top twenty per cent of households received over forty per cent of public expenditure on theatres, sporting events and other entertainments while the bottom twenty-five per cent received just four per cent.[17] Thus the pattern I have been pursuing is completed, for recent work has shown that 'Almost all public expenditure on the social services in Britain benefits the better off to a greater extent than the poor' (*The Strategy of Equality*, p. 43).

The location of culturism within welfare capitalism helps to explain the attention to Shakespeare and the assumption of State responsibility. The further factor – the accompanying radical identity – derives from the particular orientation of the left in England in the late 1950s and early 1960s. This we may call 'left culturism': the belief that socialists must now concern themselves with 'the quality of life' in the society. Richard Hoggart in *The Uses of Literacy* (1957) argued that traditional working-class culture was being debased by the commercial pressures of mass entertainment, concluding that 'the freedom from official interference ... seems to be allowing cultural developments as dangerous in their own way as those we are shocked at in totalitarian societies'.[18] Raymond Williams explored this argument powerfully in *The Long Revolution* (1961), pointing to 'the central fact that most of our cultural institutions are in the hands of speculators, interested not in the health and growth of the society, but in the quick profits that can be made by exploiting inexperience' and arguing that despite difficulties, 'the amount of capital and effort required, to make any substantial change, can come only from public sources'.[19] Williams extended this argument specifically to theatre (pp. 368–9) where, because of the decline in traditional theatre consequent upon first cinema and radio and then television, discussion was already advanced (the English Stage Company had been receiving subsidy since 1956 and the first season of the National Theatre began in 1963). The issue gained special purchase through the commitment of Arnold Wesker in his plays, his other writings and his founding of Centre 42.

The origins and impetus of left-culturism may be understood. For the right of the Labour Party, the post-war boom seemed to bring the traditional economic and political goals of the labour movement within sight of achievement and, at the same time, produced disillusionment with the resulting society. For the left, Cold-War paranoia and a proper revulsion from Stalinism inhibited the development of Marxist thought, whilst the apparent complicity of the working class with capitalism raised the question of culture as the agency by which proletarian consciousness was being subverted. From the present perspective, left-culturism seems to have been diversionary, for it narrowed the scope of political action and impeded appreciation of the political potential of subordinate cultures. Nor is it clear that it had much impact on the working class which were its ostensible concern. But it did help to construct a dissident intelligentsia, and its significant political activity is here.

It is often asserted that England has no intellectuals, but intellectuals should be defined by their social function, by their relation to the productive process. On this definition, intellectuals have increased greatly in number and confidence since the Second World War – students, workers in finance, advertising, the civil service, teaching. Precisely how we should analyse the class position of intellectuals is disputed. In Gramsci's view they elaborate and transmit the ideologies of classes to which they attach themselves; therefore they should be regarded as social categories within the class they serve.[20] According to Alvin Gouldner and others, they have become a 'new class' or class fraction, roughly divisible into a humanistic and a technical intelligentsia.[21] It does seem that during the 1960s in England and North America a distinct intellectual fraction of the middle class developed, and that it can be identified both by its relation to the production process and by a specific ideological slant. Gouldner shrewdly proposes that it shares a 'culture of critical discourse ... in which there is nothing that speakers will on principle permanently refuse to discuss or make problematic' (p. 28). This surely captures something of the technocratic discourse of government and business, which seeks to convince us that alternatives have been weighed; and of the liberal discourse of higher education and literary journalism; it suggests the spirit in which one might properly attend the RSC.

Whether this means that intellectuals are necessarily disposed towards radicalism, as Gouldner suggests, seems extremely doubtful. This must depend on specific relations with other classes at a particular conjuncture, and also on the specific concerns of intellectuals.[22] Frank Parkin in an analysis of the Campaign for Nuclear Disarmament published in 1965 found a commitment to some left causes (those more individually oriented) and not others (trades unions, for instance).[23] This was 'middle-class radicalism', but with the stimulus of the Vietnam War it became clearer and more purposeful. I have argued elsewhere (*Society and Literature 1945–1970*, ch. 6) that the theatre, from the opening of the English Stage Company in 1956, was a cultural site where a new, youthful, left-liberal intelligentsia identified itself. Parkin found a link between his subjects and the theatre (*Middle Class Radicalism*, pp. 99–104), and Williams had already noted that the new life in the English theatre was based on 'an important growth of middle-class dissidence' (*The Long Revolution*, p. 293). The major matrix in which this dissidence developed was higher education, which expanded rapidly in the period. It afforded the institutional bonding in which a culture of critical discourse, respect for high culture, and left culturism could cohere. Here the youthful left-liberal intellectuals found their structural role and their sense of validity. State support for 'the arts', and for Shakespeare especially, seemed an obvious extension of their experience, their concerns and, indeed, their political commitment.

The RSC can be observed feeling its way towards this class fraction. Hall realised that he needed a differently-constituted audience if he was to dispense with the conservative middle-class theatre tradition of Shakespeare which he regarded as moribund. In January 1963 he said: 'We want to run a popular theatre. We don't want to be an institution supported by middle-class expense accounts. We want to be socially as well as artistically open. We want to get people who have never been to the theatre – and particularly the young – to see our plays' (Addenbrooke, p. 63). By March 1965 the 'popular' and the 'open' had been refocused entirely in terms of 'the young' and particularly those in higher education: Hall saw that this was a growth area in English society and that it was creating the RSC's obvious new reference point:

There is now an extraordinary and dangerous division in our audience – between what (roughly speaking) those over 45 and those under 45 want. ... There is a new generation who do not think of the theatre as a high-brow, intellectual and difficult institution. They only object when it is a middlebrow, safe and intellectually specious. ... it is an audience that is growing and growing fast – as fast as our new universities, as fast as the large sale of LP records and paper-back books. (Addenbrooke, p. 112)

Of course, 'those over 45' had to be catered for while the new audience was constituting itself, and this no doubt accounts for much of the vagueness in stance of the RSC. But the crucial convergence was with the other audience, which was perceived by Hall in the image of the RSC: involved in high culture, concerned with the radical and relevant, prepared to demand State support.

'They only object when it is middlebrow, safe and intellectually specious', Hall said: that 'only' indicates the problem with the radicalism of the mid 1960s youthful intelligentsia. The state of England in general and the theatre in particular seemed so desperately stultified that any challenge to customary pieties seemed to be going in the right direction. It was difficult to envisage, let alone expect, specifically socialist policies. This was the feeling which Harold Wilson's rhetoric picked up and amplified: 'We are living in the jet-age but we are governed by an Edwardian establishment mentality. Over the British people lies the chill frost of Tory leadership. They freeze initiative and petrify imagination. ... We want the youth of Britain to storm the new frontiers of knowledge, to bring back to Britain that surging adventurous self-confidence and sturdy self-respect which the Tories have almost submerged by their apathy and cynicism.'[24] When Labour came into government in 1964 (and boosted Arts Council and RSC grants) the inadequacies of this programme quickly appeared and, together with the Vietnam War, this helped to focus a more strenuous interrogation of the ills of modern society.

Hall's direction of David Warner as Hamlet in 1965 affords access to the complexity of this cultural formation. Warner (rather like Jimmy Porter before him) invaded one cultural milieu with the lifestyle of another: 'his lank blond hair ruffled, a rust-red scarf looped about his neck, and his cloak rucked up like a belted grey mackintosh, reminds us of a drama student, or an inconspicuous undergraduate, or a worried young man leaving a coffee-bar in the King's Road' (quoted in Berry, *Changing Styles*, p. 97). This was something with which to disturb the A level teacher! For Hall, the production evoked a scepticism about political action which, we have seen, was his own – but he attributed it to young people: 'the young of the West, and particularly the intellectuals, have by and large lost the ordinary, predictable radical impulses which the young in all generations have had' (programme note).[25] But the effects of cultural production are always negotiated in the particular conditions of reception. The young in the audience found in the performance something they could use more positively: they showed, wrote J. C. Trewin, 'by their overwhelming cheers at the close that David Warner was the Hamlet of their imagination and their heart' (Wells, *Royal Shakespeare*, p. 36). They saw Warner's Hamlet not as a figure of apathy but as one of rebellion or, at least, refusal: he refused the corrupt world of Claudius and Polonius. True, he had little but style with which to resist, but this might contribute a necessary initial independence of stance; as Warner observed, 'This was a young man who made his own rules and did not mind appearing ridiculous or eccentric' (Wells, *Royal Shakespeare*, p. 34). There was a stronger radical impulse in his young intellectuals than Hall had realised. By 1968, when he yielded the directorate of the RSC to Trevor Nunn, the conditions of political radicalism in society and in the theatre were changing rapidly.

The eruption of extraparliamentary political activism which we associate with 1968 (but which of course was a more gradual and uneven process) had a major impact on theatre, for it involved especially the youthful intelligentsia who had supported theatrical innovations in the 1960s and it manifested itself partly through the growth, almost from nothing in 1966, of fringe groups, venues and plays.[26] The wider breakdown of consensus politics, initially in the move to the right of the Heath Conservative administration of 1970 and then in the Tory leadership of Margaret Thatcher, placed in question RSC hopes of taking its conservative and radical audiences along together. The opening by the company of its own 'fringe' venues – with notable successes at The Place, the Other Place and the Warehouse with both Shakespeare and new work[27] – signals this split.

The response to Warner's Hamlet had already suggested that the radicalism of a part of the audience might outrun Hall's; in 1970 he deplored 'a new generation who want to shout down all opposing opinions' – he wanted to direct *The Tempest* 'because it's about wisdom, understanding and also resignation' (Addenbrooke, p. 310). Trevor Nunn's initial stance was a refusal of politics. In *Plays and Players* in September 1970 – with the nude review *Oh! Calcutta!* pictured on the front cover – Nunn said he was 'not a political animal': 'In most of our work now we are concerned with the human personalities of a king or queen rather than with their public roles'.[28] In 1969 he produced the late plays in a 'chamber' setting designed 'to work within the scale of the individual actor – to make his words, thoughts, fantasies and language seem important'; his *Hamlet* of 1970 sought 'to focus upon that man's predicament in a very domestic and familiar way' (interview, p. 17). A 'white box' set and schematic contrasts of costume suggested both a landscape of the mind and current fashion in decor, and there were explicitly religious motifs.

Nunn moved back towards the Hall–Barton mode with his productions in 1972 of Roman plays (*Coriolanus, Julius Caesar, Antony and Cleopatra* and *Titus Andronicus*). He believed that Shakespeare used Roman settings 'to conduct a less inhibited examination of political motives and social organization than was possible when he was dealing with English history' and that these plays 'are speaking directly to us now' (Addenbrooke, pp. 317, 174). But Nunn's reading of the current political situation manifested the same generalised nihilism that we saw previously – in the programme for *Titus Andronicus* he suggested: 'Shakespeare's Elizabethan nightmare has become ours ... are we already in the convulsion which heralds a fall greater than Rome's?' Despite the explicitness of some of the modern political parallels – Rome in *Julius Caesar* was a police State controlled through black-shirted soldiers – Nunn laid himself open to charges that his main concern was with stage effect, style and spectacle (he had installed lighting and stage machinery of unprecedented sophistication). In 1974 Nunn restated the original RSC programme: 'I want to be concerned with a theatre that is determined to reach beyond the barriers of income, I want an avowed and committed popular theatre. I want a socially concerned theatre. A politically aware theatre' (Addenbrooke, p. 182).

In fact RSC policy swung to and fro in the 1970s and early 1980s. In 1974 John Barton produced a doctored 'relevant' *King John*: 'Our world of outward order and inner instability, of shifting ideologies and self-destructive pragmatism, is also the world of King John'.[29] In 1977 Terry Hands' *Coriolanus* was remarkable for the extent to which the production diminished the political implications of the play (see Berry, *Changing Styles*, p. 33). The main theatre responded intermittently to the Women's Movement: after Barton's 1970 production of *Measure for Measure* it became common for Isabella to indicate a lack of enthusiasm for the Duke's final proposal of marriage. Michael Bogdanov in 1978 even managed a feminist interpretation of *The Taming of the Shrew*. He turned the play as it has traditionally been understood on its head, simply by making it clear that what the men say and do is morally repugnant; in a brilliant and moving conclusion he made Petruchio and the other men flinch in horror from the destruction of Katherine which they have achieved. Yet very many productions seemed mainly opportunist – deploying the battery of staging devices developed during the 1960s for merely immediate effect.

The Hall–Brook convergence of the 1960s, confused as it was, grew up in direct dialogue with the political conditions of that decade. But since then it has seemed that the mannerisms of radical relevance are being reused without even that initial purchase in social change, and without even the original analysis, limited as that was, of how they were supposed to signify. The strongest evidence of this tendency is productions which are intended to address political and historical matters, and which in some respects do that, but which at the same time make contradictory gestures towards a purportedly transcendent reality. In such cases Hall and Brook don't just converge, they jostle and hamper each other. In 1974 Barton, with Barry Kyle and Clifford Williams, directed *Cymbeline*. On the one hand, they suggested 'that the play, so far from being a fairy-tale to its Jacobean audience, dealt seriously with the political issues of empire and internationalism', and to this end the Roman scenes were elaborated. But on the other hand they gave major characters symbolic attributes which implied a Brookian vision of an interior experience which is also some kind of ultimate reality: 'the Queen was a practising sorceress whose spell-working filled the stage with smoke; while the King wore a cloak of senility from which, on the news of the Queen's death, he burst, like a butterfly'.[30] The powerful *King Lear* of 1982, to take another instance, was meant, according to its director Adrian Noble, to be relevant in the political climate produced by the Falklands War and to show 'the potential for violence which you get within an absolute state'.[31] In some respects the production demystified conventional notions of transcendence – 'Ripeness is all' was shouted, desperately, over the drum of the preparing army in turbulent lighting; when Lear woke at Dover he was wearing pyjamas rather than the flowing robes of an Old Testament prophet/penitent; an emphasis on touching inhibited the blind/sight imagery from setting up a dichotomy between mundane and transcendent vision. But at the same time, contradictorily, the storm and the Fool were offered as projections of Lear's state of mind and the analysis of a society in dissolution was transformed into the universe in apocalypse ('*Lear* versus *Lear*', pp. 10–11). The 1960s proclamation and abrogation of the political persists, and apparently without much attempt to develop a new analysis – Noble actually invoked Jan Kott.

Alan Sinfield

The political confusion of the RSC since 1970 has been, finally, a confusion about its audiences and roles. As a liberal, consensual institution in a society which was polarising, it received criticism from both left and right. For the left, it was a victim of its own success: it seemed part of a new establishment – liberal, but an establishment nevertheless (like the BBC, parts of the churches and much of the education system). It employed between five-hundred and six-hundred people and if it was not quite, as Hall had feared, the ICI of the theatre, it had many features of a medium-sized business. One might say it was like a family, but perhaps that was not a good thing: 'the traditional implications hold true. The Company remains a male-dominated hierarchy, with those who are definitely parents and those who are definitely children (and if they happen to be secretaries and women, which is most often the case, they will be servicing their wise, humanist "fathers" with cups of tea or coffee)' (Chambers, *Other Spaces*, p. 17). This kind of critique developed alongside a more theoretical kind of socialism, which denied that the State could protect culture or anything else from the impact of capitalism – seeing the State rather as the essential instrument of capitalism. From his position as director of the National Theatre Peter Hall perceived in all this criticism of the RSC 'a perfect metaphor of how the radical dreams of yesterday become the institutions of today, to be fought and despised'.[32]

At the same time, the waning of governmental commitment to the welfare-capitalist principle of State support for the arts increased the company's economic difficulties and forced it to listen to criticism from the right. In 1975, when Britain in general and the RSC in particular were thought to be in great danger from inflation (attributed to the OPEC increase in oil prices – the external threat to the kingdom is relevant), it seemed a good idea to start the season with *Henry V*. The Duke of Edinburgh expressed his hope that the 'marvellous spirit of the play' would inspire courage 'to overcome the menace of rising costs and inflation in the years ahead'.[33] The struggle which Terry Hands faced as director was to give a positive reading of the play which was not so clumsily patriotic as to violate the company's political identity. The war was offered, to me shockingly, as an opportunity for individuals to become 'aware of their responsibilities, both to themselves and to each other, voluntarily accepting some abdication of that individuality in a final non-hierarchic interdependence – a real brotherhood' (*RSC Henry V*, p. 15).

The theme of brotherhood was difficult to square with the text (*RSC Henry V*, pp. 59, 70) and it was not picked up by the critics. They either heralded 'a gutsy, reviving production at a time of national adversity. And, boy, do we need it' (*Daily Express*) or accepted the idea of 'troops driven to the limit to enable the king to achieve self-realization' (*The Times*; *RSC Henry V*, pp. 253, 250). That the RSC was being forced back on to the audience which Peter Hall had tried to resist is indicated by the letter of a company director who had bought six tickets for a gala performance 'but was horrified to learn from a friend that the performance of *Henry V* is to be given with the actors dressed in boiler suits or similar garb. I cannot believe this is true for such a performance, especially with royalty present ...' (*RSC Henry V*, p. 262).

With the Thatcherite government policy of commercial funding for the arts (as for other services which since 1945 have been generally taken to be the responsibility of the State), this voice is presumably being heard more insistently. Nevertheless, after a period of great uncertainty the government has made special provision (earmarked Arts Council money) to maintain the RSC in its established form. The company's subsidy in 1984–5 is an increase of 36 per cent on the previous year (most organisations are getting less than three per cent). This witnesses, of course, to the ideological power of established institutions (the RSC and Shakespeare) in England. Whether, as well, it represents enlightened support for a company whose reputation has still a radical edge, or a further incorporation and blunting of that edge, remains to be seen.

We have surveyed a whole period of cultural change, a complex institution, and a range of productions by different people working from different theories. What is constant, as we follow it all through, is the importance of being Shakespeare. It is that name which has made so much of it possible, let alone important. Hence the insistence by all the directors that what they are presenting is *really Shakespeare*. Even Bogdanov's feminist *Taming of the Shrew* was offered by him as a rediscovery of Shakespeare's true intentions: 'In this world where bodies are sold to the highest bidder Kate's attempt to establish independence challenges the regime and the preconceived ideas of a woman's role in society. Does Shakespeare *really* believe that this is the way that society should behave or is he asking for an egalitarian society of equal rights and opportunity? I believe the latter.'[34]

Despite the frank acknowledgement of Hall and Barton that their rewriting in *The Wars of the Roses* must be considered dubious in principle, Hall announced their belief that 'there are

Alan Sinfield

important – and, we think, Shakespearean – values embedded in' the plays (*Wars of the Roses*, p. ix); both his Tillyard and Kott convictions are given, always, as discoveries about Shakespeare ('Shakespeare believed ... I realised that Shakespeare's history plays were full of ... Shakespeare always knew ... Shakespeare recognises ...' – pp. x, xii, xiii). And Barton writes of the introduction of Princess Elizabeth in *Richard III* as if it were something Shakespeare unaccountably overlooked: 'We tried as economically as possible to *stress* and *clarify the* importance of the young Princess Elizabeth in *Richard III* (*Shakespeare leaves her out* of the play). To present her and explain her function seemed essential if we were to *bring out the* historical and thematic point' (p. xxii; my italics). Brook's position is only apparently more complex. In an interview published in 1977 he denied '"serving" Shakespeare', insisting instead that 'there is only one service, which is to the reality which Shakespeare is serving'. But this comes to rather the same thing, because 'you've got the greatest channel to it (i.e. reality), through the greatest creator in this form, which is Shakespeare' (Berry, *Directing Shakespeare*, p. 123).

My point is *not* that the RSC should have stayed closer to a true idea of Shakespeare. It is that the whole business of producing Shakespeare in our society, and all the cultural authority which goes with that, depends upon the assumption that through all the metamorphoses to which the plays are subjected we still have the real presence of Shakespeare. He justifies public and private expenditure of resources and ensures the scope and quality of attention; he is the cultural token which gives significance to the interpretations which are derived from him. Rival productions are, in effect, contests for the authority of Shakespeare, rival attempts to establish that he speaks this position rather than (or, at least, as well as) that.

The range of existing interpretations might seem to embarrass the notion of Shakespeare's essential presence in them all, but there is an answer to this: it is characteristic of his genius that he is endlessly interpretable. Peter Hall declared: 'He has everything: he is domestic as well as tragic, lyrical *and* dirty; as tricky as a circus and as bawdy as a music hall. He is realistic *and* surrealistic. All these and many other elements jostle each other in rich contradictions, making him human, not formal. That is why you can now read Samuel Beckett in *Lear*, or the Cuban crisis in *Troilus*' (*Crucial Years*, p. 14). Peter Brook proclaims: 'The history of the plays shows them constantly being re-interpreted and reinterpreted, and yet remaining untouched and intact' (Berry, *Directing Shakespeare*, p. 117).

The other strategy which maintains the essential Shakespeare through all interpretations is an appeal to the unevenness of the received text. Michel Foucault in his paper 'What Is an Author?' exposes the dubiousness of the whole concept of the author, which he sees in part as 'a principle of unity' serving to neutralise contradictions, a construct through which 'any unevenness of production is ascribed to changes caused by evolution, maturation, or outside influence'.[35] The case of Shakespeare is more subtle, for the unevenness of the received text (attributable to early work, collaboration, the conditions of the Elizabethan and Jacobean theatre, unsatisfactory copy texts and printers' eccentricities) is emphasised and used to justify directorial inventiveness which claims, always, to retrieve the real Shakespeare from behind the unevenness. For his production of *Henry V* in 1975 Terry Hands cut the speeches in which the Archbishop of Canterbury elaborates upon the sudden and total reformation of Henry V upon his father's death (I.i.25–59) – they conflicted with Hands's wish to stress 'the doubts and uncertainties inherent in the role of Henry' (*RSC Henry V*, p. 15). Hands' explanation complains about the thematic and dramatic implications of the passage and concludes: 'Furthermore it is not well written. It is over written. Shakespeare could write badly, especially for special occasions. This may be one of them. Accordingly we treated it as a later insertion and cut it' (*RSC Henry V*, p. 103). Two arguments for the imperfection of the text are run together – that Shakespeare was writing below his best and that the speeches are later insertions (for the latter there is no scholarly warrant). And, of course, Hands believes that in the rejection of the 'saintly' king he is recovering the true Shakespeare, 'the specific unity explored in the play itself' (p. 15). The central idea of Shakespeare, so far from affording some control over what it is that the plays might represent, is actually used to justify at least sufficient interpretive scope to secure relevance. Then, conversely, the relevance of any particular production is guaranteed by the fact that it is Shakespeare, who is always relevant. The circle seems unbreakable.

The RSC has, from the start, fostered this potent combination of relevance and the real Shakespeare by announcing its respect for the scholarship which seems to authenticate the process. John Barton's academic credentials are often mentioned. Hall declared: 'you should approach a classic with the maximum of scholarship you can muster – and then you honestly try to interpret what you think it means to a person living now' (Addenbrooke, p. 129). The outcome has been a convergence of the academic and theatre Shakespeares which is without precedent – and which corresponds neatly to the concerns of the higher-educated audience. The company's programmes characteristically sustain this effect: they consist of a collage of scholarly materials – bits from Shakespeare's sources, original contextual gobbets, even discussion of the provenance of the text – spliced in with modern material, especially quotations of political significance and commentary from modern critics (the main device is quotation, which seems to guarantee authenticity). John Elsom walks right into the trap when he remarks: 'The search for social relevance could obviously get out of hand, but at the RSC it was tempered by a concern for textual accuracy and scholarship' (*Post-War British Theatre*, p. 171). Precisely: this is the combination which cannot be faulted.

Not *any* interpretation will pass as Shakespeare, of course. A major role of theatre criticism is to police the boundaries of the permissible (which is perceived as the consistent or the credible), judging whether or not particular productions fall within the scope of Shakespeare as currently recognised. All the productions discussed in this chapter provoked dispute about their legitimacy, and several points about this preoccupation may be made quite quickly. First, the discourse of the acceptably Shakespearean shifts, and interpretations which initially seem too adventurous become acceptable with time (this is excellently shown by Ralph Berry in his book *Changing Styles in Shakespeare*). Second, the main outcome which this kind of commentary secures is the continuance of criticism: it is its function to engage in such discussions. Third, such controversy does not necessarily damage audience figures – people like to join in and make their own assessment of the limits of Shakespearean production. Fourth, dispute about a particular interpretation does not undermine the principle of interpretation, for it assumes that there are limits within which interpretation is good; and fifth, what is certainly not brought into question is Shakespeare, for he is the given against which particular instances are measured.

For all these reasons, disputes about the scope of interpretation are finally unimportant – part of the conditions for the continuance of the game. But there is a persistent note of deep anxiety about productions which diverge too far from conventional understanding of the plays, and the reason for it is this: if you push the Shakespeare-plus-relevance combination too hard, it begins to turn into a contradiction. Then its force is lost, and questions about the whole enterprise start to formulate themselves. This became more likely and more disturbing with the break up. of consensus from 1968, as some directors attempted a more purposeful and precise radicalism. Jonathan Miller provoked disputes with his productions of *The Tempest* (Mermaid Theatre, 1970) and *Merchant of Venice* (National Theatre,1970) by presenting Ariel, Caliban and Shylock as members of oppressed racial minorities (Miller held nevertheless that he was producing Shakespeare: 'The mystery of Shakespeare's genius lies in the fact that innumerable performances of his plays can be rendered, few of which are closely compatible with one another' – Berry, *Directing Shakespeare*, p. 9 and *passim*).

Benedict Nightingale, among others, took on the critic's supervisory role, disallowing Miller's interpretations: 'his view seems to be that Shakespeare's plays are fair game for the vivisectionist. It is, he thinks, interesting to see what can be done with them; how far the daring director-surgeon is able to go without the experimental animal expiring'; yet 'Shakespeare must be at least nominally responsible for everything we hear'.[36] Nightingale seems to be anticipating my point, but in fact he is not prepared to question the underlying structure of Shakespeare-plus-relevance, as we can see from the care with which he proceeds. He declares that Miller's *Tempest* is a savage reduction ('Caliban, a tattered field nigger, incapable of progress; Ariel, the educated black, preparing to take over the country after independence' – *Theatre 71*, p. 157), and responds with his own idea of the play: 'a celebration of youth and spring, an unsentimental declaration of faith in the future, a marvellously mellow confession of love and charity for men' (p. 159). Nightingale does not push this particular reading at all dogmatically: he does not need to, he has offered an acceptable enough 'relevant' theme, and so can safely repudiate Miller's. But the *Merchant* does seem to be anti-semitic, and that is not the kind of relevance that is required; Nightingale observes: 'it is pro-Christian and, though it offers him a certain, paradoxical sympathy, anti-Shylock – while Miller is anti-Christian and pro-Shylock. This is, of course, an emphasis any good contemporary radical would prefer. Just now, it looks like the play Shakespeare ought to have written. The only trouble is that he didn't' (*Theatre 71*, pp. 158–9). In the present climate of opinion anti-semitism cannot be brushed aside, although 'Just now' almost permits that, so Nightingale allows: 'It could be that Miller made a better and bigger play of the *Merchant*' (p. 159). This is a very unusual move: faced with a discrepancy between the production and the usual understanding of Shakespeare, Nightingale suggests that Shakespeare had not in every respect the superior wisdom. But the *Merchant* is not a central play (how could it be, when it so resists the dominant ways of producing Shakespeare?) and anti-semitism is very tricky. So rather than stretch intolerably the scope of interpretation – which could bring into disrepute the whole strategy of Shakespeare-plus-relevance – Nightingale is prepared to withhold from this play the full authority of Shakespeare. The main enterprise is rescued at the expense of one relatively insignificant part. Even then, Nightingale still has a formula which could be used to retrieve the *Merchant*: 'It could be that the relevance he [the modern director] is rightly trying to achieve is of too limited a kind. It could be that it is too merely social. It could be that he is forgetting that the reason Shakespeare has survived is that he speaks to generation after generation, not merely or mainly about the public issues that happen to preoccupy them, but about the elemental, lasting problems of human nature' (*Theatre* 71, p. 161). Nightingale does not say whether he would prefer to regard anti-semitism as a 'merely social' preoccupation. What is clear is that if we read the *Merchant* for some 'elemental, lasting problems' we will get the anti-semitism as well. Neither Nightingale nor Miller can obscure totally the contradictions in the dominant construction of Shakespeare.

The reason for adjusting Shakespeare to radical ends is that he is an established cultural token – this is Margot Heinemann's argument in a later chapter. But it is precisely that establishment status which proves, always, a hindrance. In the work of the RSC we may perceive a strain of opportunism, or at least a wish to sustain the company itself, but there has also, no doubt, been a great deal of genuine radical purpose. But within the culturalist ethos of 'Royal Shake-speare', one either makes an acceptable compromise with received ideas of the play and the radical purpose is ineffectual, or, like Bogdanov with the *Shrew*, one goes for political explicitness which is easily set aside as 'not Shakespeare'. The problem, of course, is *Shakespeare* – the whole aura of elusive genius and institutionalised profundity. For even when the resistances set up by received notions of the plays are overcome and a genuinely radical interpretation is rendered persuasive (and it is not clear that this has ocurred), the idea of the real Shakespeare from which it all emanates nevertheless registers cultural authority, and implies that every innovation has been anticipated. The underlying pressure is towards deference and inertia.

It is the cultural, and therefore political authority of Shakespeare which must be challenged – and especially the assumption that because human nature is always the same the plays can be presented as direct sources of wisdom. One way of doing this is to take aspects of the plays and reconstitute them explicitly so that they become the vehicle of other values. Brecht in *Coriolanus*, Edward Bond in *Lear* (1971), Arnold Wesker in *The Merchant* (1976), Tom Stoppard in *Rosencrantz and Guildenstern Are Dead* (1966) and Charles Marowitz in a series of adaptations[37] have appropriated aspects of the plays for a different politics (not always a progressive politics). Even here, it is possible that the new play will still, by its self-conscious irreverence, point back towards Shakespeare as the profound and inclusive originator in whose margins we can doodle only parasitic follies.

The other way is proposed by Michael Billington in an interview with Bogdanov about the *Shrew*: 'To us, it may seem repugnantly chauvinist: treat it as an Elizabethan play and it reveals a lot about social attitudes to women'.[38] This proposal is repudiated by all the directors whose work has been discussed here: it amounts to treating Shakespeare as a historical phenomenon, implicated in values which are not ours but which can in production be made to reveal themselves, can become contestable. The relevance then develops through our critical response to that representation, the questions about modes of human relationships which it provokes. Productions designed to do this would seek explicitly to share cultural authority with Shakespeare; they would be instructive, and, at the least, they would stimulate awareness of change instead of submerging the range of historical and future possibilities into a permanent human wisdom author-ised, allegedly, by Shakespeare.

Notes

1 Richard Findlater, *The Unholy Trade* (London: Gollancz, 1952), p. 57.
2 Peter Brook, *The Empty Stage* (Harmondsworth: Penguin, 1972), p. 51
3 Charles Landstone, *Off-Stage* (London: Elek, 1953), p. 180.
4 Trevor Nunn in Ralph Berry, *On Directing Shakespeare* (London: Croom Helm, 1977), p. 56
5 David Addenbrooke, *The Royal Shakespeare Company* (London: Kimber, 1974), p. 66.
6 Sally Beauman, *The Royal Shakespeare Company* (Oxford University Press, 1982), p. 273; Ralph Berry, *Changing Styles in Shakespeare* (London: Allen and Unwin, 1981), p. 7.
7 John Barton with Peter Hall, *The Wars of the Roses* (London: BBC, 1970), p. x.
8 Jan Kott, *Shakespeare Our Contemporary*, 2nd edn. (London: Methuen, 1967), p. 37.

9 See Alan Sinfield, ed., *Society and Literature 1945–1970* (London: Methuen, 1983), pp. 97–100.
10 Charles Marowitz, Tom Milne and Owen Hale, eds., *The Encore Reader* (London: Methuen, 1965), p. 251.
11 Royal Shakespeare Company, *Crucial Years* (London: Reinhardt, 1963), p. 22.
12 Charles Marowitz and Simon Trussler, eds., *Theatre at Work* (London: Methuen, 1967), p. 134.
13 See Sinfield, *Society and Literature 1945–1970*, pp. 186–7.
14 John Roberts's review in *Plays and Players*, vol. 18, no. 1 (October 1970), 43, 57.
15 Interview in *Plays and Players*, vol. 18, no. 1 (October 1970), 18, 19. See further David Selbourne, *The Making of A Midsummer Night's Dream* (London: Methuen, 1982).
16 C. A. R. Crosland, *The Future of Socialism* (London: Jonathan Cape, 1956) p. 519.
17 Julian Le Grand, *The Strategy of Equality* (London: Allen and Unwin, 1982), p. 158. See also Sinfield, *Society and Literature 1945–1970*, p. 180.
18 Richard Hoggart, *The Uses of Literacy* (Harmondsworth: Penguin, 1958), p. 345.
19 Raymond Williams, *The Long Revolution* (Harmondsworth: Penguin, 1965), p. 366. For a powerful argument by Wesker see *The Encore Reader*, pp. 96–103.
20 Antonio Gramsci, *Selections from the Prison Notebooks*, ed. and trans. Quintin Hoare and Geoffrey Nowell Smith (London: Lawrence and Wishart, 1971; New York: International, 1971), pp. 5–16. The relationship between intellectuals and the petty bourgeoisie is uneven and must be argued in terms of specific conjunctures. Cf. pp. 142–6 above, and Nicos Poulantzas, *Classes in Contemporary Capitalism* (London: New Left Books, 1975), pp. 252–7.
21 Alvin W. Gouldner, *The Future of Intellectuals and the Rise of the New Class* (London: Macmillan, 1979).
22 See Tom Bottomore's comments in *Schumpeter's Vision*, ed. Arnold Heertje (Eastbourne and New York: Praeger, 1981), pp. 36–8; Robert J. Brym, *Intellectuals and Politics* (London: Allen and Unwin, 1980).
23 Frank Parkin, *Middle Class Radicalism* (Manchester University Press, 1968), chs 2, 7, 8. Also Michael W. Miles, 'The Student Movement and Industrialisation of Higher Education', in *Power and Ideology in Education*, ed. Jeromc Karobel and A. H. Halsey (New York: Oxford University Press, 1977).
24 Harold Wilson, *The New Britain: Labour's Plan* (Harmondsworth: Penguin, 1964), pp. 9–10.
25 Stanley Wells, *Royal Shakespeare* (Manchester University Press, 1977), p. 25.
26 See Catherine Itzin, *Stages in the Revolution* (London: Eyre Methuen, 1980).
27 See Beauman, pp. 308–14, 319–21, 329–30, 333–7; Colin Chambers, *Other Spaces* (London: Eyre Methuen and TQ Publications, 1980).
28 'Director in Interview: Trevor Nunn talks to Peter Ansorge', *Plays and Players*, vol. 17, no. 12 (September 1970), 16. See also Addenbrooke, pp. 170–2.
29 John Elsom, *Post-War British Theatre*, 2nd edn. (London: Routledge, 1979), p. 171.
30 Richard David, *Shakespeare in the Theatre* (Cambridge University Press, 1978), p. 187.
31 Alan Sinfield, 'King Lear versus Lear at Stratford', *Critical Quarterly*, 24 (Winter 1982), 5–14; pp. 7–8.
32 *Peter Hall's Diaries*, ed. John Goodwin (London: Hamish Hamilton, 1983), 5 July 1973.
33 *The Royal Shakespeare Company's Production of Henry V*, ed. Sally Beauman (Oxford: Pergamon, 1976), Foreword.
34 Michael Bogdanov with Joss Buckley, *Shakespeare Lives!* (London: Channel Four TV and Quintet Films, 1983), p. 5.
35 Michel Foucault, *Language, Counter-Memory, Practice* (Oxford: Basil Blackwell, 1977), p. 128.

36 Benedict Nightingale, 'Shakespeare Is as Shakespeare's Done' in *Theatre 71*, ed. Sheridan Morley (London: Hutchinson, 1971), pp. 159, 157.
37 Charles Marowitz, *The Marowitz Shakespeare* (London: Marion Boyers, 1978) – *Hamlet, Macbeth, The Taming of the Shrew, Measure for Measure, The Merchant of Venice*. On Bond, see Sinfield, '*King Lear* versus *Lear* at Stratford'.
38 'Why Old Bill needs rejuvenating', *The Guardian*, 30 December 1982, reprinted in Bogdanov, *Shakespeare Lives!*, p. 4.

I have profited from the advice of Ralph Berry, Linda Fitzsimmons, Mark Sinfield, Peter Stallybrass.

Radical potentiality and institutional closure: Shakespeare in film and television

I

Whereas the BBC TV Shakespeare series could be regarded as a characteristic expression of the cultural policies of the producing corporation, cinematic reproduction of Shakespeare constitutes at best a marginal dimension of film history. The primary function of cinema as a cultural industry in a bourgeois economy is to reproduce and naturalise dominant ideologies; and by contrast with the theatre, the plays of Shakespeare seem to have offered few opportunities for the prosecution of that function. The relation between 'Shakespeare' and 'film' is very much that suggested in our Introduction to Part II (p. 132): the exchange of cultural authority between institutions in a reciprocal process. The repute of cinema art and of the film industry can be enhanced by their capacity to incorporate Shakespeare; the institution of Shakespeare itself benefits from that transaction by a confirmation of its persistent universality. Shakespeare films exist on that important but peripheral fringe of cinematic production, where the values of high art can be held to justify or compensate for the lack of commercial success (they are probably screened more often and witnessed by more spectators in the form of 16mm prints hired by institutions of education than in the commercial cinemas), and they can scarcely be regarded as central to the mainstream practice and development of the cinema.

This essay has no space to attempt a general survey of Shakespeare films (which can in any case be found in some excellent full-length studies);[1] but will instead confine itself to two basic problems: the position of Shakespeare films within what has been defined as the ideological function of the cinema in society; and the existing status and potential value of films within the dominant practices of literary education.

Writing from within the embattled domain of 'Literature' teaching and criticism, we are likely to assume that any translation of a

Shakespeare text into a 'live' dramatic form – theatrical performance, film adaptation, television production – will automatically
constitute a progressive act. Such translation seems inevitably to
entail a liberation of the *play*, a text for reproduction or recreation in
performance, from the fetished holy writ of the *text*; and any move to
challenge the hegemony of that dominant form of ideological
oppression must, surely, be welcomed.

Theatrical, film and television productions have always been
accorded a place and a potential value within the broad conspectus
of a literary education: the question is what place, and what value?
Are such things ancillary to the essential critical labour, marginal
diversions to the study of texts? Traditional 'Literature' must keep
them peripheral, since when they became a central focus they tend to
displace the text from its central role in constituting the nature of the
subject; tend to render the discipline itself unstable, open to question, vulnerable to change. Useful evidence of the tension created
when film is introduced into the institution of Literature can be
found in GCE O level examiners' reports (I offer a few instances from
many examples):

> Imaginative interpretations of texts can be misleading. The visual
> impact of films and productions of plays was often stronger than the
> impact of Shakespeare's or Hardy's words.[2]
>
> Films and stage-productions are not always entirely helpful. Lady
> Macduff bathing her son, Macbeth's soldiers attacking her maids,
> Lady Macbeth leaping from the battlements, Macbeth's mutilated
> body scattered across the stage, were so commonplace that it seemed
> fortunate that productions of *The Crucible* were less easily available.
> (1973, p. 9)
>
> ... most candidates appeared to know *Macbeth* well. Some, however,
> were handicapped by having seen a film version ... candidates should
> remember that it is Shakespeare's text which is being examined.
> (1977, p. 9)

'Literature' here encounters 'Film' as a subversive influence to be
resisted, marginalised or suppressed. Is the adoption of Shakespeare
by the cinematic medium in educational practice, if not in the
commercial cinema, inherently radical?

Catherine Belsey, in a very interesting article,[3] proposes exactly
the opposite: in her argument, both the literary text and a theatrical
production under Elizabethan stage conditions are potentially
productive of plurality of meaning: whereas films operate to close
the plural work into a single dimension of significance:

[183]

> In the Elizabethan theatre there is no proscenium arch, no painted
> back-drop defining a setting in perspective, but a stage projected out-
> wards into the auditorium, with the audience placed on at least three
> sides of it and possibly four. There is no single place to which the
> action is addressed and from which it is intelligible. The introduction
> after 1660 of the proscenium theatre with perspective backdrops
> radically changed the relationship between the audience and the
> stage ...
>   ... Film is the final realisation of the project of perspective staging.
> The framed rectangle contains a world which is set out as the single
> object of the spectator's gaze, displayed in order to be known from a
> single point of view ... Through the intervention of the camera, which
> monitors what we see and therefore what we know, the film collects
> up meanings which may be lying around in the text, and streamlines
> them into one single, coherent interpretation which it fixes as
> inescapable. It arrests the play of possible meanings and presents its
> brilliant rectangle full of significance to and from a specific place, a
> single and at the same time inevitable point of view.

This passage represents a body of opinion which forms, to my
original thesis, the antithesis: that film is an inherently *conservative*
medium, which inevitably exercises a despotic ideological control
over the spectator's responses, closing off the work's potentiality for
multiplicity of significance, depriving the audience of an opportunity
to participate in a collaborative construction of meaning. 'Film', in
the words of another writer, 'overwhelms the mind with a relentless
progression of visual and auditory impulses ... all other arts liberate
the imagination, film entraps it.'[4]

In terms of this latter view, the medium of film itself can only be an
invisible, apparently innocent communicator of ideology. Like the
naturalist stage, it purports to provide the spectator with a transparent window on to experience: isolated in the darkness of an
auditorium she or he is overwhelmed with an enormous concentration of visual imagery insistently signifying its irreducible reality.
Belsey offers as illustrations two films, both of which are said to offer
ideology a free, unhampered passage: Joseph L. Mankiewicz's *Julius
Caesar* (1953) transmits the liberal dilemma of a bourgeois-democratic society; while the *King Lear* (1970) of Peter Brook communi-
cates a 'theoretical nihilism': '... like *Julius Caesar*, this film also
makes a political statement: that the struggle for change, however
heroic, is doomed in a world where all law, morality and justice are
finally illusory'. Mankiewicz's film is of course a piece of thorough-
going film naturalism, alternating close-ups of the main characters
with long-shots of crowd scenes, all played against a 'realistic'
Roman background. Belsey acknowledges, in an enthusiastic

critique, that the cinematic techniques of *King Lear* are stylistically very different: she lists the grainy black-and-white photography, stylised acting, direct addresses to camera, lightning changes of focus, rapid superimpositions, violations of screen direction. She could have added the Brechtian titles, the absence of music, the distorted images, zoom-fades, blurred visions, surreal apparitions; the 'disjointed and staccato quality, elliptic camera-work, and violent mannerist cutting;'[5] all devices which estrange the film's techniques from naturalism and from familiar screen conventions. Can a film constructed from such alienating, deconstructive devices really be a vehicle for the smooth and uninterrupted passage of ideology; can such discordant techniques really operate to naturalise ideology, obediently miming its chosen language?

Consider Brook's handling of a particularly complex dramatic moment, Gloucester's attempted suicide. Grigori Kozintsev in his film of the play felt that this scene was essentially a theatrical gesture, and avoided it by cutting. Brook, with Beckett and Jan Kott in the background, embraced the moment as a central thematic and dramatic focus of the work.

> The director duplicates in cinematic terms Shakespeare's blend of blatant stage artifice and imaginative reality ... a long shot shows Edgar and Gloucester struggling along a flat plain. But then, in a series of tight, low-angle close-ups, Edgar and Gloucester seem to climb. The sound of the waves in the distance accords with Edgar's description, and following film convention it makes us imagine an off-screen reality. Set on 'the extremest verge', Gloucester bids farewell to poor Tom, and his final speech of despair is filmed in low-angle close-up ... as he falls forward, however, Brook jolts us with an illusion-shattering cut to an extreme overhead long-shot. From this godlike perspective, we watch a tiny old man take a silent pratfall on a barren stretch of sand. (*Shakespeare on Film*, p. 240)

The complex effects of this filmic montage can't adequately be summarised either in terms of Belsey's 'political statement', or of Jorgens's 'absurdist pantomime'. The director has certainly composed and edited his shots to expose the distinction between Gloucester's physical tumble and his psychological fall down mountains of the mind; and the final perspective is that of a god dispassionately watching a wanton boy killing flies. But the effect of, for example, the low-angle close-up of Gloucester's face (described by Jorgens as 'one of the most savagely beautiful shots of a human face ever put on film'), a frame from which the character towers over the spectator in the tragic dignity of suffering, is *complicated* but not *negated* by the jump-cut to an overhead long-shot of his pathetic fall.

Moreover the fracturing of naturalist conventions increases the spectator's awareness of the camera as a constructive device, not a window opening on reality, but a mobile and changing point-of-view which can choose to record in a spirit of empathy or of alienation. The primary function of alienating devices, in this film or any other, is to intensify the viewer's awareness of the mechanisms by which this simulated reality is being produced; to impede the free transmission of ideology by discouraging unconscious, empathetic involvement and encouraging a vigilant and self-conscious curiosity, both about the object of the medium, and about the medium itself.

Belsey's identification of film with naturalist staging, though suggestive, is potentially misleading. Though the proscenium-arch perspective stage is very obviously a *selector* of reality, it can only *appear* to be an innocent *constitutor* of the reality: the spectator's point of vision is fixed, the access to the stage's simulated reality circumscribed, the window on to experience absolutely static. The film camera, by contrast, can do either: it can, like the proscenium arch, efface itself in a privileging of its object, constituting reality as objective in the illusionistic manner of naturalism; or it can, by violating those naturalist conventions, by emphasising and exploiting its mobility, call the spectator's attention to the mechanisms of its own perception. Without employing alienation devices, the naturalist stage can *only* offer itself as the *premise* of a simulated reality; the film can be seen to operate as a moving *commentary* on its object, releasing the viewer from the tyranny of empathetic illusion to a freer consideration of reality and of the artifice which produces it.

Considering Shakespeare films in the light of this most fundamental distinction in the whole of film theory – between naturalistic, illusionist cinema and its opposite – we can conclude that certain filmed adaptations of the plays operate simply as vehicles for the transmissions of ideology. Other films block, deflect or otherwise 'work on' ideology in order partially to disclose its mechanisms. The same method of evaluation will reveal which films are potentially more valuable for mobilisation in the educational context; and which can only work to reinforce and familiarise conventional attitudes to Shakespeare. Again, the object of this essay is not to attempt such evaluation across a wide range of films, but rather to suggest, with the help of particular illustrations, methods of procedure and analysis appropriate to such investigation.

In addition to describing the formal characteristics of the medium, some account must be taken, in however abstract a fashion, of the audience itself: which is not, after all, entirely created by the particular work of art it happens to be witnessing. A film of Shakespeare is never experienced in total vacuum, because of the ubiquity, the universality of Shakespeare as a cultural phenomenon. A film's 'arrested play of meanings' will enter into conflictual or co-operative relationship with certain ideological premises, certain cultural assumptions, certain definite levels of knowledge. The school students rebuked by the JMB examiners were witnessing a film *in the light of* some knowledge of the play as literary text. The film may be experienced in a context of other encounters with the play – a TV or theatrical production perhaps, or another film (most of the 'great' Shakespeare plays have been filmed several times). Or the film may simply reinforce or subvert an inherited cultural concept of 'Shakespeare' – the familiar associations of costume drama, perspective staging, unintelligible plots, projected delivery. It is this body of assumptions that an effective film transliteration is likely to subvert: clashing with the spectator's preconceptions to produce a liberating dialectic, to foster that very 'play of meanings' which art can press ideology to deliver.

I have chosen to concentrate my analysis on two examples of ideology-resistant Shakespeare film treatment: Akira Kurosawa's *Throne of Blood* (1957), and Peter Hall's 1969 production of *A Midsummer Night's Dream*. Hall's own conception of how a Shakespeare play should be filmed was expounded in an interview with Roger Manvell:

> The greatest influence on me, or my generation, was Leavis, who believed above everything in a critical examination of the text, the search for meaning and metaphor ... Too much normal film art contradicts the techniques of the plays, at least as far as their most important element, the text, is concerned. But the medium of film can certainly be used to communicate the text most effectively, even to the extent of making its meaning clearer than is sometimes possible in the theatre ... This is not a film *from* a stage production or a film *based* on the play. It attempts to bend the medium of the film to reveal the full quality of the text. (*Shakespeare and the Film*, pp. 121–6)

Hall insists that the film should be a visual embodiment of the text, fleshing the verbal structure with the concrete reality it signifies, but subordinated absolutely to the authoritative structure and rhythm of the text. In practice, the experiment produced something entirely different. Hall thought the film was probably 'not a film at all', but an incarnation of literary language; in fact the director's 'textualist' ideology enters into sharp and disruptive conflict with the film medium to produce one of the most inventive and valuable of all the Shakespeare films.

[187]

The film opens with a deliberate disruption of naturalist film convention: superimposed on an English neo-classical country house, surrounded by images of order and authority, appears the title 'Athens'. The assurance customarily guaranteed by film techniques which confirm our normal habits of perception, is subverted: what we see on the screen may well be deceptive. The 'Athenian' court is set in a chaste, barren and colourless environment, shot with a telephoto lens to make the images two-dimensional. The movement away from the court towards the forest is signalled by further disruptive devices, as the narrative rhythm of the text clashes against the essentially cinematic technique of *montage*: 'Momentum, regular rhythm and continuity are provided by the text while jump cuts disrupts our sense of realistic space. A tension is established between what sounds like a conventional, clearly articulated stage performance and visuals which whisk the star-crossed lovers from the grey interior to a flat boat pond ...' (*Shakespeare on Film*, p. 55). These sequences were filmed with hand-held camera: the slight movement imparted to the shots calls attention to the camera as a recorder of these simulated events. The actors address the camera directly, demolishing the naturalistic 'fourth wall'. In the wood itself, the conjuring tricks of the photography and editing emulate Oberon's magic: Puck appears and disappears, disjunctive editing confuses the reality of time and space. Puck's concluding invitation to the audience to

> Think but this, and all is mended,
> That you have but slumbered here
> While these visions did appear.
> And this weak and idle theme
> No more yielding but a dream

is spoken in darkness.[6] Puck snaps his fingers, and it is morning. Which is the reality, which the illusion: daylight and the solid facade of Theseus' rationalistic Athens, or the 'magic' of the forest conjured by the film's 'radical cinematography'? In this way the film foregrounds its constructive devices, offering the spectator an open awareness of the medium as a conjuring and simulating power which makes 'reality', yet renders itself visible in the act of making.

Ultimately, however, the film is pulled back into an ideological resolution. When Hall's 'rustics' present their play, the courtly audience is thoroughly involved in a shared experience of festive celebration. Despite his reverence for the text, the director cut the courtiers' condescending comments, and filmed a scene which suggests that the lovers have benefited by their flirtation with the occult, and can take their places in a society united into community by the combined magic of supernatural agency, enthusiastic popular theatricals and *avant-garde* film: a liberal resolution which almost reconstructs Leavis's 'organic community'. Finally the film's subversive and self-reflexive experiment is pulled towards a resolution expressing the well-balanced harmony of the formalist's literary text.

Akira Kurosawa's *Throne of Blood* (1957) is the most complete translation of Shakespeare into film. The text is abandoned altogether, not even translated; the action shifted from medieval Scotland to feudal Japan; a western Renaissance tragedy becomes an Oriental samurai epic. This most celebrated of all Shakespeare films has been praised particularly for the completeness of its transformation of drama into cinema: 'the great masterpiece' (Peter Brook), 'the finest of the Shakespeare movies' (Grigori Kozintsev). Critics have stressed the *independence* of play and film: Frank Kermode called it 'an allusion to *Macbeth*', and Peter Brook asserted that it 'doesn't come into the Shakespeare question at all'. J. Blumenthal calls it 'a masterpiece in its own right', wholly liberated from 'the dreaded literary media'.[7] Clearly, if play and film occupy entirely different spaces and cannot even be compared, much less evaluated, against one another: not only do the separate 'masterpieces' enjoy their independent prestige, but the film is rendered incapable of violating the integrity of 'Shakespeare', unable to interrogate or subvert the play's immortal and immanent identity. If this proposition were accepted, *Throne of Blood* would disappear from 'the Shakespeare question' altogether and would offer the possibility of meaning only in relation to Kurosawa's other work and to Japanese culture, ideology and society.[8]

The most substantial critical objection made against the film is that it robs Shakespeare's play of its tragic form and style: 'Kurosawa's Macbeth is not grand';[9] 'His crime is not against God but against Society';[10] 'Kurosawa has betrayed the power of the play'.[11] In fact this is clearly a fundamental aesthetic strategy of the film, which begins in a style more epic than tragic, with a chorus commenting on the images of a ruined castle and a grave: 'Behold within this place now desolate stood once a mighty fortress, / Lived a proud warrior murdered by ambition, his spirit walking still. / Vain pride, then as now, will lead ambition to the kill.' The film's narrative is thus framed by an artistic device which contains the story in an explicit moral meaning offered for consideration, to an epic rather than a dramatic audience. Epic detachment is also characteristic of the film's visual style, which is largely structured by the conventions

Graham Holderness

of Japanese Noh drama. Acting and *mise-en-scène* are conventionalised rather than naturalistic; 'Noh is ritual drama, and the world of the Noh is both closed and artificial' (*The Films of Akira Kurosawa*, p. 117). The camerawork, as Kurosawa himself declared, entailed a deliberate avoidance of close-ups (*ibid.*, p. 121). The effect of this technique is detachment: 'the camera and chorus maintain an aesthetic distance from the action' ('*Throne of Blood*: Kurosawa's *Macbeth*', p. 16); or as Donald Richie terms it, 'alienation': '... alienation is one of the effects of moving the camera back just as moving it forward suggests empathy. The full-shot reveals everything, ... it disengages the viewer and allows him to see cause and effect' (*The Films of Akira Kurosawa*, p. 121).

What can this cinematic interpretation tell us about Shakespeare's *Macbeth*? To begin with, it locates the problem of regicide (*ge-koku-jo*) into a very specific historical and social context, parallel with Duncan's feudal Scotland but radically unlike Shakespeare's England or the modern world. The film displays a militaristic society with an elaborate code of loyalty, expressed in conventionalised social rituals: the intensely-stylised social intercourse of samurai and lord seeks to control the power and violence by which such a society exists. 'Ambition' in this society is not some eccentric personality-disorder, but a central historical contradiction: a natural extension of the militaristic violence which is both liberated and restrained by the feudal pattern of authority. 'What samurai does not want to be lord of a castle?' Washizu (Macbeth) asks Miki (Banquo). The question cannot be explained away in psychological terms, nor collapsed into a universalist moral system. It has meaning only within the historical world of the film. To adopt a similar perspective on *Macbeth* would entail a focus on the play's reconstruction of a distant society, observed not as a shadowy presage of the present, nor as a universal, providentially-established natural kingdom of the past. *Macbeth* opens with a startling contradiction: between the ugly, violent butchery described by the captain, in his account of Macbeth's killing of Macdonwald; and the elaborate rhetoric of chivalry and courtesy used by Duncan to control that power. Macbeth is bound to Duncan by that language of trust, loyalty, honour; but also by a social relationship which depends on a vulnerable and unstable division of authority and power. When Duncan declares Malcolm his successor (a declaration which indicates that this is *not* a hereditary dynasty) he is simultaneously creating a hierarchy and rendering it open to assault by suppressing the very power, vested in the thanes, which sustains his authority.

Critics have complained at the film's understanding of tragic 'inevitability' as social rather than psychological or supernatural: 'Washizu is given social and biological excuses for what can only be put down to unfathomable greed in Shakespeare's Macbeth' ('Shakespeare, Kurosawa and *Macbeth*', p. 357). But it is evident that *both* Kurosawa's film *and* Shakespeare's play can be seen primarily as *social* tragedies, set within a distanced historical context in which social problems and contradictions can be rendered visible and fully intelligible to the audience's *curiosity*. Furthermore, tragedy narrated with such aesthetic detachment becomes 'epic'. The *tragedy* of Macbeth involves some degree of empathetic involvement by the spectator in the protagonist's experience; like Malcolm, we identify with Macbeth in order to live imaginatively through the knowledge of evil in a cathartic purgation. *Throne of Blood* denies the spectator that experience, and offers in its place, in the epic style, a detached scrutiny of certain actions and events within a certain social context. The choreographed artifice of Noh drama can certainly express a sense of constraint and predetermined destiny: but the artifice is visible, self-evident and self-conscious; the actors are acting out a stylised performance, not miming an inevitable process of psychological development. Again, it is valid to see *Macbeth* itself as an epic rather than a tragic drama. A performance of the play in Elizabethan stage conditions would have possessed certain qualities evident in the film (excluding of course the film's location sequences): bare sets, conventionalised acting, certain possibilities for detachment and alienation (consider Macbeth's self-reflexive characterisation of himself as a 'poor player'), and the acting-out of a well-known story the outcome of which is known beforehand. Even the soliloquies, so highly privileged by modern psychological interpretations, would not have been played as intense self-communings but as colloquies, dialogues between actor and audience. This is no mere academic speculation: Trevor Nunn's 1976 television production of *Macbeth* brings out these qualities of the play with startling distinctness: using a bare studio, actors visible *as* actors, nondescript costume, direct addresses to camera; all techniques which foreground the 'epic' rather than the 'tragic' dimension of the play.

I am not attempting to argue that Kurosawa has discovered and expressed the *true meaning* of Shakespeare's play: that would be to acknowledge that the text has an authentic, immanent meaning released by a particular act of interpretation. *Throne of Blood* is self-evidently *not* Shakespeare; and therein lies its incomparable value for strategic use in a radical exploration of the play. If the text can be reproduced in a virtually unrecognisable form, then the plurality of the text is proved beyond reasonable doubt. This bastard offspring, the play's *alter ego*, can then be brought back into conjunction with the text, to liberate some of its more radical possibilities of meaning.

I have offered reasons why some films should be regarded as possessing deeper radical possibilities than others. Ultimately, though, the *political* potentiality of these film adaptations depends on their strategic mobilisation in the educational rather than the general cultural context. As the same assertion will be made about television Shakespeare, the point can be made as a final conclusion.

II

'Television constitutes the only really "national" theatre our society is likely to have.'[12] The medium of television would appear to offer unique opportunities for a democratic recovery of Shakespeare: a reappropriation of jealously-guarded fortresses of high culture for the popular audience which initially embraced and fostered the Elizabethan drama. Television is (unlike the Elizabethan theatre) a national institution in a genuinely universal sense; its place that fundamental space of social life, the home; its mode of communication direct, populist and general; its content largely constituted by the 'entertainment' and information widely regarded as the staple necessities of our contemporary culture. Some writers have drawn a close parallel between television and the Elizabethan theatre: a cultural comparison which appears to underlie the BBC Shakespeare series. Terry Hawkes actually proposes the television medium as a successor or reconstitution of the Elizabethan theatre's cultural potentialities;[12] and John Wilders, literary adviser to the BBC Shakespeare series, follows this analogy to propose that TV reproduction of Shakespeare's drama can emulate or at least approach the freedom and flexibility of Shakespeare's contemporary stage.[13]

Whether in practice television adaptations of Shakespeare genuinely fulfil these ambitions – and, indeed, whether the Elizabethan theatre can be properly regarded in retrospect as the central focus of national culture – remains open to question. A different kind of populism emerges from within the BBC itself: where academics envisage television as a means of reconstituting the Elizabethan theatre, producers think more in terms of translating theatre into the familiar discourse of television itself. For Cedric Messina, the original producer (replaced after the first two years by Jonathan Miller) the 'primary purpose of the series' was 'to provide good entertainment ... because that's what Shakespeare wrote them for'.[14] 'The guiding principle ... is to make the plays, in permanent form, accessible to audiences throughout the world.'[15] Within this alliance of academics and broadcasters there naturally arose a certain tension, between, on the one hand, scholarly and educational concerns, and on the other the values of popular entertainment; with the TV medium usually imposing its own solution, as John Wilders indicates: 'The television equivalent of Shakespeare's stage would be an empty studio ... I am now certain however that we were right not to adopt this style ... to the television viewer, accustomed as he is to such representations of reality as football matches, news films, and thrillers filmed on location in California, the opening scene of *Macbeth* would not have been 'an open place' but Studio 1 of the Televison Centre, White City' ('Adjusting the set', p. 13). None the less, within that alliance of the camera and the pen, these discrete ideologies, the scholarly/ democratic and the media-populist, seem to have coalesced into unity: and the tendency of the resultant approach to Shakespeare must necessarily move towards a devolution of cultural power, an undermining of 'Shakespeare' as a symbol of cultural authority.

The argument for 'accessibility' is greatly strengthened by the (now familiar but actually very recent) developments in the manufacture and marketing of video technology. Broadcasting itself makes the complex and expensive products of an intensely central-ised culture immediately available to the whole of a society; but the availability remains at the mercy of centralised planning bodies and not at all subject to popular participation or democratic control. Video technology increases that availability enormously, and (however severely constrained by restrictive copyright legislation and the absence of a licensing system) confers much more power on the consumer. The planners of the BBC Shakespeare had this in mind from the outset: Cedric Messina accepted the suggestion that one hope of the planners was for the creation of 'a library of Shakespeare video productions that will last for quite some time'. This aspiration involved commercial as well as cultural considerations: '... the plays are actually starting to pay for themselves. The plays are selling already around the world ...' ('Cedric Messina discusses *The Shakespeare Plays*', p. 135).

It has already been argued in relation to film that in one sense, and particularly for those operating within the educational apparatus of 'Literature', the translation of Shakespeare into a non-literary form must necessarily be *potentially* radical: subverting the cultural hegemony of literature itself, disturbing the equilibrium of received cultural traditions. Similarly, if one symptomatic strategy of bourgeois culture is to preserve certain figures of cultural authority for specialised participation by a social and intellectual elite, then the

extension of participation in Shakespeare to a much wider constituency *via* that audience's most familiar medium, must necessarily
exert some pressure on the bases of cultural power. But these
propositions bring us up against the truly fundamental question: is
the extension of high culture to be seen as a democratic appropriation of cultural wealth by the people; or simply as an extension of
centralised cultural power by the transmission of authority, in the
form of an art which *cannot choose but* be reactionary and
pacificatory in its ideological effects? After all Matthew Arnold, and
the *Newbolt Report*, and *Scrutiny*, all spoke of the desirability of
taking Shakespeare to the masses, often in a rhetoric of intense
radical populism: but they were certainly not fostering or proposing
a radical cultural politics.

Although productions of Shakespeare on TV are nothing new, the
project of the series, in its ambitious scope and scale and massive
investment of cultural capital, clearly represents the most significant
intervention to date into the reproduction of Shakespeare on the
screen. And other, more material investment was required to get the
series off the ground: the BBC entered into partnership with the
American company Time-Life TV, which in turn raised financial
backing for the series from three big private corporations in the USA
– Exxon Corporation, Metropolitan Life Insurance Company and
Morgan Guaranty Trust Company of New York. This alliance
between the BBC and American private enterprise indicates how the
series was generated from the very highest levels of economic and
cultural power. Clearly it is inadequate to write the series off as a
predictable symptom of its institutional and capitalistic origin: but it
is important to trace and measure the constraints and determinants
built into the series itself as a consequence of its economic and
institutional basis.

The scale of investment and the nature of commercial underwriting (as distinct from commercial *sponsorship*) imposed one very
obvious requirement on this enterprise: it should be economically
viable; that is, give an economic as well as a cultural return on capital
investment. This condition necessarily entailed the preservation of
the plays in a consumer-durable form (video-cassette) rather than
restriction to one-off transmission, and an international marketing
operation. Conscious of this dependence on the market rather than
on patronage and subsidy, the planners insisted that productions
should aim for 'high quality' and 'durability'. What 'high quality'
originally implied in such a context is predictable: 'great' directors,
'classical' actors, 'straightforward' productions: '... these productions will offer a wonderful opportunity to study the plays per-

formed by some of the greatest classical actors of our time' (Messina, *Richard II*, p. 8). This insistence on building into the productions that isolating quality of 'excellence' is familiar from the Arnoldian practices of literary criticism: though it is perhaps unusual to find critical excellence and market value, the common pursuit of true judgement and industrial quality control, quite so firmly identified. The concept of 'high quality' in fact entailed a conservative respect for 'traditional' values in Shakespearean production. Jonathan Miller has described the 'problems' he inherited in taking over the series, among them '. . . the original contract with the American co-producers – it had to be so-called traditional . . .'.[16] Cedric Messina had accepted this constraint even more readily, in the belief that only 'traditional' productions would 'stand the test of time': 'We've not done anything too sensational in the shooting of it – there's no arty-crafty shooting at all. All of them are, for want of a better word, straightforward productions' ('Cedric Messina discusses *The Shakespeare Plays*', p. 137).

Despite expressed reservations, Jonathan Miller accepted the executive producership of the series after the second season. Whatever his capacities as a stage director, Miller believes in the absolute determinacy of the television medium, which imposes its own constraints on dramatic production. Television is incurably naturalistic and translates everything into naturalism.[17] Miller is therefore averse to any attempt to theatricalise television: TV productions should display no manneristic theatrical styles, no expressionistic acting and no mixing of conventions. It is impossible to reproduce Elizabethan theatre conditions in a television presentation: 'What is characteristic about the Elizabethan stage condition is that the audience is part of that condition . . . In television you automatically eliminate the audience. It isn't present at the production. It's absolutely hopeless to try and reconstitute the wooden "O" inside the electric square' ('An interview with Jonathan Miller', p. 9). Olivier's film version of *Henry V* was therefore mistaken in trying 'to set up within one medium the conventions of another'. Miller's consistent adherence to naturalism is admitted as an explicit commitment to illusionist representation: the audience should be 'unaware of the fact that they're in the presence of an art-form'.

In fact there is greater diversity of production styles in the series than these theoretical pronouncements would suggest. But there can be little doubt that overall a conservative 'drag' is applied by a combination of factors: the constraints of commercial underwriting; the consequent concern of the BBC to build high-quality prestige into the series; the conservative cultural views of the original producer

and the willing submission of his successor to the dominant naturalistic style of television drama. The conservatism of the whole series
can best be measured against one remarkable exception, Jane
Howell's production of the first historical tetralogy.

The most appropriate contrast of detail to be made is that between
the productions of the second historical tetralogy (which belong to
the first and second 'seasons' of 1978–9), directed by David Giles
under the producership of Cedric Messina; and the 1982 productions of *Henry VI* and *Richard III*. Messina foregrounded the
English history cycle, allowing these plays to dominate the first two
seasons (*Richard II* and *Henry VIII* in 1978; the *Henry IVs* and
Henry V in 1979). These programming decisions suggest a
nationalistic desire to celebrate the course of English history; but the
'British' quality emerges also from Messina's thoroughly conventional view of the plays: 'These histories are a sort of curse of the
House of Atreus in English'. This view was supported by an ancillary
broadcast featuring right-wing pundit Paul Johnson: 'According to
the orthodox Tudor view of history the deposition of the rightful and
anointed king, Richard II, was a crime against God, which thereafter
had to be expiated by the nation in a series of bloody struggles . . .'.[18]
Messina wanted to organise the plays into a coherent historical
totality: and it was originally the producer's hope that the plays
would share a uniformity of style, knitting them even more closely
together into an integrated unity: asked by an interviewer what he
would be doing to 'assure continuity', Messina spoke of maintaining
character castings, and indicated that he thought it would be 'right
and proper' to keep the same director ('Cedric Messina discusses
The Shakespeare Plays', p. 137).

This didn't, in the event, happen: and the consequences are
instructive. The second tetralogy is a characteristic example of
conventional 'high-quality' Shakespearean production: performed,
in Messina's words 'by a splendid company, including many of the
leading names in our classical drama' (Messina, *Richard II*, p. 9).
The central actors tend to be classical old stagers or modern stars:
John Gielgud, Wendy Hiller, Anthony Quayle, Derek Jacobi and Jon
Finch. The overall style of production is overwhelmingly naturalistic; the director David Giles was chosen as an experienced *television* director regarded as 'adept at dealing with English history and
the English character' (e.g. *The Forsyte Saga*) (*ibid.*, p. 19). The
combat-scene in *Richard II* (I.iii), a formalised heraldic ritual which
hardly invites naturalistic presentation, was done in this mode: 'You
can't do it realistically in a television studio and yet we didn't want it
to get too stylized: that's why we used real horses. If we had gone too

stylized with the list scene we would have had to stylise the play all the way through, and stylization on television is very difficult' (David Giles, *ibid.*, p. 20).

The second tetralogy emerges from this production as a constituent element in an inclusive and integrated dramatic totality, illustrating the violation of natural social 'order' by the deposition of a legitimate king. The plays are produced in 'classic drama' style with predominantly naturalistic devices of acting, *mise-en-scène*, and filming. Actors are identified wholly with their roles, growing old in them; settings are more naturalistic than conventionalised; camera movements and angles always 'straightforward', with no 'arty-crafty' shooting.

In the case of Jane Howell's productions of the first historical tetralogy, the director's whole conception of the Shakespearean history play diverges strikingly from that propounded by Cedric Messina and evidently accepted by David Giles. Where Messina saw the history plays conventionally as orthodox Tudor historiography, and the director employed dramatic techniqes which allow that ideology a free and unhampered passage to the spectator, Jane Howell takes a more complex view of the first tetralogy as, simultaneously, a serious attempt at historical interpretation, and as a drama with a peculiarly modern relevance and contemporary application. The plays, to this director, are not a dramatisation of the Elizabethan World Picture but a sustained interrogation of residual and emergent ideologies in a changing society.[19] Commenting on Talbot's dilemma in *1 Henry VI*, IV.v-vi, Howell defines the drama as a disclosure of the contradictoriness of chivalric values: 'When Talbot finally comes face to face with his own son who will not leave the battle although he knows he is going to get killed, then Talbot has to come face to face with his own values; because if the values of chivalry mean you have to sacrifice your son ...' (*1 Henry VI*, p. 31). At the same time Howell wanted to explore the plays' potentiality for contemporary signification: 'We felt it shouldn't be too mediaeval ... we talked about Northern Ireland and Beirut and South America, about warlords and factions'.[20] This awareness of the multiplicity of potential meanings in the play required a decisive and scrupulous avoidance of television or theatrical naturalism: methods of production should operate to open the plays out, rather than close them into the immediately recognisable familiarity of conventional Shakespearean production.

Howell's basic conception of the plays entailed a refusal to attempt naturalisation: Jonathan Miller's insistence that the TV medium *enforces* naturalism, and that the conventions of theatre would not work within it, seems to have been systematically ignored: 'At the outset she had made the clear decision to avoid any attempt to scale down the action to make it more "televisual". The energy, she felt, was essentially theatrical and she therefore made a number of theatrical decisions – the company would double parts as they do in the theatre; the action would all take place on a single set, which would change in mood from play to play ...' ('Dialogues of Dis-integration', p. 20). One important consideration here was a his-torical one: Howell felt that the plays would work better in the kind of theatrical situation they were originally produced in, on a relatively bare stage with minimal, emblematic props and scenery, by a company of actors operating as an *ensemble*. The set, modelled on an adventure playground in Fulham, was designed to suggest the loca-tions of popular drama – 'we thought of fairgrounds and circuses and mystery plays' as well as familiar modern environments, a children's playground or a burnt-out building site. It was con-structed to appear deliberately non-naturalistic: thus allowing the play to express both historical and contemporary meanings. Oliver Bayldon, the set-designer, explained his decision to use a modern parquet floor as a deliberate violation of illusionist representation: 'It stops the set from literally representing ... it reminds us we are in a modern television studio'.[21] Stanley Wells commended this aspect of the production: 'Jane Howell has dared to encourage us to remember that the action is taking place in a studio'.[22]

It will be apparent to what extent Jane Howell's practice con-tradicts or negates the definitive pronouncements of Cedric Messina and Jonathan Miller, on how Shakespeare should be televised. This director found it possible to reject television naturalism in favour of the theatricalising of television; to mix the conventions of one medium with those of another; and to recreate some of the radical potentialities of the Elizabethan theatre. Even Jonathan Miller's persuasive point about TV's elimination of the audience was solved here by constituting members of the cast, for certain scenes, as a vociferous and participating audience (e.g. the Jack Cade scenes in 2 *Henry VI*); as well as by extensive use of the direct address to camera, the equivalent of actor–audience dialogue.

All these devices are defamiliarising, estranging, 'alienating'; they induce the kind of alert and vigilant curiosity sought by Brecht's 'epic' theatre. The actors double parts, thus preventing any illusion-ary identification of actor and character. Nor are the actors the familiar Shakespearean stars of the BBC *Richard II*, their personali-ties so subdued to what they work in that they appear to *be* characters from Shakespeare. Furthermore, under the director's influence there is a general rejection of Stanislavskian method: her advice to her actors insistently recalls Brecht (see *BBC 2 Henry VI*, p. 24). This 'epic' style provides much greater flexibility and freedom to the actor, who is no longer imprisoned within the naturalist concept of a coherent psychological identity, but able to play out those psychological incoherences which can disclose sociological truths (see *BBC 1 Henry VI*, p. 30).

III

The radical potentialities of television Shakespeare, evident enough from these examples, are in practice systematically blocked, suppressed or marginalised by the conservatism of the dominant cultural institutions. Overall the BBC Shakespeare series operates to confirm the cultural authority which in turn confers the status of high culture upon the BBC itself, and on those powerful capitalist corporations which financed it – a circular process which effectively closes out the people for whom the series is supposedly produced. Once the production becomes completed and packaged in video-cassette form it becomes universally available, but also permanently fixed, unchangeable: the radical and subversive potentiality of performance is translated back into something closer to the authoritarian dominance of the literary text. The BBC Shakespeare series is in fact the most perfect consummation to date of a process which commenced in Shakespeare's own time, with the Tudor government's systematic destruction of the national religious drama, the professionalising of theatre by the licensing of a few acting companies and the building of the first purpose-built playhouses; the privileging of metropolitan over national culture, and the incorporation of the drama into the cultural structure of an emergent bourgeois nation-State. A 'national' culture is, in bourgeois terms, the production by a centralised cultural apparatus, operating from the capital, of high-quality aesthetic objects which are then transmitted to the 'nation', which in turn acts as passive recipient of a pre-packaged cultural commodity. The active, democratic participation and intervention of the Elizabethan audience actually generated a process which reduced that audience to an inert constituency loyally consuming liberal doses of what one is tempted to call, following Peter Brook, 'deadly television'.[23]

Film and television reproduction of Shakespeare are in essence no different from other forms of reproduction, in theatre or education: they have specific commercial and cultural functions within the economic and ideological apparatus of a bourgeois-democratic society. Spaces are created within that cultural apparatus for radical intervention, and such opportunities have to a limited extent been seized. The most promising space for cultural intervention remains, despite systematic attacks on the system, that of education; where film and television productions can be introduced into literature courses, posing fundamental cultural questions, liberating radical possibilities of meaning, and contributing to the much needed politicisation of the 'Shakespeare' institution.

Notes

1 Roger Manvell: *Shakespeare and the Film* (South Brunswick and New York: A. S. Barnes, 1979), is encyclopaedic and full of useful interviews, comments from directors, etc. The best *critical* book is Jack Jorgens: *Shakespeare on Film* (Bloomington: Indiana University Press, 1977).
2 Joint Matriculation Board *Examiners' Reports*, vol. 1. *Arts and Social Sciences* (1974), p. 9.
3 Catherine Belsey: 'Shakespeare and Film', *Literature/Film Quarterly*, XI (spring 1983), no. 2
4 S. D. Lawder: 'Film: Art of the Twentieth Century', *Yale Alumni Magazine* (May 1968), p. 33.
5 David Robinson: *Financial Times* (23 July 1971). Quoted by Jorgens, *Shakespeare on Film*, p. 244.
6 Harold F. Brooks, ed., *The New Arden Shakespeare: A Midsummer Night's Dream* (London: Methuen, 1979), V.i.410–14.
7 Peter Brook: 'Shakespeare on Three Screens', *Sight and Sound*, 34 (1965), 68; Grigori Kozintsev: *Shakespeare, Time and Conscience* (New York: Hill and Wang, 1966), p. 29; Frank Kermode: 'Shakespeare in the Movies', *New York Review of Books* (10 October 1972); J. Blumenthal: '*Macbeth* into Throne of Blood', *Sight and Sound*, 34 (1965), 191.
8 The film has been very usefully discussed in this latter context by Ana Laura Zambrano: '*Throne of Blood*: Kurosawa's *Macbeth*', *Literature/Film Quarterly*, II (summer 1974), no. 3.
9 Donald Richie: *The Films of Akira Kurosawa*, (Berkeley and Los Angeles: University of California Press, 1965), p. 117.
10 Zambrano, *op. cit.*, p. 269.
11 John Gerlach: 'Shakespeare, Kurosawa and *Macbeth*', *Literature/Film Quarterly* I (fall 1973), no. 4, p. 352.
12 Terence Hawkes: *Shakespeare's Talking Animals* (London: Edward Arnold, 1973), p. 231.
13 John Wilders: 'Adjusting the set', *Times Higher Educational Supplement* (10 July 1981), 13.
14 'Cedric Messina discusses *The Shakespeare Plays*', *Shakespeare Quarterly*, 30 (1979), 137.
15 Cedric Messina: 'Preface' to *The BBC TV Shakespeare: Richard II* (London: BBC, 1978), p. 8.
16 Ann Pasternak Slater: 'An interview with Jonathan Miller', *Quarto*, 10 (1980), 9.
17 Tim Hallinan: 'Jonathan Miller on *The Shakespeare Plays*', *Shakespeare Quarterly*, 32 (1981), 134.
18 Paul Johnson: '*Richard II*', in Roger Sales, ed., *Shakespeare in Perspective* (London: BBC/Ariel Books, 1982), p. 33.

19 Henry Fenwick: 'The Production', *The BBC TV Shakespeare: Henry VI Part One* (London: BBC 1983), pp. 22–3.
20 Henry Fenwick: 'Dialogues of Disintegration', *Radio Times* (1 January 1983).
21 *The BBC TV Shakespeare: Henry VI, Part Two* (London: BBC 1983), p. 20.
22 Stanley Wells: 'The History of the Whole Contention', *Times Higher Educational Supplement* (4 February 1983), p. 105.
23 See Graham Holderness, *Shakespeare's History* (Dublin: Gill and Macmillan, 1984), Introduction 3: 'Drama and Society'.

I am grateful to the staff of the British Film Institute Library, and of the Library at University College Swansea, for providing material relating to this study; and also to my friend and colleague Christopher McCullough, to whom the essay is deeply indebted.

How Brecht read Shakespeare

Notes on the material

Brecht didn't live to bring his writings on Shakespeare together as he had once planned to do. We have to pick up his approach and his ideas for production from short essays, sections of longer works (the most important being in the *Messingkauf Dialogues*, itself compiled posthumously from his drafts and still incomplete), adaptations, plagiarisms, notes and jokes, the last two providing some of the most thought-provoking examples – over two hundred separate references in all. Not only do the ideas change over time, but even at the same period Brecht will emphasise one side of a contradiction in one piece and a different side in another, according to the point being argued over. For instance, the stress in *A Short Organum for the Theatre* is different from that in *Messingkauf*, the first more concerned with *dissociating* Brecht from Shakespearean tradition, the second with emphasising the *power* of Shakespearean dramaturgy and how much can still be learned and made from it. It would be not merely pointless but distorting to try to construct a single closely-co-ordinated, fully consistent argument out of all this rich material, whose multi-faceted fragmentary nature reflects Brecht's flexible, experimental approach. A general way of seeing does however stand out, and the notes and sketches seem to me to stimulate our thinking about 'political Shakespeare' perhaps all the more for being unfinished and provisional.

I have organised the analysis in three main sections: (1) Brecht's double view of the plays and their historical setting; (2) his ideas for performing them today; (3) some Shakespeare productions after Brecht.

Shakespeare and the Chancellor

Even sophisticated readers used to the idea that there's no one 'right' interpretation of Shakespeare may well have been slightly startled to see the recent appreciation of him by the Right Hon. Nigel Lawson MP, Mrs Thatcher's Chancellor of the Exchequer, when interviewed about his own political philosophy:

'People are different, not equal. The appeal of egalitarianism is I think wholly destructive. It's an appeal to envy – one of the strongest emotions, one of the seven deadly sins too. It is I think something which is damaging in economic terms and in social terms too, because it can never be realised and so people feel permanently dissatisfied. ...'

Mr Lawson has occasionally quoted those lines from *Troilus* which say:

Take but degree away, untune that string,
And hark what discord follows.

Why did he like those lines?

'The fact of differences, and the need for some kind of hierarchy, both these facts, are expressed more powerfully there than anywhere else I know in literature.'

So Shakespeare was a good Tory? 'Shakespeare was a Tory, without any doubt.'

Could he give another example? 'I think that in *Coriolanus* the Tory virtues, the Roman virtues as mediated through Shakespeare are ... it's written from a Tory point of view....

'I am not a great believer in progress, in the sense of an inevitable upward movement. ... Man doesn't change. Or man's nature doesn't change. The same problems are there in different forms.'[1]

It's appropriate to begin with Mr Lawson because it puts the discussion of 'political Shakespeare' into perspective, estranges it as it were. To hear Shakespeare cited directly in the context of cutting the health service and reducing taxation on the well-to-do is unnerving, a kind of alienation-effect. We see more clearly what the struggle over the meanings of Shakespeare is really about: or at least it concentrates the mind.

It's interesting of course that to make his point Mr Lawson has to remember his examples so wholly out of dramatic context, disregarding entirely the conflicts of values and action that surround them in the plays. Ulysses may talk about the sacredness of hierarchy and order, but the setting shows him as a cunning politician whose behaviour undercuts what he says here, as indeed does the whole play. Coriolanus is a hero, yes, but one whose pride makes him not only an exemplar of Roman virtues but a traitor to his country. And if Shakespeare was as anti-egalitarian as the Chancellor, how did he come to write *King Lear*, where both Lear and Gloucester realise too late that the wealth of the rich should have been shared with the poor, of whose sufferings they have taken too little care? 'So distribution should undo excess, / And each man have enough.'

But crude though it may be, the argument needs to be taken seriously. For, as the right knows if the left does not, Shakespeare is *there*, deeply embedded in the culture, the language, the media and the educational system of Britain. Moreover, to those depressed by a sense of national decline the reasons for which they don't understand, it means something that his plays still work in theatre and film in every part of the globe. Shakespeare has become part of the way that literally millions of people, consciously or unconsciously, imagine and fantasise and think about the world. If we're seriously concerned about politics, we need among other things to think freshly about the plays and how to present them, not hand Shakespeare over as a reactionary writer to be used or misused by the defenders of capitalism in decay. And for this we can find stimulus in the work of Bertolt Brecht, not only 'the strongest, most influential, most radical theatre man of our time',[2] but one of its most perceptive Shakespeare critics.

Drama for cannibals? or truth of life?

Brecht's attitude to Shakespeare is double, contradictory – and, like all his attitudes, changing through time. He once said, 'one has to grapple [*sich auseinandersetzen*] with Shakespeare as one does with life'. And though he has been criticised for the imprecise and romantic nature of this statement, it seems to have been exactly what he meant. It was above all the contradictory, unpredictable, dialectical element in Shakespeare that he felt was 'close to life', to historical processes, raw material to be worked on, a problem not yet solved. In Germany almost as much as in England, Shakespeare was the backbone of the classical theatre repertory. As such he was also, for the young Brecht, the centre of reaction in the drama, everything that his own theatre needed to break away from. Not only the 'plaster-monumental' style of production, the bourgeois-philistine audience with its weekly season-tickets escaping from mercenary reality in the plush seats, but the mighty magnetic presence of the noble hero, portrayed by a great star, with whose doomed sufferings every smug petty bourgeois could identify – all this was anathema to him and remained so. 'The classics no longer work. They're war casualties, our war sacrifices.'

On the other hand, paradoxically, he consciously drew from Shakespeare and the Elizabethans much of what was new and innovative in his own dramatic methods and attitudes to the theatre – what he calls first 'epic' theatre and later develops into 'dialectical' theatre.[3] He seems from the first to have been deeply fascinated and attracted by the plays, even though critical of their 'dead' and outdated aspects and repelled by most of the productions he had seen. This is clear in the earliest jottings on his reading of *The*

Merchant of Venice for instance: 'Here we have the story of an immoral contract ... Here is a battered, violated, spat-upon fellow who wants to break some damned neck with the help of the law, and what the law does is to help dislocate his wrists for him. It is a father whose only daughter has been stolen. He is not particularly nice ... One need is satisfied by this play: the need for justice. The man knows we have invested something in it. We shan't look this horse in the mouth. We enjoy demolishing. The pretext: he's so immoral.'[4] Already it is the dialectical, contradictory aspect of the play that interests him. Is the law a force for justice? We like to think so – Shylock is cheated, but since he's a nasty man who threatens our comfort we're pleased that he gets punished. What a modern producer like Jonathan Miller might do with the play is already hinted at in this cryptic note. See also Brecht's diary for August 1920, when he was 22: 'I've read Shakespeare's *Antony and Cleopatra*, a splendid drama that really gripped me' (*Diaries 1920–1922*, p. 15).

Brecht's critique refers only partly to Shakespeare himself as a writer of emerging bourgeois individualism (at a time when that world-view still had some heroic and iconoclastic qualities which it no longer has in the age of large-scale late capitalism). More often it turns out to be a critique of the mode of reading and interpreting him by romantic critics, and of modern theatre productions which reinforce that view.

From the time when he is beginning seriously to study Marxism in the late 1920s, Brecht revolts against Shakespeare as it's produced at the heart of the classical repertory, seeing it as concerned purely with naked individualism, with the isolated hero, not at all with the social causes of catastrophe or with people as social beings.

> The great individuals were the material that produced the form of this drama, the so-called dramatic form; and dramatic means: in tempestuous movement, passionate, contradictory, dynamic. What was its aim? You can see it clearly in Shakespeare. Through four acts Shakespeare drives the great individual, Lear, Othello, Macbeth, out of all his human connections with family and state out on to the heath, into total isolation, where he must show himself great in his ruin.... The object of the exercise is the great individual experience. Later times will call this drama a drama for cannibals.[5]

Thus performed, Shakespeare is of little or even negative value to modern spectators, who unlike Lear or Hamlet are small people, whose destinies are controlled not by fate or their own personal characters or actions but by the behaviour of collectives, large masses, social classes. If this exaltation of the heroic doomed individual was once progressive and liberating, it is so no longer. Indeed it may actually intensify the spectator's passivity and help-lessness and his or her willingness to acquiesce in injustice – as Brecht still insists twenty years later:

> The theatre as we know it shows the structure of society (represented on the stage) as incapable of being influenced by society (in the auditorium). Shakespeare's great solitary figures, bearing on their breast the star of their fate, carry through with irresistible force their futile and deadly outbursts; they prepare their own downfall; life, not death, becomes obscene as they collapse; the catastrophe is beyond criticism. Human sacrifices all round! Barbaric delights! We know that the barbarians have their art. Let us create another.[6]

But this purely negative view is immediately contradicted, based as it is on the distortions of romantic criticism and modern productions. Against a radical critic (Döblin) who argues that the drama can't represent life truthfully at all, that 'one can never learn about life from a play, only about the dramatist's state of mind', Brecht says that while this may be true of most German drama, Shakespeare's theatre and drama were very close to a form that could preserve 'the truth of life itself', the life that is of his own time.

> With Shakespeare the spectator does the constructing. Shakespeare never bends the course of a human destiny in the second act to make a fifth act possible. With him everything takes its natural course. In the lack of connection between his acts we see the lack of connection in a human destiny, when it is recounted by someone with no interest in tidying it up so as to provide an idea (which can only be a prejudice) with an argument not taken from life. There's nothing more stupid than to perform Shakespeare so that he's clear. He's by his very nature unclear. He's pure material.[7]

When Brecht calls Shakespeare 'a great realist',[8] as he repeatedly does from this time onwards, he of course means something very different from naturalism. As he says in the *Messingkauf Dialogues*, 'True realism has to do more than just make reality visible on the stage ... One has to be able to see the laws that decide how the processes of life develop';[9] and for this naturalism is too restrictive. Shakespeare is a great realist firstly because he's a great observer, because of his ability to embody so much contradictory material and to tell a story convincingly. 'He always shovels a lot of raw material on to the stage, unvarnished representations of what he has seen'[10] – as much in a single scene as would make a whole modern play, and yet nothing is missing. This material is not tidied up or harmonised in accordance with a preconceived idea, and can therefore preserve some of the complexity, irregularity and contradictory movement of history itself.[11] And because character and action are shown as contradictory and relative, it's possible for the director by changing the stress to highlight a different aspect of the contradiction, even with little or nothing added or changed in the text, to engage a modern audience.

Placing Shakespeare in history: between two worlds

Brecht is interested in explaining *why* Shakespeare's theatre could be 'close to life' in this way. It's not that he simply transcended a class outlook – no one can stand above the struggle because no one can stand outside his or her own time. Brecht relates it tu two causes, the nature of Shakespeare's theatre and his particular situation in history.

Historically, Brecht sees Shakespeare and the Elizabethans as living between the two worlds of declining feudalism and nascent capitalism, and embodying the conflicts and clashes of values of that moment. Shakespeare represents the decline of feudalism and of 'great ruling classes' as tragic.[12] At the same time the new rising classes with their individualist ethos make new demands – in love, ambition, thinking, family relations – which challenge feudalism: 'From the feudal point of view the new love (Romeo, Antony), the new thinking (Hamlet), the new demand for freedom (Brutus), the ambition (Macbeth), the new self-regard (Richard III), are deadly. From the bourgeois point of view the feudal-type restrictions are deadly, and the new way of behaving triumphs through its indifference to this death in view of the satisfactions it affords.'[13]

It's these 'valuable fracture points' (*wertvolle Bruchstellen*),[14] where the old in the period collides directly with the new, that Brecht sees as particularly illuminating. The collisions, he says, happen not only between characters but within them.

> *The Philosopher*: Lear, tied up in his own patriarchal ideas; Richard III, the unlikeable man who makes himself terrifying; Macbeth, the ambitious man swindled by witches; Antony, the hedonist who hazards his mastery of the world; Othello, destroyed by jealousy; they are all living in a new world and are smashed by it.
> *The Actor*: That explanation might spoil the plays for a lot of people.
> *The Philosopher*: But how could there be anything more complex, fascinating, and important than the decline of great ruling classes?
> (*Messingkauf Dialogues*, p. 59)

Whereas critics like Goethe and Hegel and modern actor managers represent Shakespearean heroes as consistent, monolithic (*aus einem Guss*), at one with their inevitable destinies, Shakespeare's characters as Brecht sees them are inconsistent, relative, and hence more like life, where development depends on contradiction. Actors who think it's more effective to simplify, to present a character as wholly and utterly ambitious rather than relatively ambitious, must learn to get their effects with something that's less unlikely to happen in real life.

> The Actor: A nice Macbeth that would make: sometimes ambitious and sometimes not, and only relatively more ambitious than Duncan. And your Hamlet: very hesitant, but also very inclined to act too hastily, no? ... Romeo: relatively in love.
> The Dramaturg: Yes, more or less. You needn't laugh. In Shakespeare he's already in love before he's seen his Juliet at all. After that he's more in love. (Messingkauf Dialogues, p. 61)

For while we have to show the behaviour of individuals as taking place within particular economic and social conditions, this doesn't mean that the individual ceases to be the focus of theatrical interest. The laws of causality in history, as Marxism understands them, are laws of trend and statistical probability, applying to the behaviour of masses of people: not of absolute causality determining the behaviour of each individual.[15] 'The audience should see not simply people who do their own deed ... but human beings, shifting raw material, unformed and undefined, that can surprise them.' Only this will encourage them to think about what they see. 'There are certain laws that apply to class. They apply to the individual only in so far as he coincides with his class, i.e. not absolutely; for the concept of class is only arrived at by ignoring particular features of the individual. You're not representing principles, but human beings' (Messingkauf Dialogues, p. 80).

Shakespeare's theatre: 'full of alienation effects'

Shakespeare is able to represent so much of these complex movements because of the particular nature of his theatre, summed up by Brecht in some of the most brilliant pages of the Messingkauf as 'a theatre full of alienation effects' (pp. 57–64). For one thing, it was an informal theatre with a very mixed public, popular and educated, close to both 'beer-gardens and colleges' and using the language of both. Since illusion was impossible anyway, with daylight performances, boys playing girls and so on, it was easy to include direct address to the audience, narrative and commentary; and the action could move freely from one place or country to another on the unlocalised stage, so that remote as well as immediate causes could be represented and distant opponents brought into confrontation.[16] The wealth of contrasting raw material, Brecht thinks, arose partly from dramatising existing sources and especially the chronicles, so that particular known incidents had to be included because otherwise people would have missed them. And a collective of theatre people probably worked on each play, which made 'epic' construction ('each scene for itself') and montage effects the most appropriate and easiest form.[17] The dramatic technique this led to – 'a naive surrealism', Brecht calls it at one point – is practised not only by Shakespeare but by at least twenty of his contemporaries, 'not all of them geniuses'. Some of these conditions – the informality and absence of illusion, the assumption (not always realised in practice) of an audience drawn from both 'beer-gardens and colleges',[18] the use of white light, songs and narrators, the collective work – Brecht attempted to borrow directly for his own theatre.

Recognising the scientific spirit of discovery and experiment as the greatest bourgeois virtue, he sees Shakespeare as an experimental writer trying out different ways to tell a story, and compares his work with that of Galileo and Bacon at the same period, the heroic age of Renaissance thought and of bourgeois science. Plays and scenes are in one sense *Versuche*, experiments or models of reality, like the hypothetical models made by physicists to explain physical processes. Alternative experiments and models are thus in order; why shouldn't one experiment with a writer himself so experimental?[19]

While he consistently analyses Shakespeare in terms of the class situation, however, Brecht's is not the kind of 'Marxist' criticism that stops at that point, as if to place a writer in his time meant that we have nothing more to learn from him. Thus he writes scathingly in his diary of a 'somewhat bloodthirsty' discussion he's read between two Soviet critics as to whether Shakespeare and Tolstoy are to be treated as apologists for their class or for humanity. 'The public prosecutor is called in to exonerate Shakespeare from the suspicion of being a writer for the aristocracy ... The tone is horrifyingly unproductive.' His own resolution of the question is at once Marxist and humanist: 'In the dispute whether the great bourgeois writers represent humanity or the bourgeoisie a dialectician would find no difficulty. They represent humanity and the bourgeoisie, since they are at the same time human and bourgeois, that is contradictory beings. They represent humanity as bourgeois and the bourgeoisie as members of humanity as a whole' (*Arbeitsjournal*, 16 October 1943).

The discoveries of the Renaissance are not simply written off: the 'heritage' is positive as well as fettering. As the *Messingkauf* (p. 63) has it (provocative as usual):

Margot Heinemann

We too are at one and the same time fathers of a new period and sons of an old one; we understand a great deal of the remote past and can still share once overwhelming feelings which were once stimulated on a grand scale ... Man is the sum of all the social conditions of all times, as the [Marxist] classics have it. All the same, there is a lot in [Shakespeare's] works that is dead, distorted and empty. This can continue to be printed; for all we know it may be shamming dead ... I would almost sooner call your attention to the wealth of living elements still to be found in such works at apparently dead junctures. An infinitesimal addition, and they spring to life, specifically now, specifically not till now.

How to play Shakespeare in the progressive theatre

All his life Brecht keeps returning to the problem of how to produce and act Shakespeare ('without whom a national theatre is almost impossible') for a modern audience. It's not enough if the director transmits something like the original production or throws light on the age when the play was written; it has to say something meaningful to modern spectators, not just to be part of a respectable cultural heritage. But to modernise effectively is not simple. It's not just a matter of dressing Hamlet in a dinner-jacket or Caesar in Wilhelmine uniform, which merely introduces a different set of anachronisms. 'It's a costume piece either way.'

But how important is Shakespeare anyway to the progressive theatre? Brecht seems to answer this question in different ways at different periods. In the mid–1920s, after the experience of war and famine, inflation and counter-revolution, he often expresses a sweeping revulsion against 'the classics', which have come to seem irrelevant. Working later (1929–33) with youth and workers' theatre groups and speech choirs on 'Lehrstücke' (teaching plays) for performance at mass meetings or in schools, at a time of rising tension and economic crisis which the left expected to lead inevitably to communist revolution, he argued that actors and audiences would learn too little from performing Shakespeare to make it worthwhile. The interest is in explicitly revolutionary drama, in practice largely for the converted, and this coincides with a period of little interest in Shakespeare and little writing about him. Unemployment and hunger would soon lead the people to reject social democracy and liberalism anyway. So they did: but it was the Nazis who triumphed, thanks partly to the deep divisions among anti-fascists, to which the go-it-alone sectarianism and over-confidence of the Marxist Left, active and heroic though it was, contributed their share.

After Hitler's seizure of power and the violent repression of the Left, reduced to 'the exile's trade of hoping', watching for a mass resistance in Germany that didn't come, Brecht grappled with the problem of 'how to represent the present-day world in the theatre' in its most bitter and tragic form. At this point he read and re-read Shakespeare, and found new possibilities in the plays which he thought he could make use of. His writings and diaries in exile are full of Shakespearean notes and illustrations. And finally after the war in the GDR we find him arguing for young playwrights to study the many-sided, dialectical,argumentative style of Shakespeare as an antidote to the flatness, dullness and over-simplification of much contemporary socialist drama, a new and more exciting kind of realism.[20]

His whole approach assumes that ordinary people can enjoy Shakespeare and learn from him,[21] though at present they may need help from the director if they're not simply to identify with outdated attitudes (bullying servants or bashing Jews). The incongruity of old customs may need to be underlined: we can't just rely on the traditions and expectations that people bring with them (in a capitalist society these will be largely capitalist expectations, in a society recently Fascist they will still be Fascist). But audiences can learn and enjoy learning, and he looks forward to a time when their more developed sense of history will make such additions unnecessary.[22]

> B. We want to have and to communicate the fun of dealing with a slice of illuminated history. And to have first-hand experience of dialectics.
> P. Isn't the second point a considerable refinement, reserved for a handful of connoisseurs?
> B. No. Even with popular ballads or the peepshows at fairs the simple people (who are so far from simple) love stories of the rise and fall of great men, of eternal change, of the ingenuity of the oppressed, of the potentialities of mankind. And they hunt for the truth that is 'behind it all'. (From *Coriolanus* discussion, *Brecht on Theatre*, p. 265)

Yet after the war, when Brecht finally acquired a company of his own in East Germany, he was held back from producing Shakespeare not only by the urgent need to stage his own and other contemporary plays but also by the conviction that neither the audience, the actors nor the authorities were ready for Shakespeare as he wanted to do it.

For one thing, the responses of audiences and cultural authorities were deeply affected by the immediate Nazi past and the realities of existence in their defeated country. For instance, when the Communist producer Gustav von Wangenheim staged *Hamlet* at the Deutsches Theater in 1946, he knew very well (says the GDR scholar A. G. Kuckhoff) that Shakespeare's ending is *not* one of immediate optimism — Fortinbras may be the right man for this moment, but certainly not for setting right the time that is out of joint. 'But at this moment of complete collapse that could not be the end of an evening in the theatre. It would have intensified the despair, resignation and passivity which weighed on people then.'[23] Hamlet's downfall could not be so shown as to 'puzzle the will'; it was felt that the spectator had to be stirred to identify with his plans for the future. The strongest actor in the company was therefore cast as Fortinbras, standing above the bloody conflict in bright costume, with every light and spotlight trained on the stage: 'So immediately after the death of the protagonist the scene was transformed to a hopeful, forward-looking present.' This finale may sound absurd to our more sheltered ears, and even at the time may well have been counter-productive. Among the gaunt ruins of Berlin, without electricity, machinery or manpower to clear them, with little to eat for many but dry bread and potatoes, it's hard to say what the effect on an audience would be. But the motive is at least intelligible: soon afterwards Brecht himself was composing the youth song: 'Away with the ruins, and build something new! / We've got to look after ourselves, and come out against us if you dare!'

Theatre doesn't take place in a vacuum. When *King John* was produced in Dresden in 1950, the episode where Hubert prepares to blind Arthur became the central scene of the play, which, as Kuckhoff says, it certainly isn't in Shakespeare. Yet the audience wept and was deeply moved — how not, five years after the Gestapo barracks and the concentration camps?

The reception in 1951 of Goethe's *Urfaust* and Lenz's *Hofmeister*, classical plays on which Brecht had worked, suggested that his kind of Shakespeare was still not on. Official cultural policy was to stage the classics 'positively', so as to bring out the progressive-humanist heritage, not critically or iconoclastically, and his *Urfaust* was heavily criticised by the cultural authorities as too negative. Brecht for his part sharply attacked 'the traditional style of performance which is automatically counted as part of our cultural heritage', on the grounds that 'what gets lost is the classics' original freshness, the element of surprise': 'where the classics are full of fighting spirit, here the lessons taught the audience are tame and cosy and fail to grip. This leads of course to a ghastly boredom.'[24]

Nor were the pressures only external. Brecht himself seems to have felt that the time was not yet ripe for him to produce some of his own plays, let alone a dialectical Shakespeare. Actors and audience had not yet enough knowledge and understanding of history, especially the Fascist past, to appreciate the deadly clowning in *Arturo Ui* (though he thought they might take the more straightforward *Fear and Misery of the Third Reich*), or the complexity of sympathy in *Coriolanus*. It remained his steady aim to 'cut the way through to Shakespeare' by preparatory work with actors and audiences on other classical plays.

Two ways of staging Shakespearean tragedy

The problem in presenting Shakespearean tragedy as usually conceived (and here Brecht is responding directly to Goethe's and especially to Hegel's reading[25]) is that it is based on the *acceptance* of evil and disaster as fated, unalterable, eternal. 'Fate is mastered, but through adjustment to it; the evil is endured, and that is the mastery.'[26] The hero is essentially passive: 'His character is built up by showing what happens to him ... Lear reacts to the ingratitude of his daughters ... Hamlet to his father's demand to avenge him ... The question is posed by "fate", it only releases the trigger, it is not subject to human activity, it's an "eternal" question ... The people act under compulsion, according to their "character", their character is "eternal", it has no causes that human beings can understand' (*GW*, 15, p. 332).

If the aim of the performance is for us to enter into and identify with the hero's experience (*Einfühlung*, empathy), the spectator will feel as helpless as he does. 'It is scarcely possible to conceive of the laws of motion if one looks at them from a tennis-ball's point of view.'[27]

This passive acceptance has become altogether too dangerous and inappropriate in the age of atomic science. Wars are accepted as mysterious and inevitable, like earthquakes. 'The same attitude as people once showed in face of unpredictable natural catastrophes they now adopt towards their own undertakings' – whether nuclear explosions or factory closures. And the new theatre has to help to break this attitude down, by encouraging a critical understanding of why such catastrophes happen:

> *The Philosopher*: The causes of a lot of tragedies lie outside the power of those who suffer them, so it seems.
> *The Dramaturg*: So it seems?
> *The Philosopher*: Of course it only seems. Nothing human can possibly lie outside the powers of humanity, and such tragedies have human causes. (*Messingkauf*, p. 32)

In the old theatre, based on empathy, we're not encouraged to think that character or predicament might be altered by social change. 'Hamlet's mother has committed a crime, it can only be answered by another crime ... Macbeth's king didn't become king as any ordinary person might – as Macbeth might – Macbeth can never become such a king as he was' (*GW*, 15, p. 333). It's the audience's acceptance of these unquestionable assumptions that has to be jolted. 'The new theatre ... exposes any given type together with his way of behaving, so as to throw light on his social motivations. ... Individuals remain individual, but become a social phenomenon. The individual's position in society loses its God-given character and becomes the centre of attention' (*Messingkauf*, p. 103). For a critical attitude to develop, people must be able to imagine the characters acting differently from the way they do. 'You can represent the famous opening scene in *Lear*, where he divides his kingdom between his daughters according to the measure of their love for him, and gets the measure quite wrong, in such a way that the audience says: "He's going about it quite the wrong way. If only he hadn't said that, or had noticed this, or at any rate thought twice."' Performed in this way, the play might still be tragic, but it would be a different *kind* of tragic experience. The audience would not simply 'plunge into those dream-like figures up on the stage, there to take part in the crescendos and climaxes which "normal" life denies us'; it would be thoughtful and critical.

The politics of empathy

Brecht's deep hostility to *Einfühlung*, total emotional identification as the main basis of performance, can't be seen as purely an aesthetic preference; it is historical and political. As he wrote in 1940: 'Already in the last years of the Weimar Republic, the German drama took a decisively rationalistic turn. Fascisms's grotesque emphasising of the emotions, and perhaps no less a certain decline of the rational element in Marxist teaching, led me personally to lay particular stress on the rational' (*GW*, 15, p. 242, Willett, *Brecht on Theatre*, adapted). It's not a question of eliminating *feeling* from the theatre. Empathy is only *one* kind of feeling, and not, says Brecht, one that the Shakespearean drama itself (as distinct from its modern interpreters) relies on very much.[28] Shakespeare's theatre was more concerned with telling stories, whereas modern interpreters are no longer interested in making the sequence of events credible and concentrate on making us share the inner life of the characters. Empathy in Shakespeare's theatre was 'a contradictory, complicated, intermittent operation': now it is taken as central. And this can pave the way for passive acceptance of Fascist demagogy.

Thus Hitler's emotional appeal to a mass audience is shown to be based on theatrical identification of exactly this kind, furthered at mass rallies by evocative lighting, hypnotic sound effects and colour-symbolism. The Führer personalises his fight, his enemies, flies into rages with them and so on, and the intensity of his feeling carries the hearers along with him, so that they cease to have an independent critical consciousness, but simply experience what he experiences and do as he does.[29] Film and television are of course splendid media for this kind of self-identification (as we know from recent examples in Britain). It's the same habit of passive, uncritical empathy that Brecht perceives in the 'culinary' theatre, especially perhaps in the intense, irrational emotionalism and subjectivism of much pre-Hitler Expressionist drama and film.[30]

True, in Shakespeare productions of the 1980s an uncritically sympathetic presentation of the hero is hardly the problem. We have long come to expect hysterical Hamlets, senile Lears and ethnically-inferior Othellos. What misleads, however, is not the degree of sympathy so much as the excessive concentration of interest and causation on the central character's mind and motives alone, and the magnetisation of the audience so that its own powers of judgement are paralysed: 'If I want to see Richard III, I don't want to feel like Richard III. I want to see this phenomenon in all its strangeness and incomprehensible quality' (GW 15, p. 189).

Historicising (or distancing) Shakespeare

In Brecht's view one must play these old works historically, which means 'setting them in powerful contrast to our own time'. He criticises modern directors who slur over what divides us from the past. '... We need to develop the historical sense (needed also for the appreciation of the new plays) into a real sensuous delight. When our theatres perform plays of other periods they like to annihilate distance, fill in the gap, gloss over the differences. But what becomes then of our delight in comparisons, in distance, in dissimilarity – which is at the same time a delight in what is close and proper to ourselves?' (Appendices to *Short Organum*, *Brecht on Theatre*, p. 276). If the director shows *only* what the past has in common with our own time, he will represent human nature and the past itself as timeless and unalterable, and our present social arrangements and behaviour as fixed and inevitable – the opposite of what Brecht wants from the theatre. As he says in the *Short Organum*: 'We must drop our habit of taking the different social structures of past periods, then stripping them of everything that makes them different; so that they all look more or less like our own, which then acquires from this process a certain air of having been there all along, in other words of permanence pure and simple. Instead we must leave them their distinguishing marks and keep their impermanence always before our eyes, so that our own period can be seen to be impermanent too' (para. 36).

This doesn't mean, however, that the characters should become dehumanised, archaeological figures. Our sense of their social situation, the inescapable pressures on them, makes their actions and feelings credible and human to us without our having to pretend to react like Elizabethans, which of course we can't do. 'The spectator cannot simply feel: that's how I would act, but at most can say: if I had lived under those circumstances' (*Short Organum*, para. 37). This is the guiding idea for a Brechtian approach to producing the plays.

When Brecht calls *Lear*, for instance, a 'barbaric play', he doesn't mean that it has to be scrapped, only that the audience have to be encouraged to 'keep their heads', not to identify with social and class attitudes quite alien to them. 'What you cannot have is the audience, including those who happen to be servants themselves, taking Lear's side to such an extent that they applaud when a servant gets beaten for carrying out his mistress' orders, as happens in Act I Scene 4' (*Messingkauf*, p. 62). And again: 'The spectators at the Globe theatre, who three centuries ago saw King Lear give away his kingdom in pieces, pitied honest Cordelia, who didn't get one of the pieces, not the thousands of people who were thus given away. But we ourselves even now scarcely make any protest about the way they were treated.'[31] So Lear's rage is not to be represented as timeless and universal, but as related to its time (*Zeitgebunden*). To feel its full impact we have to be aware of Lear as patriarch, father, feudal monarch, maddened by a defiance he has never been taught to expect either from daughters or from servants. We have to observe this not simply from Lear's point of view, or even from Kent's or Cordelia's (that is from within the society), but from our own, which does not accept the whims of princes as sacred; and we may need a nudge to ensure this. Thus to emphasise Lear's tyranny, Oswald could be made to stagger out after Kent has beaten him 'with every sign of having been hurt'. The arbitrariness of Lear's division of the kingdom could be stressed by having an actual map torn up: 'Lear could hand the pieces to his daughters in the hope of ensuring their love that way. He could take the third piece, the one meant for Cordelia, and tear that across once again to distribute to the others. That would be a particularly good way of making the audience stop and think' (*Messingkauf*, p. 63).

So, again, Othello's jealousy is not just a universal passion, but is set in a particular possessive, competitive world. He doesn't only possess Desdemona, he also possesses a post as general, which he has not inherited as a feudal general would, but won by outstanding achievements, and presumably has snatched from someone else; he must defend it or it will be snatched from him. He lives in a world of fighting for property and position, and his relationship with the woman he loves develops as a property relationship.

If we show it like this in the theatre, the passion of jealousy is not reduced but deepened, and the suggestion arises that social change might alter things. Of course, Brecht adds, to show this is not the whole purpose of performing *Othello*, but it does make a successful performance possible.[32]

Hamlet is still often read in terms of sick psychology. Either Hamlet has a paralysing fixation on his mother; or it is, to quote Olivier's film, 'the tragedy of a man who could not make up his mind', the intellectual constitutionally incapable of acting. Or else, with Hegel, 'In the background of Hamlet's soul, death is already present from the first. The sandbank of finite condition will not content his spirit' (*Shakespeare in Europe*, p. 87). Brecht will have none of this. He sees Hamlet historically, between two worlds, unhappy with the dark revenge duty, yet unable to find another way to act. The Protestant University of Wittenberg has taught him to rely on reason and conscience – in the bloody business of feudal revenge reason merely impedes him. The idea of 'valuable fracture points' is crucial here: 'What a work this *Hamlet* is! The interest in it, lasting over centuries, probably arose from the fact that a new type, fully developed, stands out as totally estranged in a mediaeval environment that has remained almost entirely unmodified. The scream for revenge, ennobled by the Greek tragedians, then ruled out by Christianity, in the drama of *Hamlet* is still loud enough, reproduced with enough infectious power to make the new doubting, testing, planning appear estranging' (*Arbeitsjournal*, 25 November 1948). Bourgeois *Hamlet* criticism, says Brecht, usually grasps Hamlet's hesitation as the interesting new element in the play, but considers the massacre in the fifth act, with the sweeping away of hesitation and the turn to action instead, as a positive solution. We, however, can see just the delay as sensible, for the act is an act of horror, a relapse. The play can be read in other ways, of course, but the theatre has to speak for the interests of its own time, and this reading might interest a modern audience, 'still threatened by relapses of this kind' into pointless bloodshed.

This is the point of the little 'parallel scene' Brecht wrote for actors
in rehearsal. Hamlet, on his way to England in Act IV, reaches the
coast and learns from the ferryman that relations between Denmark
and Norway have now been settled by a treaty, whereby Denmark
gives up the piece of coastline in dispute and Norway contracts to
buy Danish fish, so that a war has become unnecessary. Hamlet
approves this change from old feudal to modern bourgeois behaviour. 'The new methods, friend. You find that now all over the
place. Blood doesn't smell good any more. Tastes have changed.'
The idea is not to act this to the audience, but to make the
rehearsing actor aware that Hamlet is living in a time of changing
values, and has a real choice. He must be played as full of doubts
about taking revenge, till the chance encounter with Fortinbras'
army decides him to revert to unthinking 'heroic' action and the
barbaric virtues of the blood-bath. Brecht sums it up in a sonnet:

> Here is the body, puffy and inert,
> Where we can trace the virus of the mind.
> How lost he seems among his steel-clad kind
> This introspective sponger in a shirt.
>
> Till they bring drums to wake him up again
> As Fortinbras and all the fools he's found
> March off to battle for that patch of ground
> 'Which is not tomb enough to hide the slain.'
>
> At that his too, too solid flesh sees red.
> He feels he's hesitated long enough.
> It's time to turn to (bloody) deeds instead.
>
> So we nod grimly when the play is done
> And they pronounce that he was of the stuff
> To prove 'most royally', 'had he been put on'.[33]

Is Brecht being thoroughly and provocatively un-Shakespearean
here, or does he open up and make explicit contradictions which are
deep in the play as Shakespeare wrote it? Clearly, I think, the latter:
there's so much in the text which sustains this kind of reading, once
one thinks about it, and which indeed could hardly have got there by
accident. Thus when Hamlet, shamed by the willingness of
Fortinbras and his army to die 'even for an eggshell ... when
honour's at the stake', resolves to pursue revenge at any cost, there is
surely some kind of irony involved in the unreserved approval of
killing for honour, coming as it does after Falstaff in *Henry IV* and
(more significantly) near *Troilus*, where Hector, defying his reason
and conscience, continues the war for 'honour and renown' which
ends in his own butchery. Hamlet's conclusion here doesn't neces-

sarily have to be the spectator's, and a post-Falklands audience is likely to be at least divided about it. So, probably, would the popular London audience in 1600.

Again, Shakespeare deliberately contrasts the simple passions and values of the older revenge drama (displayed in the player's Hecuba speech and in the play presented before Claudius) with the appalling complexity of the contradictory issues and feelings that arise with such events in real life. And he seems fully confident that he can make the audience feel the difference between the two, as they hardly would if they all took medieval values for granted. Brecht's interpretation appears to be working with, not against, the grain of the play.

Alterations and adaptations

Should one rewrite or alter Shakespeare for performance? No objection in principle, says Brecht, if it's necessary and one can do it successfully. 'Sacrilege sanctifies': if the plays hadn't been used and misused over ages by schoolmasters to squeeze out morals and by commercial entrepreneurs to make a profit, they would have died long ago. 'I think we can alter Shakespeare if we can alter him.' But it has to be done very carefully, not arbitrarily, if we're not to spoil the play. And there's always a risk that unsuitable alterations may 'mobilise all Shakespeare's excellences against you'. In the *Coriolanus* discussion[34] we see Brecht resisting some suggested alterations that he thinks would have this effect.[35]

His experimental use of the 'great realist' varies. Sometimes, especially in the earlier writings, he treats the plays primarily as 'a mine of discoveries as rich as life', from which one can loot scenes, speeches or plots for a modern play much as (he insists) Shakespeare himself did with other writers. At other times he's concerned not only with raw material, but with Shakespeare's dialectical structure for the play as a whole, which will be destroyed if one alters it too much. And in the last resort – especially after working on *Coriolanus* – he's more and more impressed by Shakespeare's own command of contradiction and causation. 'Couldn't one do it just as it is, only with skilful direction?' This, referring to *Coriolanus*, is the last entry in his working diary.

The practice scenes he wrote for *Hamlet* (see above), *Romeo* and *Macbeth* are exercises for rehearsing actors, not meant for inclusion in performance, though they do throw light on the interpretations. More significant are those adaptations which allude to, incorporate or parody famous scenes or parts of plays in order to show up and undermine contemporary bourgeois values and assumptions (rather as T. S. Eliot alludes to the meeting of Antony and Cleopatra on the Nile to contrast with squalor of the modern London river in *The Waste Land*). Thus in *Arturo Ui* the theatricality of Hitler's oratory is mockingly exposed when the gangster-Führer takes lessons in elocution from an old ham actor, who appropriately trains him on Antony's speech to the crowd in *Julius Caesar*. And the unresisted take-over of Austria (the Anschluss) is represented by a scene in which Ui woos the Chancellor's wife, first in the style of Faust wooing Gretchen, then as Richard III woos his murdered victim's widow over her husband's coffin. Both scenes are very funny and very frightening.

Although episodes like these are exaggerated caricatures of the originals, Brecht nevertheless often makes explicit subversive ideas which seem to be already there, half submerged, in Shakespeare's text. Thus in *Round Heads and Pointed Heads*, which began as a reworking of *Measure for Measure* (regarded by Brecht as Shakespeare's most progressive play), he throws a new and sinister light on the conflict between Angelo, Isabella and Claudio (here called Guzman), who is threatened with death as a grandee of inferior race for seducing a Round Head (= Aryan) girl. To save her brother, Isabella unwillingly agrees to keep a rendezvous with the corrupt police chief Angelo Iberin. But when she goes to consult a prostitute for professional advice on how to behave, the brothel-keeper is shocked that a lady should even think of doing such a job herself, and for a handsome payment arranges for the appointment to be kept by one of her girls. (The whore is paid her usual plain time-rate, the madam pocketing the difference, and in the event gets beaten up.)

Of course this is not exactly what happens in *Measure*, since Mariana, who stands in for Isabella there, was once betrothed to Angelo and still wants to marry him: yet Mariana too is vulnerable and desperate because she's poor, her dowry having been lost at sea. And Brecht's main dramatic point, that the gentry can usually find someone else to suffer the unpleasant experiences for them, is hinted at again in *Measure* in comic form, when the Duke hunts around for a low-class convict to be executed so that his head can be sent to satisfy Angelo: it's only because Barnardine, the stroppy drunkard, refuses to get up in the morning to be hanged that this plan collapses. Beneath the surface of Shakespeare's reassuringly happy ending lurks a very nasty underworld of sexual and commercial exploitation of inferiors, which is never cleaned up, only played down and obscured. In Brecht's rewriting this side of the contradiction becomes the central impression.

The one major adaptation that Brecht completed was his *Coriolanus* (1952–5), 'the only at all topical Shakespeare with which we have a reasonable chance of filling the house'. It was a play he greatly admired for its dialectical power. As he wrote of the opening scene: 'All these great and small conflicts thrown on the scene at once: the unrest of the starving plebeians together with the war against their neighbours the Volsces: the plebeians' hatred for Marcius, the people's enemy; together with his patriotism; the creation of the people's Tribunes – together with Marcius' appointment to a leading post in the war. How much of that do we get in the bourgeois theatre?' The alterations he made ('of course we will have to change the behaviour of the plebs') have to be seen in their historical context, so soon after Hitler's war.[36] Spectators many of whom were still under the influence of Nazi myth and glamour, brought up in SA or Hitler Youth, could all too easily see the story in terms of the true patriot and military hero, stabbed in the back by the cowardly masses under Red labour leaders. The production must show that no leader, however talented, is indispensable.

It's not necessary, says Brecht, and given Shakespeare's genius not possible, to leave out or blunt the tragedy of pride, even if the tragedy of the single individual interests us much less than that of the commonwealth caused by the individual. 'As far as the enjoyment of the hero is concerned, we've got to get beyond mere identification with the hero Marcius to arrive at a richer enjoyment. We must be able to experience not only the tragedy of Coriolanus but also that of Rome and the plebeians'. 'Society is set in irreconcilable conflict with this hero, and the production has to make that possible and indeed enforce it.' Brecht, however, resists the temptation to make Coriolanus a wholly unsympathetic or contemptible militarist. He has to be shown as a hero who would be valuable to his country if he were not prevented by pride and narrow class outlook. At the same time Brecht never accepts the notion (put forward by Georg Brandes, and later endorsed by Günther Grass in attacking Brecht) of Shakespeare's 'hatred of the plebians': 'Brandes may be right that he was portraying his English class equals rather than the Roman plebs ... But theatrical criticism of the common man need not arise, as Brandes thinks, from snobbish hatred.'[37]

Brecht's work on the opening scene with the crowd – the most impressive and stimulating record we have of him as a director of Shakespeare – shows him building on what's already there with little verbal alteration.[38] Most of the new ideas refer to the visual impression the crowd is to make or to stage directions which explain their behaviour. They are not to be an amorphous mass: their weapons may be improvised out of fire-irons and broom-handles, but they should look effective – these are after all the people who make weapons for the army. And their political attitudes are carefully differentiated and individualised. In particular, Brecht introduces a new character, 'man with a child', who takes over some of First Citizen's lines: originally he was going to emigrate, but in the new more democratic Rome he decides to stay, and the people's growth in political confidence is later shown through him. Again, a disabled ex-serviceman, who embraces the wounded patrician Lartius on his crutches, demonstrates the temporary unity between patricians and citizens, based on 'the naive patriotism that's so common among ordinary people, and so often shockingly abused'.

The main changes, which for Brecht are relatively minor ones, are, first, that the plebeians are more consistent and organised. It's their determination to resist (the majority volunteering to defend the city), rather than simply Volumnia's persuasion, that induces Coriolanus to turn back to his own destruction. The tribunes, in Shakespeare shabby politicans who envy Marcius and manipulate the people, become their spokesmen and at times genuine leaders. And Menenius, who could be seen in Shakespeare as a reconciler, [39] is here merely a twisty patrician using soft-soap rhetoric. This disposes of the possibility that the conflict could be avoided if Coriolanus would only be more tactful; it's now a class struggle, and what persuades the people to disperse in Act I, scene i is not Menenius' oratory but the greater conflict of the Volscian war.

The revised version (as modified by Wekwerth and Tenschert) was a tremendous success in Berlin and London in the 1960s. Yet Brecht was never satisfied with his years of work on it. A late entry in his diary shows him still grappling with the problems, leaning (as Shakespeare did) on Plutarch:

> I transcribe the scene of the murder of Coriolanus. Feel tempted to make another version of the scenes I've altered. When the feeling for history is more strongly developed, and when the masses have more self-confidence, everything can be left more or less as it is. The plebs is still very weak after the abolition of the monarchy, and the existence of the nation (city state) is exposed to the blackmail of men like Coriolanus. The patricians have to order everything under their own control if they do not want to fall into slavery like neighbouring states. Coriolanus tries to extort new or old privileges for his class during the incessant wars, and turns back in the interests of his class. In West Germany the piece could be performed today just as it is.
> (*Arbeitsjournal*, p. 594)

This raises a problem with all Brecht's adaptations (much more those of most modern directors). If, as he says, the power of Shakespeare's dramaturgy lies in the contradictions, the doubleness of character and action, and our conflicting response to it which compels us to think, don't the adaptations tend to harmonise and flatten out the effects, much as he convicts the bourgeois theatre of doing?

Some Shakespeare productions after Brecht

If Brecht's work on Shakespeare is to be useful to modern theatre people, it's certainly not a matter of copying his own adaptations and alterations, designed for a particular audience at a particular moment in time, which is not ours. What can be valuable is the dialectical method, the sense of a whole historical world surrounding the hero, and the insights into particular plays.

'Brechtian' has become a cliché. Any production that changes scenery or costumes in sight of the audience, reminds us that we're in a theatre, shocks our expectations or reduces properties to a minimum is apt to be called Brechtian. This however is wrong. Brecht's distancing effects – including alienation effects that work by surprising us – are, as he said, deliberately combative, *political* effects.

Thus in Peter Brook's famous production of *Lear* with Paul Scofield – a production often called Brechtian because it alienated our view of the king – the director deliberately cut out the servants who stand up to Cornwall and Regan and try to help the blinded Gloucester, because he wanted to prevent 'reassurance' being given to the audience. The world of *Lear* must be shown as *wholly*, unchangeably (not relatively) black and evil, and so the crucial turning point, when the oppressed common people begin to resist the bullies and torturers, has to go – which means the forces which, however feeble as yet, will one day alter this world have to go too. Cutting the contradictions like this is positively *anti*-Brechtian.[40]

Again, when John Barton did a much admired *Henry V* with Alan Howard, the two Archbishops who open the play started in modern civilian clothes, gradually putting on their vestments while they spoke their lines. The device may be borrowed from the robing of the Pope in Brecht's *Galileo*, but in this context it ruined an essential dramatic point, since the audience could not register their remarks as those of bishops at all. Thus the director sacrificed Shakespeare's own alienation effect, for in these speeches the bishops are planning to tell Henry he has a just claim to the French throne and encourage him to invade France, partly in order to divert him from taxing the wealth of the Church at home. This cynical calculation allows the whole subsequent action to be seen, intermittently at least, in the cold light of Realpolitik. To cut it out helps to enforce the ideal-istic–militarist view of the play that Lord Chalfont (himself an establishment politician), while recognising it as one-sided, would still wish to emphasise: 'Henry had revived the pride of Englishmen in being English and had by his own example inspired them to believe that there are still values worth fighting for and worth dying for.'[41]

True, Brecht cuts properties to the minimum: only what is essen-tial to the action will appear on the stage. But note the trouble taken to ensure that Weigel's props, for instance, should look real and used, or the care given by Caspar Neher to selecting every chair, weapon or instrument.[42] Respect for manual work and the people who do it is expressed in the conviction and accuracy with which a canteen wagon is fitted out, a chicken plucked, a sleazy bar-room mounted. Compare this with the kind of Boar's Head tavern we often get at Stratford, without so much as a chair or a table in sight to allow the actors to suggest the easy attraction of pub life, so that while drinking they must either stand propping up the wall (Hal and Poins) or sprawl in the straw on the floor (Falstaff and Doll). This may seem to be merely following a harmless fashion for empty stages, but it makes the visual representation of historical context and class contrast very difficult.

One way of trying to modernise is to scale down Shakespeare's representation of great historical processes to the merely private, personal and naturalistic – a tempting method for the small screen, where talking heads are so much easier to show than large groups. In the histories and Roman plays the politics may be treated as irrelevant, and the heroes seen as interesting only because, while they may *think* they stand for political ideas or the social interests of their class, they are really motivated only by petty vanity, jeal-ousy and spite just as we in the audience are. Thus the recent introduction to the BBC's *Julius Caesar*: 'When [Brutus and Cassius] die, it is a tragedy, not because their strategies collapsed, not be-cause some great ideal perished with them, but because they were rather ordinary, vulnerable human beings, almost pathetically trapped in power, who overreached themselves' (Jonathan Dimbleby, *Shakespeare in Perspective*, vol. i, p. 59). But this kind of thing, however well-intentioned in debunking politicians, is not at all what Brecht wanted from the Shakespearean histories. 'Miserable philistines will always find the same motive force in history, their own' (*Messingkauf*, p. 48). 'People don't change much', says the philistine spectator, who doesn't want to know about any life or aspirations going beyond his or her own; whereas in the history plays (the closest of all to life, as Brecht puts it) Shakespeare succeeds in dramatising so much of the complexity of real historical events.

The acid test, probably, for a production that has assimilated the most important elements of Brecht's thinking is how it deals with crowds, servants and the lower orders generally. The extra weight and attention given by him to these 'famous forebears' in itself alters the dialectics of the plays.[43] In Shakespeare's own theatre, the common people must have been immediately recognisable by their dress, and by vernacular idiom and local dialect, in contrast to the elevated speech of aristocratic heroes. And they are, of course, often given the most searching comments on the heroic action. The Gravediggers, Pompey the bawd, the soldiers before Agincourt, represent one of the most important means of distancing the main action and enabling the audience to judge it. Often, however, in modern productions these characters are routinely presented as gross, stupid and barely human – rogues, sluts and varlets with straw in their hair, whose antics the audience can laugh at but whose comments it can't be expected to take seriously. Indeed, the combination of Loamshire dialect and dated jokes often makes the comments unintelligible anyway.

Thus in a recent TV *Measure*, Pompey was a grotesque from some unimaginable lower depths, wearing a coarse tunic like an Ancient Briton and covered with debris from the stable: whereas in the text he's a barman in a tavern-cum-brothel much patronised by the gentry, a quick-witted Cockney making a living in a trade which would be legal if the law would allow it, and clever enough to run rings round the police. If he is either sentimentalised or degraded below the level of human discussion, we lose the alienating effect of his comic dialogue with Escalus about sex and the law.

So too Doll Tearsheet must be played as a prostitute past her best, not a witch-like harridan with elf-locks, if her farewell to the ageing Falstaff is to have its necessary moment of pathos, and her arrest by order of virtuous Hal is to sharpen our sense of class hypocrisy and injustice. Hamlet's gravediggers may be called 'Clown' in the margin, but they are not to wear baggy trousers and funny hats: they are not slapstick comic relief but commonsense countrymen, one of whom at least can articulate the wisdom of uneducated people to the admiration of the Prince.

A revealing contempt for 'low' characters is shown when directors of our national companies make them all walk with their feet wide apart and their bottoms stuck out, in contrast to the aristocracy who stand up properly. It's not a question of idealising them. But if Pistol's boy looks like that, what becomes of the shudder of horror when we hear that 'the boys and the luggage' have been slaughtered?

Crowds are of course a problem. You can't present the crowd in Shakespeare's Rome as if they were the modern, organised industrial working class (though this visual equation was actually made in Dimbleby's TV Prologue to *Caesar*, where the Roman crowd was paralleled with trade unionists marching behind an anti-racist banner). The fickleness of this mob, which is the main thing Shakespeare shows about it, is a real characteristic of a pre-industrial city crowd, united only temporarily to riot over a specific grievance;[44] if you make them into modern miners or dockers you merely confirm the Lawson stereotype of trade unionists motivated by inferiority and envy, incapable of uniting for any constructive change.

What the director *can* do is present the crowd with respect, as people driven to desperation by poverty and extortion. Jack Cade can be a credible peasant leader, not just a comic drunk; his millenarian visions take on a different colour if we bring out the arrogance of his noble opponents. And indeed Shakespeare provides a basis for this in Cade's death scene. On the other hand, it's no use to prettify scenes of crowd violence – as was done in the play about the Paris Commune described in *Messingkauf* (p. 34): 'To begin with we showed a shop being smashed up in the course of the rising. Then we dropped that, as we didn't want to suggest that the Commune was hostile to small tradespeople. It made for an extremely unrealistic popular rising.'

Effective crowds come expensive, though they need not be vast. But it's hard on Henry V if the RSC economises on extras to the point where he has to storm Harfleur with scarcely any troops except the comics. In this respect perhaps the most 'Brechtian' production of our time has been Grigori Kozintsev's film of *Lear* (influenced as much by Meyerhold as by Brecht) which took the imagery of beggars, outcasts and oppressed peasants in the text and made it into marvellous images of the masses which framed the great people's story. In Kozintsev's own words: 'There is no "desert" in *Lear*, the world of tragedy is densely populated ... We had not to take away the landscapes but to move the characters forward into life ... The scenes of courtly life, the life of politics, villages, war – tragedy takes place not among landscapes but among people ...'[45]

Historicising Brecht

Nearly all Brecht's work comes out of the 'dark times' of which he so often writes, when 'a word without anger is stupid; a smooth forehead is a sign of insensitivity; a conversation about trees is almost a crime because it involves silence about so many horrors'. And his work on Shakespeare has the urgency of that time, which can look like crudeness if one sees it outside history and from a more sheltered position. The times explain why there are relatively few comments on the festive comedies or the late plays: the tragedies, the histories and dark plays like *Measure* seemed more productive for a contemporary audience. It was the conflicts and contradictions, rather than the element of Utopian humanist vision, that he needed to emphasise. The heroic determination that made him go on studying and working on Shakespeare as well as his own plays, even at a time when he had no theatre to stage them in and didn't know if he ever would have one again, also made him focus his interest in terms of the immediate struggle, recognising that in some ways this narrows it. 'Even anger against injustice / Makes the voice hoarse.'[46] And at times he wondered: 'When will the time come for the kind of realism that dialectics makes possible? Even to represent situations as latent balances of intensifying conflicts today comes up against enormous difficulties. The very purposefulness [*Zielstrebigkeit*] of the writer eliminates too many tendencies in the situation to be described' (*Arbeitsjournal*, 31 January 1941, written in Finnish exile). It is unfortunately too soon for us to look down with forbearance on Brecht's deficiencies as part of the 'dark time we have escaped'. For the horrors are still there, though they may take new forms. It's more to the point so to present Shakespeare now, in theatre and in education, that we can say with Brecht: 'I could not do much, but without me / Those in power would have sat safer, so I hoped.'

Notes

1 From an interview with Terry Coleman, *Guardian*, 5 September 1983.
2 The phrase is Peter Brook's in *The Empty Space* (Harmondsworth: Penguin, 1972).
3 The other major influence, very different in kind, was Japanese and Chinese theatre.
4 Brecht, *Diaries 1920–1922*, trans. John Willett (London: Methuen, 1973): entry for 2 October 1921, p. 129.
5 Cologne radio discussion, 15 April 1928, in Brecht, *Gesammelte Werke* (Frankfurt, 1967), 15, p. 149.
6 Brecht, *Short Organum for the Theatre*, trans. and ed. John Willett, *Brecht on Theatre: the Development of an Aesthetic* (London: Methuen 1974), p. 33.
7 Extract from an introductory talk given by Brecht before the broadcast of his radio version of *Macbeth* on Berlin radio, 14 October 1927, in *Gesammelte Werke*, 15, p. 119.

Margot Heinemann

8 Brecht uses the term consistently from the mid-1920s, long before the Socialist Realism controversy with Lukacs and Zhdanov – it's not a defensive use.

9 Brecht, *Messingkauf Dialogues*, trans. John Willett (London: Methuen, 1977), p. 27.

10 *Ibid.*, p. 63.

11 As he says in the prologue to his radio version of *Macbeth*, 'this illogicality of events, the way in which a tragic sequence of events is continually interrupted, is not characteristic of our theatre, it's characteristic only of life'.

12 *Messingkauf Dialogues*, p. 59.

13 Brecht, *Arbeitsjournal*, ed. W. Hecht (Frankfurt, 1974): 7 January 1948, p. 507.

14 Willett translates 'useful junction points', but this seems unsatisfactory, since the collision is the main concern of the metaphor.

15 *Messingkauf Dialogues*, p. 35. See also GW, 15, pp. 279–80, 'Causality in Non-Aristotelian Dramaturgy': 'We would think the individual lacking in something ... if he were to accord too readily to the laws governing the movement of masses'. For an excellent account of Brecht's views on this question see Erich Speidel, 'The Individual and Society', in *Brecht in Perspective*, ed. G. Bartram and A. Waine (London: Longman, 1982).

16 How to represent remote causes is for Brecht a crucial problem of the modern drama. In a world where one can press a lever in America and kill 12 or 12,000 people in Ireland, it seems to people as if their own decisions no longer matter. But 'of course it only seems': ways have to be found to make the connections visible (*Messingkauf Dialogues*, p. 32).

17 See also GW, 15, p. 335, *Shakespeare Studien*.

18 Compare Peter Hall, who in his early days at Stratford dreamed of creating a theatre for a wider audience of 'young people, poor people, working-class people', but later came to think this 'curiously naive' because 'anyone who wants to go the theatre is today well able to do so' – *Peter Hall's Diaries: the Story of a Dramatic Battle*, ed. J. Goodwin (London: Hamilton 1983): 22 July 1972, p. 14.

19 For example, he suggests that *Hamlet*, Act IV, is experimental: there was a problem about how to bring this sensitive, philosophical character to perpetrate the final massacre. There may be alternative scenes: perhaps after the scene with Fortinbras's captain Hamlet was to go straight back and do the killing, or perhaps he was to hesitate to the end. Perhaps Shakespeare came with a different scene every day, like Brecht himself.

20 Brecht, *Schriften*, I, 938.

21 It is perhaps easier for Brecht, as a German, to avoid thinking of Shakespeare as an irredeemably elitist experience; for he is far more accessible to ordinary audiences in translation (even the old ones of Schlegel and Tieck) than in the archaism and compression of the original English. Of course, they miss a lot, but they also understand a lot.

22 Brecht has been attacked by some English directors, themselves university-educated, for his 'pedagogic' approach, the emphasis on teaching, which in their view means passing *down* information and judgements, 'the art of the superior to the inferior'. But to assume that workers will never want to acquire any actual *knowledge* (as distinct from gut-reactions) is surely far more patronising and anti-revolutionary. It might be called the 'pull-up-the-ladder, Jack' school of socialist criticism.

23 A. G. Kuckhoff, 'On the Reception of Shakespeare in the GDR, 1945–80', *Shakespeare Jahrbuch*, 118, 1982. As this interesting article shows, fashions in Shakespeare production there have gone through some striking changes and reversals since 1945.

24 *Sinn und Form* (Potsdam, 1954), in Willett, *Brecht on Theatre*, p. 273.

25 Hegel: 'Shakespeare supplies us with the finest examples of essentially stable and consistent characters, who go to their doom precisely because of their tenacious

hold upon themselves and their ends. . . . This onward movement of a great soul . . . is the main content of some of Shakespeare's most interesting tragedies'; from *The Philosophy of Fine Art*, cited in *Shakespeare in Europe*, ed. O. Le Winter (Cleveland and New York: Meridian, 1970; Harmondsworth: Penguin, 1970), p. 86.

26 Cf. the views of tragedy much cited in university courses on the subject, e.g. in Clifford Leech's textbook *Tragedy* (London: Methuen, 1969): 'Shakespeare was not attempting to justify the ways of God to men . . . He was writing tragedy, and tragedy would not be tragedy if it were not a painful mystery' (A. C. Bradley); 'In a tragedy, nothing is in doubt and everyone's destiny is known. Tragedy is restful, and the reason is that hope, that foul, deceitful thing, has no part in it' (Jean Anouilh).

27 GW, 16, p. 930; in Willett, *Brecht on Theatre*, p. 275.

28 See *Short Organum*, para. 12. See also 'A Little Private Tuition for My Friend Max Gorelik', in Willett, *Brecht on Theatre*, p. 161.

29 'Über die Theatralik des Faschismus', from *Politik auf dem Theater*, ed. W. Hecht (1983), pp. 41–9; trans. the present writer.

30 Some left Expressionist writers, like Kaiser and Toller, remained anti-Fascists. Others succumbed to the demagogy of the right. Brecht's former close friend, the dramatist Arnolt Bronnen (author of the violently emotional play *Vatermord*), went over to the Nazis, as did Hans Johst who became head of the Nazi writers' organisation. It was from painful experience that Brecht advised us to 'be very suspicious of people who wish to exclude reason in any way from artistic work', denouncing it as cold, inhuman and hostile to feeling.

31 *On Non-Aristotelian Drama, Schriften*, I (1933–9) 315.

32 From 'Stanislawski Studien', GW, 16, 847–8.

33 'On Shakespeare's Play *Hamlet*', trans. John Willett in Brecht, *Poems*, ed. John Willett and R. Manheim (London: Eyre Methuen, 1976), p. 321.

34 GW, 16, 869.

35 For instance, a suggestion that the First Citizen should turn out to be the newly-appointed tribune Sicinius. This, says Brecht, would be excessive, even though it doesn't involve rewriting. There's such a thing as the specific weight a character has in the action, and we must not arouse an interest that can't be satisfied later. Anyway we must not lessen the role of the Volscian danger in establishing the tribunes. Again, when it's suggested that Coriolanus should welcome the news of a bloody war, 'like Hindenburg', Brecht warns that this is a different kind of war which led to the unity of Italy under a (temporarily) democratic Rome. 'One thing's clear to me, Marcius must be shown as a patriot. Only the tremendous events shown in the play turn him into a deadly enemy of his country.'

36 There is no evidence that the authorities wanted these alterations. They seem indeed to have preferred Shakespeare and Goethe done 'straight', as part of the cultural heritage (see above).

37 Interestingly, after Brecht's death his collaborators, Wekwerth and Tenschert, made further changes in his version before performance, believing that he had idealised the behaviour of the people.

38 See 'Study of the First Scene in Shakespeare's *Coriolanus*', in *Dialectics in the Theatre*, in Willett, *Brecht on Theatre*, pp. 252–65.

39 This, however, is an arguable interpretation, though dear to 'liberal' teachers. Shakespeare may well have meant him to appear as Brecht suggests.

40 The influence mainly at work here is of course not Brecht but Jan Kott. See above, pp. 162–4 and p. 180, note 12.

41 Conclusion of his *Perspective* talk, introducing the play on BBC television: *Shakespeare in Perspective*, I, ed. R. Sales (London, 1982), p. 137.

42 See Brecht's poem 'Weigel's Props'. See also his praise of Neher's work in *Messingkauf Dialogues*, pp. 84–6.

Margot Heinemann

43 I remember seeing a memorable *Timon* by the theatre of Karl Marx Stadt (formerly Chemnitz), otherwise fairly conventional, where the whole effect was transformed by the playing of the servants, dressed in brown to distinguish them from the aristocracy in white and the city magnates in black. The faithful steward, but especially the old house servants, made redundant and going out silently into a jobless future, gave the thing a poignancy one hardly ever feels in performance of this play.

44 See Eric Hobsbawm, *Primitive Rebels* (Manchester University Press, 1971), pp. 103–25.

45 Grigori Kozintsev, *King Lear: The Space of Tragedy: The Diary of a Film Director* (London: Heinemann, 1977), p. 82.

46 References in this paragraph are to Brecht's poem 'To Posterity' (*An die Nachgeborenen*), *GW*, 10, 722. This poem, written around 1938, historicises Brecht much more effectively and movingly than I can do. It is translated by Willett in Brecht, *Poems*, p. 318.

Raymond Williams

Afterword

Recording a certain wariness, an unease, about the main title of this volume of essays, I found myself back in the North Wing of Cambridge University Library, in the autumn of 1939. I was there to pick up a couple of books on Shakespeare for an essay. My first impression of those hundreds of volumes, tightly stacked in what looked like an industrial warehouse, can be best understood if I add that this was the first time I had been in any library larger than a living room. Wandering in and out, trying to decipher (as still today) the complicated system of classification, I came across a section which induced a kind of vertigo. I don't, fortunately, remember all the actual titles, but a quick scan showed me Shakespeare as royalist, democrat, catholic, puritan, feudalist, progressive, humanist, racist, Englishman, homosexual, Marlowe, Bacon and so on round the bay. I flicked the pages of some of the more improbable ascriptions. The compounded smell of disuse and of evidence rose to my nostrils. I got out and went for a walk.

A sophisticated explanation awaited me. The central error of these laborious volumes was the isolation of speeches by particular characters as Shakespeare's own essential beliefs, and then intrapolation or extrapolation from scraps of speculative biography and contingent history. This is still said and is still, as far as it goes, true. But the academy is very skilful in solving one problem as a way of evading another. Given that such books, which are in fact diverse not only in ascription but in level and seriousness, are flawed or vitiated by a central methodological error – that of reading dramatic speech as authorial confession or assertion – what has next to be said about the evident fact that the plays are full of explicit and implicit conflicts and tests of beliefs, and that these are in many cases directly presented as elements of social and political actions?

A sophisticated explanation awaited yet again. In presenting, so often powerfully, so many incompatible beliefs, Shakespeare was saying something about belief itself. To which, even then, I replied:

Raymond Williams

go on. For there is something peculiarly seductive about 'something'. Listening to the answers, I got a range from 'something' as a sad wise recognition of the pathos and folly of all (other people's) beliefs, especially when these were at all passionately held, to a rather confident assertion that there was something called 'experience', which we and Shakespeare could share, which was before, above and beyond beliefs, but in which we could settle and enrich ourselves.

These two rather specific ideological positions, actively shaped in the academy in the 1920s and 1930s and then inertly dominant until the 1960s, are of course different from each other, though they are often indifferently combined. The first always seemed to me a rationalisation of post-liberalism, after the shocks of the Great War: a humane scepticism of all formal and established beliefs, which had then turned back on itself into what was at once resignation and complacency: a difficult mood to sustain unless – but then this was made to happen – there was the high authority of Literature and of Shakespeare himself to demonstrate and ratify it. There could then be a sharp picking-off of any rash attempts to show beliefs as active or as decisive, even where the close reading which was simultaneously recommended seemed in certain works to show just this.

This was where more serious people moved to the second position, which still has the advantage of getting near to saying something which, more precisely said, might be helpful. But again it was a matter of what this 'something' was. The constructive next move is the question: given that it is the case, in this or that play, that A, B and C argue powerfully for different, incompatible or actually conflicting beliefs, must this be taken only as a series of variations which nothing in the play transforms or resolves? Evidently not, one would have to say. Some are shown, in the whole action, to be deluded or deceived. Some are shown to be in bad or in mixed faith. Some, more pragmatically, succeed or fail, but then this cannot be directly taken as validation or invalidation, except in some generic sidestep which would allow this in the histories but not in the tragedies: the apparently decisive distinction which, on closer examination, turns out to have created the categories which are then used to ratify it.

Still, however, are the plays not evidently more than a series from A, B and C to Z and breakoff? Do not transformations and resolutions visibly occur? Does not A change, after this or that event? All these questions, if seriously pursued, lead us into detailed studies of particular plays: indeed into experience of them, through analysis, production and discourse. But although this has often happened, the shadow of that other, undefined 'experience' still often falls: a shadow often darkened, at its centre, by that simpler first position,

[232]

which is itself not experience but belief: the conviction, for indeed it is that, that all beliefs, which declare themselves as beliefs, are *a priori* inadequate to interpret or resolve the full human condition, but that still beyond them there is ... something.

It is reasonably clear now what, in that period, that something was. It was the God that did not dare to speak its name: an anxious, serious, intermittently sceptical, post-Christian metaphysic. If names were demanded, in the forecourt, they could be as it were professionally produced: Literature (the selected writings we have defined as Literature); Tragedy (authentic tragedy; tragedy proper); Experience (that term taken directly from late Protestant nonconformist meetings, in which without the intervention of dogmas or priestly authority direct, first-hand contact with the power beyond us was personally demonstrated and affirmed). These are big names, about bigger things, but in almost all cases they did not answer the questions; they deflected and contained them. Under pressure, of course, but then there were many ways of living with the pressure, some of them useful: careful and deliberately limited scholarship; empirical critical readings and interpretations; contextual studies.

Yet many of these, we can now see, were for all their local particularities still in the shadow of the belief that did not dare to speak its name. This was most evident in the scandalised revulsion which made itself heard when a later generation of students, trained in just these particularities and at their best having demonstrated their competence in them, began asking the questions again, and now in much harder, more unfamiliar, more aggressive forms. There was then a fine muddle and mutual incomprehension; each, evidently, has persisted. There were also, in some key places, bitter and damaging struggles. Not all established Shakespeareans (for this was now a category in the census of occupations, alongside Medievalist) were as genially baffled as one who asked me why 'all these young people' were writing about 'the power-structure in *Coriolanus*', remaining still genial and baffled when I suggested that they might find it one of the more obvious things to write about and that indeed, in the examination in question, they had been invited to discuss it, but under the different rubric of 'authority'.

This took me back to the time of the sophisticated answers. For while I had then complained that in a number of the plays there were political beliefs and actions that needed to be directly discussed, I soon found that in practice this was not denied. The sophisticated answers coexisted directly with *The Elizabethan World Picture*, which was recommended for our instruction. At one level this was part of a reasonable attempt to get us to see Shakespeare's plays within the beliefs of his own time, as distinct from rash attempts to transfer the beliefs and actions to our own. But at another level it was a form of containment: not only of our rashness, but of those beliefs and actions themselves, and then even more of the plays to which this singular summary stood as background. Even before we could push through to the real complications of the history and 'world-picture' that were being summarised, there was the fact of the dynamic complexity of the major plays, and their resistance to this kind of foreground-background formula. It was a problem that forced itself through, later, when we were offered summaries of the Greek View of Life, which beyond some obviously useful items of information had the effect of making the tragedies even stranger and more incomprehensible. Could anything as settled, as taken for granted, as that singular Elizabethan or Greek World Picture, really have coexisted with these dynamic, complicated, tearing actions; even their resolutions at times deadlocked, precarious, open? To study the plays carefully but then to lead them back into that corral was at its best a contradictory kind of instruction.

Unfortunately what then happened, in most cases, was that two parallel kinds of study developed, often out of touch with each other. The main kind was close reading of the texts without much attention to history. The formula was that one went to 'context' only when the 'text' enforced it. But this assumption of the availability of the text to what was then general reading, however close, was the rashest move that could have been made. Indeed it could never have been seriously pursued if there had not still been the assumption that while (some) history was undoubtedly there, and was at times relevant, the key linkage was through experience of a radically continuous human nature. Even when it was conceded that the conditions of such a nature changed, these were taken as contingent: a twentieth-century student could read the experience of a Renaissance Prince, by the more rather than the less that they had in common. Meanwhile, on the other track, this was strenuously denied. Not only the beliefs and the actions that were actually in play, of which by definition few modern readers could have anything that could be properly called experience, but the very language that was being so closely read, the specific conventions that were often not only misunderstood but not even noticed, were matters that had to be learned. In its more extreme forms, this track really did produce Shakespeareans of a specific kind: people who lived, at least while at work, in an internal exile from their own time, saturated and in some cases dazzled by that distant but technically recoverable world.

Meanwhile, at many levels, the plays were still there. There were continuing critical and textual controversies. But in two important public spheres, beyond the special conditions of academic study, the effective distribution of the plays was in other hands. The schools and the theatres were of course affected by what was happening in the universities; at times very closely. But their inescapable conditions of production were radically different. It has been instructive, throughout, to watch the difficulties of passage from the complexities of knowledge and method in professional academic work to the simplicities imposed by the set book and the examination question. This is not only so in the schools. There have been repeated complaints by Cambridge examiners that the quality of work in undergraduate examinations on the compulsory Shakespeare paper has been low, and many have added that it is much lower than the quality of the work ordinarily done in supervisions, classes and essays. But then examinations are one of the key conditions of production, at school and university. Whatever the sophistication of professional work, it is there, in that form and at that level, that what is taken as relevant knowledge is affirmed and validated.

The conditions of production in the theatres are very different. The plays have to make their way in specific social and economic conditions to contemporary non-candidate audiences. At times, as one might expect, there has been aloof reaction by the academy; or a graded aloofness, in a descent from theatre to film to television. Yet increasingly something quite different has happened. There has been direct traffic and contact between academy and performance, much of it enlivening. Yet this history is especially revealing when it is returned to arguments within the academy. Extraordinary liberties with texts, including deletions, amendments and actual insertions, have appeared to coexist happily with the ferocious minutiae of textual editing and with the disciplines of precise reading. Historical transferences and cancellations have coexisted, even in mutual congratulation, with the most detailed studies of the Elizabethan world and with stringent denunciations of the ignorance, among students and others, of the most elementary historical facts.

But this is a special case, it is at once said. Production has to be different. It has to be live. And it is easy to agree with this until the limits of the special case are encountered. For to take back any of that experimentation, that projection, that reworking to the academy itself can be to encounter, unchanged, the habits full of reasons why anything of the kind is wholly impermissible. What is then clear is that the apparent open-mindedness towards the theatre is not really an open-mindedness; it is a deference to what is at once successful and beyond the limits of an academic authority which is otherwise still stubbornly imposed.

In the last fifteen years there has been a steadily mounting challenge to these imperfect and often complacent settlements. Much of this challenge, in its earliest phase, was, however, in relatively unfamiliar terms and on relatively unfamiliar material. I remember a colleague, holding at arm's length some of the new kinds of analysis of modernist literature, saying he could only begin to take 'these young people' seriously when they applied their supposed skills to the centrality of Shakespeare. Perhaps this was a remark in good faith. For what was most clear in that phase was that a profession which had evolved its own highly specific internal vocabulary, of which only a few terms had ever achieved common currency with general readers, was outraged by the thrusting appearance and repetition of terms which were soon generalised as an alien and barbarous jargon. This was so even in the case of the mild term, 'ideology': ironically so, since one of the most frequent new uses of this difficult term was (at times unnoticed by its users) almost an exact repetition of that embedded sense of the limited and artificial character of all formulated and organised beliefs. But it was the set of the new approaches as a whole, without much discrimination of their many internal variations, which was mainly identified for hostility. I remember an eminent visitor to Cambridge, during what was called quite falsely the row about structuralism, asking, in an apparently interested way, what structuralism and post-structuralism meant, intellectually; and saying, after some quite prolonged explanations: 'Ah, I see: Marxism'. In that kind of atmosphere, the meticulous clarification of new questions and possible new answers was not exactly straightforward.

We are beyond that phase now, though not beyond its residual muddles and hostilities. A body of work is beginning to be formed, and there is a special interest in its application to works in what has been received and defined as the mainstream of English literature. Indeed, from some parts of the contemporary educational system, there is complaint that too much attention is given, is even confined, to works in that orthodox syllabus. Yet as one who has worked, over many years, in analysis of other kinds of writing and of other including contemporary cultural forms, I have always believed that the works of what has been defined, and often contained, as the mainstream simply have to go on being addressed: not only because of their own substantial importance, but also because their very formation into what has been called a canon, with implications for all the works and related forms which that significant term excludes and is at times designed to exclude, enforces, in any new analysis, direct and sustained attention to what can be known of these works both before and after this incorporating and often flattening process.

And then, from this emphasis, the matter of Shakespeare is unquestionably central. One of the most interesting features of this collection of essays is that it combines, within the same covers, studies of particular plays and of the institutions, in education and theatre, which have been built around versions of them. Either kind of study might be more completely carried through on its own, but there is intellectual as well as tactical merit in combining examples of both.

It is not for the writer of an afterword to select and direct attention to particular essays. I am glad that the studies of contemporary productions of Shakespeare, in education and performance, are so detailed and challenging. I think it is important that they, along with their implications for the realities of orthodox academic study, should be read closely alongside the historical and ideological explorations of the first part. And I am especially glad that the main direction of these explorations of the plays should be in the interest of something more significant than what is called, in one of them, the 'reversal of polarities'. For I have to say that when I first encountered what I have described as the ideology of containment of the plays, or the more active forms of their translation into singular forms of authority and order, it was radically disabling that the most evidently available alternative was indeed a reversal of polarities: a reclaiming of Shakespeare for what were then called 'the ranks of progessive writers'. There had been a dismal practice, from the 1930s, of assembling lists of reactionary and progressive writers or, under an alternative rubric, of the true, great, non-ideological writers and the narrowly political and committed rest. What was always significant, however long and complicated the lists became, was that Shakespeare was always in the approved list, though in fact that had led us to that bay in the North Wing and its serried appropriations.

The process now under way, not without difficulties, hesitations and even reversions, is in general admirably more open. Yet this is not, at its best, the weakest, most indifferent form of openness. It is, if I might try to clarify it from one of my own emphases, a radical acceptance of the inherent openness of the forms. There is a shift, beyond the world of world-pictures, and equally beyond the close readings of dramatic poems, to attention to the basic forms of drama itself and then especially to the forms of this drama.

This is not, in these essays, fully argued through, but the effects of its adoption are often evident. Moreover, given the institutional essays, there should be no danger of assuming that this emphasis on the production of a relatively open form leads us to any simple acceptance or ratification of contemporary kinds of production, just because they are on the stage. On the contrary, that orthodox division of labour – texts and contexts in the academy, production on the stage – in its mutual congratulation and deference usually hides the real problems.

Many of the new forms of analysis were founded on the problems of narrative. The status of the author was construed as the problem of the identity and stance of a narrator. Any sub-text was within or beyond an intractably linear text. But in the case of drama these problems are different from the beginning. The form is inherently multivocal. The very composition is inherently interactive. Moreover, while this is true of all drama, it is outstandingly true of these particular historical forms, which contrast with forms which include chorus or expositor as major dramatic elements, and with forms which in their relative immobility of scene and action make of the stage and stage-set an effective 'narrative' and directive position. Further, the extraordinary diversity and interaction of many linguistic (sociolinguistic) levels is a central feature of these plays, by comparison with the great majority of all other dramatic forms, before and since.

Thus certain inherent features of these plays, accentuating certain permanent features of any drama, alter from the beginning the assumptions on which many traditional kinds of analysis have been based. They alter especially that sanctified kind which is always a search for the author within or behind the work, declaring or hiding his identity: the essential Shakespeare. This search usually takes the form of a search for non-dramatic beliefs within what is then the problematically multivocal drama. But the selection and development of multivocal forms is not itself neutral, or a matter of simple aesthetic implication. It is, quite evidently, itself historical, in the observed variations between dramatic and narrative practice in different periods and cultures, and in the analysable variation, within this general unevenness, between relatively open and relatively closed dramatic forms. Once this has been grasped, the questions of meaning, whether construed as of history or of belief, are necessarily shifted into a new dimension. The reductive moves, towards the singularity of world-pictures, the continuity of essential experience, or the mere neutrality beyond all beliefs and actions, are necessarily rejected. What is left to do, with the grain of the actual material, is of course intellectually more difficult. Yet its essential congruity with the kind of practice which it is offering to analyse is good reason for expecting it to be increasingly practical and effective.

I have my own reasons for believing that the most practical and effective new direction will be in analysis of the historically based conventions of language and representation: the plays themselves as socially and materially produced, within discoverable conditions; indeed the texts themselves as history. It is already encouraging that work of this kind is beginning to appear, some of it connecting without strain to elements of an earlier scholarship. Yet it remains a condition of developing this new work, and the clarification it can make of many longstanding problems, that there should be an edge of challenge to the existing confusions and certainties: an edge which from its provocative title onwards this volume seems to me to provide.

Index

Index

Hume, David, 28
Hunsdon, Lord, 84

Itzin, Catherine, 180 n26
Izard, C., 85 n8

Jacquot, Jean, 45 n2, 45 n6, 46 n10
James I, King, 8, 16 n20, 50, 63, 65,
   110, 114–9, 125
Jameson, Fredric, 71 n36
Jardine, Lisa, 16 n6, 107 n24
Jefferson, Tony, 155 n16, 156 n33
Jenkins, Richard, 156 n33
Johnson, Paul, 196
Johnson, Richard, 52
Johst, Hans, 229 n30
Jones, Ann Rosalind, 70 n29
Jones, Howard Mumford, 71 n34
Jones, Ken, 156 n32, 157 n35, 157 n40,
   157 n42
Jonson, Ben, 130; *Irish Masque at
Court*, 63; *Oberon*, 114, 117;
Sejanus, 11, 81
Jorgens, Jack, 200 n1

Kafka, Franz, 29
Kahn, Coppelia, 17 n29, 88, 91
Kantorowicz, Ernst H., 127 n8
Kermode, Frank, 60, 69 n1, 189
Kimberley, Keith, 157
Knights, L. C., 140
Kott, Jan, 131–2, 161–4, 171, 174,
   185, 229 n40
Kozintsev, Grigori, 185, 189, 226,
   230 n45
Kress, Gunther, 15 n4
Kuckhoff, A. G., 211–12
Kuhn, Annette, 106 n1, 108 n27
Kupperman, Ordahl, 46 n22
Kurosawa, Akira, 187, 189
Kyd, Thomas, 21

Labov, W., 156 n33
Laing, Stuart, 156 n29
Landstone, Charles, 158, 179 n3
Larrain, Jorge, 16 n17
Lawder, S. D., 200 n4
Lawson, Right Hon. Nigel, 202, 226
Lawton, Denis, 156 n24, 157 n35
Leavis, F. R., 143, 189
Leech, Clifford, 229 n26
Le Grand, Julian, 180 n17
Lentricchia, Frank, 14, 17 n31
Lenz, Carolyn, 106 n2, 107 n3
Lever, J. W., 15 n3, 72, 77, 82

Levine, Mortimer, 127 n7
Longhurst, Derek, 154 n4, 155 n18
Lovell, Terry, 15 n1
Lytle, Guy Fitch, 16 n10, 127 n9

McCullough, Christopher, 201
Macdonald, Madeleine, 154 n2
Macdonald, Michael, 103–4
McIntosh, Mary, 108 n44
McLuskie, Kathleen, 11
Macherey, Pierre, 3, 155 n11
Machiavelli, Niccolò, 13, 19–23
Mack, Maynard, 30, 46 n18
Mankiewicz, Joseph L., 184
Manvell, Roger, 200 n1
Marcus, Leah, 127 n14
Marlowe, Christopher, 18, 20–1, 25, 27
Marotti, Arthur F., 127 n9
Marowitz, Charles, 145, 163, 179,
   180 n10, 180 n12
Martyr, Peter, 56
Marx, Karl, 3, 16 n12
Mary, Queen of Scots, 113
Mathieson, Margaret, 156 n23,
   157 n35, 157 n41
Messina, Cedric, 192–3, 195–6
Miles, Michael W., 180 n23
Miller, D. A., 46 n28
Miller, Jonathan, 95, 177–8, 192, 195,
   197–8, 204
Montaigne, Michel de, 19, 48, 56
Montrose, Louis Adrian, 16 n10,
   16 n11, 70 n29
Moore, Michael, 15 n4
More, Thomas, 44
Moretti, Franco, 15 n3, 17 n25
Morton, Grenfell, 70 n20
Mullaney, Stephen, 16 n11
Mulvey, Laura, 95
Munden, R. C., 128 n22

Narajan, S., 108 n25
Nashe, Thomas, 84
Neale, J. E., 46 n29
Neely, Carol, 106 n2, 107 n3
Neville, Sir Henry, 119
Newsom Report (1963), 135, 145
Nightingale, Benedict, 177
Noble, Adrian, 171
Nunn, Trevor, 158 ff, 191

Orgel, Stephen, 16 n10, 17 n21, 70 n29,
   127 n9, 127 n15, 127 n16

Parkin, Frank, 167

Index